SEVENTY YEARS OF LIFE AND LABOR

SAMUEL GOMPERS, NEW RIVER, WEST VIRGINIA
Photograph taken by a detective. 1890s.
Courtesy of George Meany Memorial Archives, AFL-CIO.

SEVENTY YEARS OF LIFE AND LABOR

AN AUTOBIOGRAPHY

Samuel Gompers

Edited and with an Introduction by
Nick Salvatore

ILR PRESS
New York State School of
Industrial and Labor Relations
Cornell University

Burgess

*HD
8073
. G6
A3
1984
copy 1*

Cover design: Kathleen Dalton

Cover photograph courtesy of
George Meany Memorial Archives, AFL-CIO

Library of Congress number: 84-10765
ISBN: cloth 0-87546-112-3, paper 0-87546-109-3

Library of Congress Cataloging in Publication Data

Gompers, Samuel, 1850–1924.
  Seventy years of life and labor.

  Bibliography: p.
  Includes index.
  1. Gompers, Samuel, 1850–1924. 2. Trade-unions—
United States—Officials and employees—Biography.
3. American Federation of Labor. 4. Labor and laboring
classes—United States. I. Salvatore, Nick, 1943–.
II. Title.
HD8073.G6A3   1984   331.88'32'0924 [B]   84-10765
ISBN 0-87546-112-3
ISBN 0-87546-109-3 (pbk.)

Copies may be ordered from
ILR Press
New York State School of
Industrial and Labor Relations
Cornell University
Ithaca, NY 14853

Printed by Braun-Brumfield in the United States of America
54321

CONTENTS

PREFACE

Sixty years after his death, Samuel Gompers remains a commanding figure in the history of the American labor movement. More than any other single individual, Gompers influenced the structure and ultimate orientation of the institutions of American workers. During the 1870s, he became a leading force in the Cigarmakers International Union at a time when that group played a central role within the young labor movement. During the 1880s, Gompers was quite active in a number of organizations, but most important, he helped to establish and then nurse through its early lean years the American Federation of Labor. In the years between 1886 and his death in 1924, moreover, Gompers was president of the federation for all but one. In that capacity, his influence upon organized workers grew far beyond his formal constitutional power within the federation and extended into areas of national politics and policy as well. More than those of any other labor leader of his era, Gompers's views on a wide variety of issues were sought by working people, politicians and, on occasion, even by corporate leaders. As American society completed its transformation into a mature industrial capitalist society, Gompers assumed the position of labor's leading representative both to workers and to the larger society.

Many of the positions Gompers took engendered serious opposition within the labor movement. The very existence of that sustained controversy ensures Gompers a prominent place in the history of the early organized labor movement, for it underscores his central role. In addition, however, the career of this early labor leader is of interest to readers primarily concerned with the contemporary labor movement. While there have been many important changes in the labor movement since Gompers's time (not the least of which was the emergence of the Congress of Industrial Organizations in the mass production industries during the 1930s), the *structure* of the modern labor movement would be immediately recognizable to Gompers today. Indeed it should, for, especially since the merger in 1955 between the federation and the Congress of Industrial Organizations, that structure reflects in both general outline and many specific details the very orientation Gompers himself helped establish many decades earlier. Thus even to critics of his legacy within labor today, Samuel Gompers remains an essential starting point for understanding the ideas that have largely influenced the development of organized labor in America.

This edition of *Seventy Years of Life and Labor* represents a little more than a quarter of the original eleven hundred pages. Despite the drastic cuts dictated by considerations of space, I have sought to include each major experience or discussion from the original volumes. As Gompers often repeated himself in different chapters, I was able to select the most appropriate examples and exclude others. In certain cases, whole chapters were omitted. Gompers's discussions of music and drama, the presidents he met, and similar chapters are not in the current text. I judged them of limited value given the need to present a relatively inexpensive edition. I have also taken the liberty of restructuring the original chapters and of connecting without ellipses passages on either side of excluded material. This edition is not meant to replace the full autobiography but rather to make available the essence of Gompers's memoirs to students of American labor. To aid those desirous of further study, I have added both a glossary of names and a selected bibliography.

I would like to thank the following friends and colleagues for the assistance they gave in commenting on the introduction or the edited text: Vernon Briggs, Stuart B. Kaufman, James Grossman, Gerd Korman, Larry Rogin, and Roy Rosenzweig. I would also thank Joyce Orzino, who prepared the final manuscript with great care and Mairead Connor, who was a valuable research assistant.

INTRODUCTION

WHEN SAMUEL GOMPERS arrived in the United States from England in July 1863, he was not a newcomer to urban industrial society. Born and raised in a working class district of London, Gompers had served by age thirteen an apprenticeship to both a shoemaker and a cigarmaker. In contrast to the majority of nineteenth-century immigrants to New York, Gompers already had experience with patterns of industrial work that a rural immigrant would yet have to acquire. Most important, through his father's membership in the British Cigarmakers' Society, the young Gompers was familiar with trade unionism and with a variety of critics of British industrial capitalism, ranging from the reform-minded Chartists to the followers of Karl Marx. The intense activity and apparent chaos of New York's streets might very well at first have intimidated Gompers. But as he mastered New York's initial foreignness, he found he possessed certain advantages over other immigrants: he knew the English language, had at least the rudiments of his craft, and was familiar with the expectations of industrial employers.

The Gompers family arrived in New York during the Civil War. Both Samuel and his father were familiar with the issues in that conflict and strongly believed in the emancipation of the slave population. In this, they reflected the attitudes of many British workers who, throughout the war years, held public meetings in Britain's industrial centers to demand that their government support the Union effort and that President Lincoln free the slaves. But other aspects of that Civil War experience, which would play a critical role in his future, were less evident to the young Gompers, as they then were to most Americans.

Despite an official laissez-faire philosophy that many Americans of all classes affirmed, relations among state and federal government and the business community had actually been quite close in the era before the Civil War. The transportation revolution in turnpikes, canals, and finally railroads, which provided the essential structure for the emergence of a national market economy, relied heavily on positive government action; manufacturing expanded to fill a market protected by federal tariffs on imports; and manipulation of the money supply helped create a proper investment atmosphere for business. Yet the Civil War years marked a deepening of these relationships. The scope of government involvement in the daily lives of citizens expanded greatly during the war years and never quite retracted in the peace that ensued. In the postwar years, Congressional committees, with an eye to potential legislation, regularly examined aspects of social relations among American citizens, a process that would have been unthinkable a generation or two earlier. The attitudes of both labor and capital, the conditions of black workers in migration from the rural South to the urban industrial North, women's work and child labor, the problems of immigrant workers and the proper federal policy toward immigration for sustained economic growth—on these and many other topics witnesses were called and the problems discussed. This massive federal inquiry found an echo on the state level as well. Try as they might to adhere to an official ideology that held to a separation between government and the business community, few businessmen of even middling size firms or labor leaders with more than a handful of members could ignore the presence of the state in the period after the Civil War.

As Samuel Gompers entered New York's world of work in 1863, awareness of these and other issues still lay before him. For the first eighteen months in America, Gompers and his father worked side by side in their tenement apartment making cigars. As Gompers recalled, he was not then very interested in the labor movement. Rather, after the day's work, he joined with other immigrant working class youths in debate societies and fraternal orders. But the realities of working class life slowly forced him to widen his perspective. On leaving the tenement for the cigar factory, he improved his work conditions and entered into a new world of ideas and visions. Cigarmakers regularly "hired" one of their co-workers to read while the others worked; in return the reader was "paid" in cigars at the day's end so that no one lost wages. The readings varied, of course, but from all accounts there was usually an emphasis on articles from the labor press and from the writings of such political economists as Karl Marx, Ferdinand Lassalle, Edward Kellogg and Ira Steward. Debate and discussion followed, and at times tempers flared. It was with little exaggeration that one historian suggested that Gompers "went to school at Hirsch's shop." Working class self-education was widespread, and Gompers was but one of many workers who discovered the world of ideas through that process.

This shop floor education reflected the intense nature of the still relatively weak labor movement in New York and other urban centers. Newspapers such as *Fincher's Trades Review, The Workingmen's Advocate, The Irish World,* and the *Labor Standard* were avidly read and handed on to other workers. The issues examined in the labor press were of fundamental importance, as they addressed both specific difficulties labor faced and broader strategies for a more thorough alteration of capitalist society. The tactics of the National Labor Union (NLU), for example, which under the leadership of William Sylvis of the Iron Molders Union sought to create an amalgamated national labor organization of both craft workers and political reformers, were repeatedly debated. The program of the International Workingmen's Association (IWA) also came under close scrutiny. To follow one branch of that movement, the one most closely associated with Karl Marx, was to emphasize the economic organization of workers into unions and to downplay, until the proper class identity emerged through those unions, independent political activity by working people. Another approach, identified with those in the IWA who followed Ferdinand Lassalle, suggested that political activity was of foremost importance and should be engaged in immediately. Each position had its adherents, and the coming of the long depression in the mid-1870s heightened the urgency of the debate. Gompers and other workers found themselves drawn by the vitality of these discussions as they occurred on the job, in saloons and cafes, and in public lectures. They discovered that they too possessed the ability to contrast current reality with a more just and humane potential.

For Samuel Gompers, a smaller discussion group of workingmen that met regularly in New York proved to be of even greater importance. Composed primarily of immigrants or, as in the case of P. J. Mc-Guire, of sons of immigrants, this group of skilled workers in various trades was predominantly of German heritage and closely associated with the Marxist wing of the IWA. While the meetings were informal, the topics discussed were far ranging. It was at these meetings and in discussions with his shopmate and mentor, Ferdinand Laurrell, that the young Gompers first systematically weighed the alternative paths of socialist politics and trade unionism. As these men were of roughly similar age, background, and experience, the personal and political bonds deepened, and they christened themselves *Die Zehn Philosophen*, or "the ten philosophers." While individual members' ideas changed on certain issues over the decade of the 1870s, they all shared a deep commitment to building a trade union movement and together vowed that they would maintain that loyalty despite future offers of more financially rewarding careers outside the labor movement. In 1878 the twenty-eight-year-old Gompers did just that in refusing a well-paid position with the Treasury Department in Washington—a striking commitment to an ideal from a young, poorly paid, overworked man with family responsibilities.

By the mid-1870s, then, Samuel Gompers was no longer the uninvolved lad who had arrived in New York a decade earlier. Prodded by his friends, his shopmates, and deteriorating economic conditions, he was deeply involved in the affairs of his union and in political activities. Older, more experienced, and far more conscious of basic issues affecting workers, Gompers began an association with the union movement that would last the rest of his life.

Gompers's active involvement with the Cigarmakers International Union (CMIU) coincided with an important change in cigar production. In 1868 a mold was invented that performed mechanically the skilled tasks that had been the core of the cigarmaker's craft. This allowed employers to utilize unskilled workers, especially recent immigrants and woman workers. Responding to this serious threat to their position, some socialists within the CMIU argued that since these un-skilled workers formed a reserve labor supply for capital and would un-dercut the potential transformation of society that skilled workers might lead, the union should not organize them. But as early as the mid-1870s, Gompers, who with Adolph Strasser led the opposition to this exclusion-ary policy, thought that economic concentration and technological inno-vation assured a more efficient means of production, were potentially beneficial for workers, and in any case were inevitable. He also force-fully rejected the utopian theme he perceived in his socialist opponents' position: until capitalism ran its course, Gompers argued, any promise that workers might escape their class position was a fantasy.

As he focused on the state of the union, the young Gompers early gave evidence of singular initiative and insight into its problems and structure. In a letter to the president of the CMIU in January 1876, he outlined three critical issues facing working people. Paramount was the necessity to include all workers, regardless of skill, in the union move-ment. The lessons learned in the debate over the mold workers in the CMIU he now applied to the whole of the labor movement. Second, he stressed the need for a reduction in the hours of work (without a reduc-tion in pay) for all workers so that they might better develop their capa-bilities as family members, unionists, and citizens. He also emphasized the importance to labor of working to raise the lowest wages in an indus-try to the level of the highest, thereby largely eliminating capital's re-serve labor supply. Finally, in a cryptic reference to a possible broader transformation of society, Gompers noted that "the fourth [issue] will be given at some future time by others if not by me."

With Adolph Strasser, Gompers was instrumental in building CMIU Local 144 in New York, and in large part due to these efforts, Strasser, with Gompers as a trusted adviser, became president of the national union in 1877. They immediately proposed three basic reforms in the CMIU's structure, which, while not approved at once, ultimately were adopted. To justify the relatively high union dues, the new admin-istration introduced traveling benefits (for members "on the tramp" in search of work), sick benefits, and unemployment compensation—all to be paid from the union treasury. Second, they borrowed from the Brit-ish experience a system of equalization of funds through which the na-tional officers might transfer money from financially stronger locals to weaker ones in crisis. Finally, they insisted on a well-financed and centralized strike fund under the control of the national officers to prevent precipitous strikes that could destroy the union but assure authorized strikers firm financial support.

Critics in Gompers's time and since have pointed to these proposals and others like them as proof that even in the 1870s Gompers was a conservative business unionist fully committed to a narrow program of unionism that encouraged the growth of a bureaucratic union structure. But the evidence from that era suggests a quite different interpretation. The overriding concern of workers in that period was to create stable union structures that could survive the severe cyclical business depressions. A frustrating pattern had already become clear by the time Gompers involved himself in the CMIU. The organizing activity of the late 1820s and early 1830s, with its dual emphasis on both political and economic action, floundered during the long depression of 1837–42; the early national unions of the trades met with similar results in the 1850s, as most were unable to withstand the depression just before the Civil War. Indeed, even as Gompers and Strasser were rebuilding the CMIU in the 1870s, the serious business downturn between 1873 and 1879, with its drastic wage cuts and widespread unemployment, leveled the organized labor movement. Gompers's search for institutional stability in the 1870s was not in any ideological sense business unionism. Rather, he sought such stability so that workers might better defend themselves against the inevitable attacks on wages, conditions, and their unions.

Gompers's resistance to independent working class political action has also generated a persistent criticism. In the 1870s and early 1880s Gompers, following Marxist thought, placed primary emphasis on the economic organization of workers. He certainly agreed with Jonathan Fincher who had argued in 1863 that, when political involvement precedes working class self-awareness, "the rights of labor are made subordinate to the claims of this or that candidate. [The worker] has not the courage to demand his rights in the shop, because he is a companion of his boss 'in the cause.'" Gompers also understood that contending political allegiances could pit worker against worker and thus detract from the effort needed to build the union. Finally, when he examined the actual political programs proposed by New York's early socialist movement, he found them highly unrealistic. The utopian theme that stressed as the ultimate goal a society of small-scale producers he thought irrelevant to the problems of industrialization; and he felt that the socialist emphasis on assuming state power, in alliance with other classes in society, was actually dangerous to workers' self interest. It would detract from their consciousness of themselves as a class and reinforce the social belief that they might escape their status. As J. P. McDonnell, an IWA member, former private secretary to Karl Marx, and a fellow member of *Die Zehn Philosophen*, commented in the 1870s on American conditions, "Our capitalist enemy resides in the breast of almost everyone."

But Gompers was by no means apolitical during this era. He was intensely interested in both political theory and electoral campaigns. Further, as the cryptic reference to broader solutions to social problems in his 1876 letter indicated, neither of the major political parties captured his imagination during these years. He publicly supported Henry George's third-party campaign in the New York City mayoralty race in 1886 and did not cast a ballot for a major party presidential candidate until 1896. Clearly, during the first two decades of his public career Samuel Gompers had a strong faith in the importance of independent political activity. What separated him from socialists at this time, however, was a question of strategy. Building the trade union was the critical task for Gompers; that accomplished, political engagement on a mass level would follow naturally. But to embroil working people in politics before the proper foundation had set was folly.

It is difficult to understand Gompers during these early years without appreciating that he was, as his friendships and associations suggest, first and foremost a skilled immigrant worker. His commitment to the working class was profound and formed a central aspect of his own self-identity. Even years later a socialist opponent could claim, in exasperation, that Gompers was "the most class conscious man I met." His immigrant background provided a critical definition of that consciousness. As Europeans knew, class identity was neither lightly borne nor easily discarded. Yet in America their pride in that class identity and Europe's rich intellectual traditions led them to be seen, even by many native-born workers, as cosmopolitan strangers who were twice-cursed, as immigrants and as class-conscious labor intellectuals, for the news they delivered to the people of the land of opportunity. It is a testament to the collective determination and intelligence of *Die Zehn Philosophen* that, as the result of their struggle to integrate their European perceptions with the complex realities of industrializing America, so many of them played such prominent roles in the American labor movement. In later years other aspects of that immigrant experience would become important to Gompers as he, like so many other immigrants, sought to distance himself from his immigrant origins in order to find acceptance and respectability. Finally, Gompers's position as a skilled craftsman was central to his development. He formed his basic concept of the trade union at a time when the mass production industries were yet in their infancy and skilled workers remained essential to employers. As his activities in the CMIU indicate, he understood the need to incorporate the unskilled into the union movement. But even then, the base of that movement was for Gompers the skilled worker.

The locale also influenced Gompers's development. He lived in a complex and still developing urban industrial society that he took to be the prototype, if not the actual reality, of the American experience. As he notes repeatedly in the autobiography, New York was for him the center of the union movement. Chicago, Pittsburgh, and Cincinnati, to say nothing of the smaller industrializing communities that dotted the American landscape, needed but to look to New York for direction and leadership. But in important ways New York was atypical of the rest of America in the years immediately following the Civil War. In other industrial communities, the immigrant population was less concentrated, the influence of Marx less evident, and industrial development more centralized than in New York's diverse and decentralized economy. Equally important, the growing national industrial work force differed substantively from that in New York. Outside that city, and one or two other urban centers, native-born Americans with rural or small town backgrounds comprised a larger percentage of the new industrial working class. Many experienced this transition from farm to city with their earlier values intact, values that pointed to the concept of citizenship, with its demand for active political engagement as part of one's duty to self and to community, as of primary importance. These men and women would in turn create organizations and leaders that reflected a different approach to such central issues as working class political activity than that developed by Gompers and his co-workers.

These and other differences would in the years ahead create severe tensions between Gompers and other labor leaders such as Terence V. Powderly, Joseph Buchanan, and Eugene V. Debs. But these tensions should not obscure the very substantial contributions Gompers made to the labor movement even in his early career. His role in revamping the trade union structure and his insistence on developing a firm class identity among workers marked an important turning point in the history of the American working class and its labor organizations.

In 1880, the organized labor movement began to recover from the effects of the long depression of 1873. The surviving unions experienced a revival, and new ones appeared, such as the United Brotherhood of Carpenters and Joiners under the leadership of P. J. McGuire. The one labor organization that claimed a national jurisdiction across craft lines, the Knights of Labor (K of L), also experienced renewed growth.

Uriah Stephens, a tailor and former student in a Baptist seminary, founded the K of L in Philadelphia in 1869. During the 1870s the K of L grew slowly, in large part because it adopted a secret ritual in order to protect the organization from employer reaction. Predominantly native-born and Protestant in its early years, the K of L nonetheless advocated the organization of all workers regardless of level of skill, sex, or racial and ethnic identity. Under the leadership of Terence V. Powderly, who became grand master workman in 1879, the K of L dropped its secret ritual and engaged in more aggressive public organizing. While the Knights opened their ranks to small businessmen and manufacturers, their primary focus was on working people who could affiliate on the local level in two ways. The trade assembly gathered together workers in the same craft. Its local organization was generally similar to the local organizations of the national craft unions, in that membership required work in the trade, but it was not necessary to also hold a card in the local craft union. The second form of local organization was the mixed assembly. As the term suggests, workers from different skilled crafts, unskilled workers ineligible for a craft union, and occasional non−working class sympathizers met together. Increasingly during the 1880s, as enough workers in the same local craft joined a mixed assembly, they broke off to form a trade assembly.

Although Samuel Gompers was a member of the Knights, the K of L's organizing efforts caused him great concern. He neither approved of the mixed assembly as a major organizing tool nor did he welcome the presence of middle class reformers in the ranks of the Knights. Even more disturbing to him was the competition the Knights presented to the development of the national craft unions. From Gompers's perspective many years later, the K of L represented a dual union as it

directly vied for the allegiance of workers already eligible for membership in the national craft unions. But as K of L organizers pointed out
during the labor struggles of the 1880s, in many of the crafts it was the
Knights, and not the national unions, who first established an institutional presence. Equally problematic for Gompers was the Knights' attraction to independent political action.

At the national level, Terence Powderly symbolized that involvement for Gompers. A skilled machinist and labor politician, the son of
Irish immigrants, Powderly served several terms as mayor of Scranton,
Pennsylvania, during his long tenure (1878–93) as master workman of
the K of L. He supported the reformist Greenback party in national
elections during much of the 1880s, spoke frequently about monetary
reform, and was a strong temperance advocate. What bothered Gompers was not primarily Powderly's political ideas, some of which Gompers shared, but rather the framework through which Powderly sought
their public acceptance. The K of L leader actively pursued cross-class
alliances, emphasized arbitration and legislation as the solutions to labor's
problems, and in frequent public speeches rejected strikes as a proper
weapon against even the most obstinate of employers. This approach,
Gompers understood, was diametric to his own emphasis on building
the trade union as an independent source of working class power. Moreover, Gompers believed, not completely inaccurately, that the Knights'
peculiar mix of loose organization, political reformist tendencies, and
lack of strict membership requirements often resulted in the K of L's
sharp attacks on the craft unions. Their primary identity was not as
workers, Gompers argued from within his immigrant Marxist-influenced
conception, and he pointed to the vicious struggle in New York between
his CMIU and the K of L's socialist-dominated District Assembly 49 to
prove his argument.

But for all the force of Gompers's criticism, his account is highly
misleading on certain central issues. Although of unquestioned importance in New York, the socialist influence was not a commanding presence nationwide in the K of L. His perception of the relationship between Powderly and the K of L is also erroneous. Gompers claims in his
memoirs that the K of L was a "highly centralized" organization directed
by Powderly, a perspective that then permitted him to criticize one man
and dismiss an organization. But as Gompers himself should have
known, had he but reflected on the persistent rank-and-file opposition

to his own leadership in the CMIU, on any given issue there is often a wide gulf between leaders and members. This was specifically evident concerning Powderly's antistrike position. While Powderly did think strikes harmful to labor's broader interests, relatively few members across the country agreed with him. In the middle of a major strike against the Gould railroads in 1886, for example, Powderly found himself in the quite awkward position of issuing a circular against the strike *after* local assemblies of the Knights throughout the Southwest had already walked off their jobs.

Similarly, Gompers's insistence on presenting the K of L in politics as a reflection of Powderly's concerns misrepresents that experience. Throughout the nation, K of L members were active in local politics primarily because their trade union activity had led these men and women to a new understanding of the interrelationship between political and economic power. It made an enormous difference, they discovered, if during a strike the local police authorities were responsive to their demands for fair treatment and justice or, conversely, if the police aligned themselves with the local employer. Despite Gompers's criticism, the Knights were rooted mainly in the nation's shops and factories. These men and women saw themselves as workers, but they also saw themselves as citizens of both the local community and the larger nation with the rights and duties of political engagement inherent in that tradition. Neither directed by Powderly nor responsive to some "unnatural" impulse, as Gompers would have it, this dual identity propelled many Knights to both political and economic activity.

Whatever the shortcomings of Gompers's retrospective arguments or the contradictions between them and his own actions at the time, it remains true that Gompers fought the influence of the K of L. This led him and other trade union leaders to create a national labor association to promote the common interests of the national craft unions. At the first meeting in Pittsburgh in 1881, which resulted in the establishment of the Federation of Organized Trades and Labor Unions (FOTLU), the Knights were present in force and active in the debates. By the time of the second meeting at Cleveland a year later, however, the K of L was all but formally excluded from participation, and the FOTLU represented only those workers who held membership in the national union of their craft. The FOTLU remained weak and underfinanced during its brief life, and its major activity focused on lobbying efforts on behalf of laws important to working people. It also served as the organizational base for the creation of the American Federation of Labor (AFL) in 1886.

The structure and guiding principles of the AFL reflected in numerous ways the often bitter struggles between the national craft union leaders and the K of L in the preceding years. From its inception, the AFL severely limited the influence of local unions unaffiliated with a national craft union, a sharp contrast with the K of L's haphazard national organization. It rejected overt institutional involvement in politics and limited its activities to support of specific legislation or individual pro-labor candidates. The AFL might support organizing drives among unorganized workers, but such efforts would respect the jurisdictional prerogatives and independent existence of the national craft unions. In an important way, the AFL founders conceived of the institution as a nationwide umbrella over organized labor, created to provide broader protection through united effort and to serve the interests of the craft unions. But the AFL was not to be strong enough on its own to withstand the opposition of those unions and their leaders.

The two guiding principles of the AFL reflected this intent. As Gompers proudly states throughout his autobiography, the AFL adhered to the philosophy of voluntarism. Applied to the institutional structure of the AFL, the concept meant that the national unions freely chose to affiliate and could, therefore, disaffiliate at any time. There existed in the AFL constitution no central force to compel or retain association. But voluntarism also contained a broader social meaning, one that addressed the nature of labor-capital relations in American society. Gompers and other AFL leaders rejected any role for the state in establishing either the general boundaries or the specific conditions of industrial relations. Employers and workers, through their unions, were the only legitimate actors, Gompers insisted, and the inevitable struggle between them would be fought directly in the economic arena without regard for political concerns. As Gompers explained to a Senate committee in 1883, the United States Constitution "does not give our National Government the right to adopt a law which would be applicable to private employments." Despite the growing regulatory power of the state and the growing presence of businessmen on the regulatory boards, these early AFL leaders concentrated on building institutions strong enough to fight employers when necessary and attractive enough to command the loyalty of their skilled members.

The second principle reinforced aspects of the first. The concept of trade union autonomy asserted the independence of the national unions within their craft jurisdictions and affirmed their right to order their internal affairs without interference from other national unions or the AFL. Agreement on this idea ensured the absence of centralized direction and a constitutionally weak office of the president for the new organization.

As the leading public advocate of these ideas within the AFL, Samuel Gompers exhibited a certain consistency with his earlier ideas and experiences. As evident in his battles with both socialists and the Knights before 1886, as well as in the long discussions among *Die Zehn Philosophen*, Gompers elected trade unionism over labor politics as the basic strategy for working people. This insight originally stemmed from his profound appreciation of the fact that even favorable labor legislation required for effective enforcement the concerted power of workers to withhold their labor. To rely on the state and not the union's ability to protect workers' interests was at best foolhardy to Gompers. But something critical changed in Gompers's formulation of this idea in the late 1880s. Although Gompers was never a Marxist in any sustained or ideological sense, he was clearly influenced by the immigrant Marxist milieu that permeated the early New York labor movement. In line with that subculture's influence, the young Gompers did indeed emphasize trade union organizing, but in a broader context that looked toward a fundamental transformation of the society. Trade union work was an essential starting point, but originally it was not an end in itself. The careers of two other of the Philosophers, P. J. McGuire and J. P. McDonnell, both of whom remained socialists and committed trade unionists after the founding of the AFL, suggest an alternative path. But for Gompers, the dialectical process that structured his earlier vision narrowed after 1886 and in time the vision would become almost a caricature of itself.

Contemporary critics were quick to point to this altered message. Daniel DeLeon's Socialist Labor Party was brutal and frequently erroneous in its criticism of Gompers, while the Socialist Party of America, led by Eugene V. Debs, was at times equally sharp in evaluating Gompers even as it sought to work with the local AFL unions. A persistent criticism also came from organized workers in AFL-affiliated unions, especially among the miners, machinists, brewery workers, and cigarmakers. These critics pointed to the Interstate Commerce Act (1887) and the Sherman Anti-Trust Act (1890) as proof of the state's increased involvement in industrial relations; and the dominance of the business community on the new regulatory boards underscored their point. Many could personally testify as well to the intimate collusion between the state and the corporate community, as they had experienced the results of it in strikes at Homestead, Coeur d'Alene, and Pullman and throughout America's coal fields. Reality, these varied critics could agree, demanded an aggressive organizing strategy and, at a minimum, the encouragement of a broad political debate to analyze these complex problems. Gompers's refusal to encourage such a program in part fostered a coalition of dissident delegates at the 1894 AFL convention that rejected Gompers and elected John McBride president.

From one perspective, Gompers himself was a captive of the organization he led. Without central power, Gompers of necessity had to rely on an ability to influence and suggest. Moreover, maintaining his position often required discovering the most common, and least controversial, denominator to resolve internal disputes, even when that result went contrary to his own understanding. His early position on the necessity of biracial organizing was a case in point. After the founding of the AFL, Gompers actively sought to enroll unaffiliated craft unions. He wooed the railway brotherhoods for many years without much success and also pressed the International Association of Machinists (IAM) to join. Founded in 1888, the IAM, like most other unions at the time, excluded black workers. In correspondence over five years, Gompers refused to grant the IAM a charter and tried to convince its leaders that the union's policy would actually hurt white machinists. But the IAM refused to budge. Finally, a compromise of sorts emerged: the IAM removed the racist clause from its national constitution and allowed for local union option on whether or not to include black workers. In exchange, the IAM received its charter, despite the widespread understanding that the local option clause was a subterfuge to maintain an all-white union. Ultimately, it was Gompers who had no option, despite his quite pragmatic commitment to biracial organizing.

In other ways, however, Samuel Gompers's own attitudes helped to foster the institutional atmosphere he at times found confining. The evolution in the meaning he gave to the concept of voluntarism suggests one aspect of this contradiction. To deny the state a role in industrial relations (and thus to deemphasize political action) did not originally require a denial of the very intimate connection between the state and the business community. Rather, the idea reflected a choice made concerning critical first steps in organizing workers. Gompers's attitude toward socialists in the early years of the AFL indicates this. He neither dismissed them as irrelevant nor thought them harmful to either the union movement or America's democratic tradition. But he did insist on the primacy of economic organizing before political involvement. During the 1890s, however, the meaning of voluntarism altered. Gompers now praised the individualistic core of that idea in ways that, if taken literally, actually threatened the philosophic justification of any group or organization. A belief in individualism, the absence of governmental interference, and the strength of a free market economy became for Gompers the criteria of both the good trade unionist and the patriotic American citizen. His earlier formulations, which reflected an appreciation of the complex political economy of industrializing America, were now rarely mentioned.

This intellectual evolution affected Gompers's ability to function as AFL president in very pragmatic ways. As he scornfully and at times viciously attacked socialists, usually without recognition of important differences among them, he found himself depending more and more on the rather conservative national officers of the craft unions. Each needed the other in their common struggle against trade union socialists, who were strong in a number of AFL unions. But Gompers could not very well then reject his allies when faced with their reticence to support organizing drives among the unskilled or among skilled workers of different racial and ethnic backgrounds.

Gompers changed in more subtle ways as well. The innovative unionist who had creatively adapted British lessons to American reality became less evident, as Gompers concentrated his energy on nurturing the AFL to stability. But there were certain consequences of this change that, while perhaps unintended, were nonetheless serious. In the same year that Samuel Gompers helped found the FOTLU, Frederick Winslow Taylor began his time-motion studies of workers and the process of work at the Midvale Steel plant. The early experiments of this industrial engineer would, within a generation, become a more systematic program of scientific management that sought to reorder the workplace along lines more attractive to management. In part, Taylor called for the reorganization of management practices to create greater efficiency. But the major focus of the movement to which Taylor lent his name looked to change the work force. Through the introduction of physiological principles to govern the worker's actual movements, new work rules to enforce the new discipline, and continued technological innovation, Taylorism promised to eliminate the employer's dependence on skilled workers. Work would be routinized, a particular skill broken down into its smallest and least demanding components—and the skilled worker replaced by a semiskilled and unskilled work force. Management, in turn, could replace these workers at its discretion since the work skills now required demanded neither extensive knowledge nor a long apprenticeship. In steel as in other emerging mass production industries, corporate executives quickly learned the lessons of scientific management and reorganized their factories accordingly.

This development presented a fundamental threat to the AFL's organizational stability. Yet Gompers and his associates were slow to respond. In his autobiography, Gompers repeatedly insists that to oppose technological change would be both wrong and suicidal for the labor movement. But that was not the fundamental question raised by Taylor's methods. As many unionists argued at the time, under Taylorism work became demeaning, the individual worker's sense of dignity and self-esteem was undercut, and there was little evidence that the obvious benefits that accrued to management and to stockholders would be shared with the workers themselves. In some industries unionists responded to this challenge by rejecting the exclusionary craft union already in place and building, often in face of opposition from Gompers, industrial unions of their own. The founding of the Amalgamated Clothing Workers of America occurred in this fashion. Others sought a broad public debate over the meaning of citizenship and democracy in a society increasingly autocratic in its economic relations. Beyond certain generalized comments about the ultimate benefit of more efficient production, however, Samuel Gompers offered little of substance.

Despite the serious problems facing the AFL, Gompers justifiably took pride in his achievements as he looked toward the twentieth century. He presided over a national organization that survived the depression of the 1890s and emerged from it with enough financial security to hire its first full-time paid organizers. Membership continued to grow, and by 1904 the AFL could claim 10 percent of the nation's wage earners. A few years earlier, the AFL moved its headquarters to the nation's capital and intensified its lobbying efforts on Capitol Hill. Gompers was more confident than ever that organized labor had secured a permanent recognition as a legitimate institution in American society. Gompers had personal reasons to be pleased as well. Reelected as AFL president after his year's "sabbatical," Gompers never again faced defeat in an election for that office. To a large extent, he had also mastered the difficult task of presiding over a group of opinionated and contentious union presidents. As his reputation grew in the larger society, his actual organizational power within the AFL also expanded. As long as it remained within certain boundaries, that power now far exceeded its constitutional limitations. But even his pride over these very real accomplishments would not efface the fundamental problems that still confronted the AFL.

The basic issue confronting American workers during the first decades of the twentieth century was quite simple. Despite the organizing gains made since the Civil War, the overwhelming majority of American employers refused to recognize the legality of the trade union. There was no legislation holding that they must. The body of case law that did exist held the opposite: the individual worker, when he or she accepted employment, entered into a voluntary contractual relation with the employer that superceded other constitutional rights the worker might possess. In *Hitchman Coal and Coke Co.* v. *Mitchell* (1917), the United States Supreme Court reaffirmed a 1908 West Virginia federal district court's judgment that the United Mine Workers of America was an illegal combination under the Sherman Anti-Trust Act. The Court argued that the union violated the company's property rights in its work force when it attempted to organize miners. The employment contract between Hitchman and its workers, which forbade workers to join unions (referred to as a "yellow dog" contract by labor), was held supreme; and, for good measure, the Court approved the use of injunctions to enforce its decree.

Hitchman v. *Mitchell* was but one of a series of disastrous court decisions for organized labor in the decade prior to America's involvement in World War I. Furthermore, the employer offensive was not limited solely to the legal arena. Individual employers and organized groups such as the National Association of Manufacturers (NAM) conducted antiunion drives nationwide on behalf of the open shop. To complicate matters further, NAM couched its argument against unions in a rhetorical defense of the individual rights and contractual freedoms of working people. By definition, NAM insisted, unions abridged these freedoms in their call for a union shop, which would compel workers to join. The philosophical justification of voluntarism now confronted Gompers and the AFL with a vengeance.

Broad alterations in American society also created difficulties for the AFL. In the years between Gompers's first term as AFL president and World War I, America received the greatest number of foreign immigrants ever in its history. In 1907 alone, nearly 1.3 million new immigrants arrived. By 1910 approximately 40 percent of New York City's population was foreign-born; the proportion for Chicago was 36 percent, for Milwaukee, 30 percent, and for the textile city of Lawrence, Massachusetts, almost 50 percent. These immigrants were mainly working class and collectively possessed little knowledge of American language and customs. Many had no prior experience with factory work, industrial discipline, or trade unions. It was precisely their lack of familiarity with the major experiences of industrial capitalist society that led many employers to welcome them. The newness of the immigrants, many presumed, would foster a malleableness that would in turn create a cheap and docile reserve labor pool of unskilled workers. Samuel Gompers and the nation's employers shared this assumption. Moreover, this change in the American work force occurred simultaneously with tremendous technological innovations in basic industry. As these developments threatened the security of the skilled worker, the semiskilled and unskilled workers needed in the restructured workplace arrived daily from Europe.

The experience in the steel industry suggests the dimensions of the problem. In the decades following the Civil War, the Amalgamated Association of Iron, Steel and Tin Workers grew into one of the strongest unions in the country, with a membership of approximately twenty-five thousand skilled workers in the industry. Composed primarily of native-born white workers, with some concentration of British, German, and other northern European immigrants, the Amalgamated ignored the increasing numbers of semiskilled and unskilled workers then pouring into American steel plants from villages in Poland, Hungary, and Czechoslovakia. Excluded from the union, these new immigrants nonetheless surprised both Amalgamated officials and steel industry executives during the bitter lockout against the union by the Carnegie Steel Company in 1892 at Homestead, Pennsylvania. Although the skilled Amalgamated members represented but 20 percent of the work force, all thirty-eight hundred Carnegie workers supported the union's demands, resisted the attack by the Pinkerton detectives, and ignored company appeals to break worker unity. This combined resistance finally collapsed in the face of the company's power to induce the governor to send in the state militia, but the solidarity expressed across ethnic and skill lines might have taught the Amalgamated officials an important lesson. Unfortunately for the union, however, it did not. The Amalgamated maintained its traditional emphasis on the skilled, despite the diminishing position of those workers in the industry, and did not change its bylaws to allow for the inclusion of the unskilled until 1910. But by that time the Amalgamated had but a shadow existence in the industry.

The problems facing Samuel Gompers and the federation were quite severe during the first decades of the twentieth century. In the economic arena, organized labor had to find a way to involve the new, largely immigrant, industrial work force at the same time it maintained the allegiance of the unions of skilled workers. Politically, the problems were even more severe. Somehow the practice of voluntarism in the political arena had to be adapted to allow organized labor to counteract the powerful corporate influence on American government and courts. To totally fail in either area could structurally weaken the AFL and possibly even lead to the organization's demise.

Gompers's position on organizing the unskilled had been constant since the 1880s. In this new crisis, symbolized by the lack of growth in AFL membership after 1904, Gompers repeated his admonitions, used his considerable influence on national union presidents, and intensified his use of the one direct organizing tactic available to him as AFL president. The original AFL constitution had allowed for the creation of "federal local unions" chartered directly by the AFL president. Similar to the K of L's mixed assemblies, these federal locals enrolled unorganized workers in various trades in a geographic area. When enough workers in a given occupation joined, the group was then attached to the appropriate national craft union. If the national union rejected the new local (because of the presence of unskilled workers, for example), the local could remain directly affiliated with the AFL. After the Homestead lockout in 1892, Gompers pressed this tactic in the steel

industry beyond his formal constitutional authority. When the Amalgamated rejected as new affiliates federal local unions among wire draw-
ers, blast furnace workers, and tube workers, the AFL grouped them together by occupation into new national unions. As important as this
tactic was in providing at least some protection to the previously unorganized, it reveals again the institutional limits of Gompers's ability to
respond to the crisis. Given the power of voluntarism and trade union
autonomy in guiding relations within the AFL, Gompers had no choice
but to fragment labor's strength in the industry. To have attempted to
force the creation of a broader industrial union, against the wishes of the
Amalgamated leaders, would have ensured the organizational breakup of
the AFL. Despite the Amalgamated's dramatic decline in membership,
Gompers of necessity still had to recognize that union's proclaimed jurisdictional prominence.

When he turned his attention to the problems in the broader political culture, Gompers also found his options restricted. His own attitudes toward American socialists had hardened since the early 1880s,
and his disagreement with them was no longer tactical. Socialists, he asserted at the 1903 AFL convention, were "impossibilists," fundamentally wrong in both theory and practice and dangerous to the interests of
working people. This scornful dismissal of American socialism reflected
both institutional constraints (there were few national union presidents
favorably disposed toward socialism) and Gompers's continuing anger
over the influence trade union socialists still exerted in numerous
unions. But it also reflected a more fundamental change in Gompers's
thought. As he reacted to the basic political crisis organized labor faced,
Gompers dismissed as impractical at best the broad political debate socialists perceived as essential to resolving the increasing tension apparent in an individual's identity as a worker and as a citizen in a democratic society. Rather, in what in retrospect appears as a two-pronged
strategy, Gompers sought to enlist some unlikely allies in the dominant
corporate and political worlds in defense of organized labor.

As Gompers was well aware, the business community in America
was anything but monolithic. Different levels of economic concentration
and power, uneven control of the market, and varying rates of technological adaptation created a diverse and at times internally inconsistent
business community. A group like NAM, for example, represented businessmen whose firms, while often quite powerful on the local and re-

gional level, commanded little national attention. In contrast, the national and international corporations in basic industry, finance, and commerce formed the National Civic Federation (NCF) to represent their interests. While neither business group welcomed unions, the NCF shied away from quick applications of direct force against workers. These corporate leaders instead pioneered in the creation of welfare capitalism. Through such programs as stock sharing, pension funds, and sponsorship of company sports teams, they sought to eliminate the appeal of the union while they preserved the full range of management rights and prerogatives. As a group, the NCF also placed a high value on mediation of industrial disputes, hoping to largely avoid the economic disruption and political tension associated with strikes.

From the founding of NCF in 1900 until his death, Samuel Gompers served as first vice president of the NCF, proudly sitting on its board with corporate executives from U.S. Steel, International Harvester, and other major businesses. Certainly Gompers was as favorable a labor representative as the businessmen who created the NCF could have discovered. He had long been on record as in favor of industrial concentration and opposed to antitrust legislation, and he had never questioned the value of technological change. Moreover, he supported noncompulsory mediation of industrial disputes and could honestly join with corporate executives to oppose government interference in the private sector of the economy. Yet the marriage was a hard one for labor. The NCF did provide support when Gompers and two associates faced jail terms as a result of a suit brought by James Van Cleave, president of both the Bucks' Stove and Range Company and the NAM, but the direct benefits to organized labor were questionable. The steel industry again serves as an example. The leading executives of U.S. Steel, including Judge Elbert Gary, the corporation's president, were quite involved in the NCF and served on a number of its committees. While they publicly praised industrial harmony and mediation of disputes as NCF members, these same executives fought the union presence in their own plants. Indeed, they conceived of and led U.S. Steel's open shop drive. The same resistance to worker organizations in *their* plants dominated the thinking of other NCF executives.

Affiliation with the NCF did not provide much direct support to organized labor, but Gompers thought it important enough to maintain despite the mounting criticism from others in the labor movement. He praised the mediation efforts conducted by the NCF in certain strikes and dismissed the strong critical reactions those settlements elicited from his labor critics in both the Pennsylvania coal strike (1902) and the New York City streetcar strike (1905). More important was his reading of the nation's political atmosphere. With reason he feared that the ferocious attacks orchestrated by NAM against organized labor might succeed. He therefore sought in the NCF allies and access to respectability and acceptance from the powerful business community. Girding this relationship was an unspoken *quid pro quo*: respectability and acceptance could be extended only to one who was presentable. In exchange, then, Gompers continued in his task of restraining the labor movement from actions deemed precipitous or radical by himself or his new allies. Fortunately for Gompers, his attitudes on basic questions frequently corresponded with those of colleagues in the NCF. Each, for example, worried over the harmful influences the immigrant community, with its surprising propensity for radical action, might exert on their respective institutions. Business members of the NCF utilized the system of welfare capitalism and the emerging field of personnel management to direct workers along the desired path. Gompers, on the other hand, saw in the organized labor movement the proper institution to police workers. Writing for a labor audience but quite conscious of his NCF associates as well, Gompers warned in 1912, after the successful strike of immigrant workers led by the left-wing Industrial Workers of the World at Lawrence, Massachusetts, that immigrant workers in the steel industry "will protest. Probably not in the same way as American trade unions . . . the Anglo-Saxon plan. But if the great industrial combinations do not deal with us they will have somebody else to deal with who will not have the American idea."

Gompers's joint message to business executive and craft unionist alike underscored the threat to each the immigrant worker represented. This theme also dominates large sections of his memoirs, as he addresses the problems he encountered in dealing with Chinese, Italian, Polish, and other non-Teutonic immigrants. The emphasis he placed on Americanization through the labor movement, "the Anglo-Saxon plan" he referred to in 1912, only hints at the importance of this theme in his personal and public life.

Gompers never felt a strong Jewish identity. A secularist, a humanist, a child of both the Enlightenment and utilitarianism, Gompers rejected religion as a superstition. But he was profoundly conscious of his immigrant origins. He came to maturity in the immigrant milieu in New York and took great pride in the intellectual abilities and skilled talents of his fellow Philosophers. As he states in his autobiography, there was a time when not only was he comfortable with the city's varied groups of immigrant workers but they were comfortable with him and regularly asked him to intervene in disputes within those organizations. His record in the CMIU, in New York State's Workingmen's Assembly, and in the FOTLU made Gompers an individual of commanding presence and importance among his fellow workers. But this occurred within a specific immigrant experience. Gompers and his coworkers might be seen as aliens, strangers in the biblical sense, but they knew they shared with each other and the dominant culture a common Teutonic background, a wide variety of industrial skills, and at the minimum some exposure to the political and intellectual traditions of Western society. But with the new mass migrations from southern and eastern Europe between the 1880s and World War I, the immigrant milieu changed completely. Largely rural if not peasant in background, without formal education, and steeped more in the traditions of their grandparents than in the varieties of Western thought, these new immigrants appeared unabsorbable to many native-born Americans and western European immigrants alike. Even a common religious tradition failed to bridge the gap. Many Jews of German, Dutch, or English heritage, for example, felt little in common with their eastern European coreligionists. Western European Jews had long felt culturally superior in Europe, and the rawness of the new Jewish immigrants, who filled the streets dressed in their frock coats and beaver hats, did little to ease relations in America. Moreover, in certain decentralized industries such as clothing and garments, the small-scale owners and subcontractors tended to be western Jews while the work force were the new eastern immigrants.

Understanding the importance of this new migration is essential if one is to comprehend a persistent theme in Gompers's *Seventy Years of Life and Labor*. Gompers's repeated insistence that he is not an immigrant and his frequent, almost bizzarre, pointing of his finger at "them," the foreign-born, as he asserts his native roots would, if taken literally, seem ridiculous. But Gompers is not denying the very immigrant background that, in another context, he proudly proclaims.

Rather, his denial is a more complicated statement whose ultimate audience is the native-born worker and especially the native-born executive and politician. In distancing himself and those he represents from the new immigrants, Gompers both praises the success of an earlier process of Americanization and offers his services as a member of the indigenous culture in this new context. Businessmen who fought him, then, opposed their own self-interest, while workers who rejected his leadership defined themselves as un-American. Like the cosmopolitan British and French Jews who, sensitive to their own tenuous status in their nations, opposed the migration of Russian Jewish refugees of the czar's programs during the 1880s, Gompers's attitude in part stemmed from a realization of labor's precarious institutional position in America. If he and the AFL might find common ground with the corporate powers, then the AFL might survive even if this was achieved at some cost to the majority of working people.

It is with this perspective in mind that Gompers's involvement with the NCF must be evaluated. Intensely aware of the hostile attitudes toward labor throughout the society, Gompers was certainly not surprised when his NCF colleagues resisted unionization of their plants. But he maintained the connection for the potential contacts and access to the powerful it provided. NCF executives conferred as equals with a succession of presidents and more often than not dominated discussions with state governors and lesser officials. These contacts, augmented by the frequent formal dinners the NCF organized, provided Gompers with that access. In his opinion, he used it well, even if he professed a certain class discomfort over the opulence of those dinners. If the price of this access was to ignore the protests from some in his own rank and file, from socialists, populists, and politically active trade unionists, to say nothing of the far less articulated pain from the mass of unorganized workers, it was a price he was willing to pay. In his opinion, defending the AFL, especially in an era of nongrowth, was the central task at the moment and the key to any future revival.

The second aspect of Gompers's strategy, moving the AFL toward overt political involvement, developed from these similar concerns. A series of court decisions between 1905 and 1909, including the Supreme Court's opinions in *Bucks' Stove and Range Co.* v. *American Federation of Labor* and *Loewe* v. *Lawlor* (the Danbury Hatters case), affirmed the prosecution of organized labor under the Sherman Anti-

Trust Act. Collectively these decisions demanded a coherent response from labor to the very real presence of the state in industrial relations. Despite the philosophy of voluntarism, Gompers could no longer ignore the political system. At first, however, he attempted to maintain the AFL's nonpartisan stance. In 1906, Gompers and other leaders presented labor's Bill of Grievances to President Theodore Roosevelt and to the Congress. Two years later, the AFL president addressed the platform committees of the two major parties' national conventions. During these years he also assigned more organizers and appropriated greater resources in an effort to reward labor's friends and punish its enemies in state and congressional elections. But political realities quickly eroded the AFL's voluntarist stance. Pragmatically, the nonpartisan component of that idea proved ineffective. The Republican party, despite the presence in it of the majority of NCF executives, rarely responded to labor's programs, and it was even hard for Gompers to get a serious hearing from Republican committees. The Democrats, on the other hand, responded more favorably, and as Gompers naturally sought to press the advantage, he found himself involved in a highly partisan alliance with the Democratic party. Philosophically as well, Gompers's commitment to voluntarism changed, despite formal pronouncements to the contrary. He recognized the involvement of the state in broad areas of labor's concern, and rather than struggling against the involvement, he searched for allies to influence its direction. While limits did exist (he refused to support government-funded unemployment compensation or social security benefits, for example), after 1910 Gompers himself perceived a broader legitimate role for the state than he had previously allowed.

As Gompers proudly recalls in his memoirs, this new approach paid handsome dividends to organized labor, its leading officials, and at far greater remove, the majority of unorganized American workers. In the last days of William Howard Taft's administration, the Republican president signed a bill establishing the Department of Labor, thus fulfilling a labor goal of many decades. But it was with the inauguration of the conservative, scholarly southern Democrat, Woodrow Wilson, as president in 1913 that Gompers's new policy came to fruition. Originally lukewarm toward Wilson's candidacy, Gompers's evaluation of Wilson soon improved. In 1914, Gompers praised Wilson without reserve for signing the Clayton Anti-Trust Act. Gompers referred to that bill as "Labor's Magna Carta" and thought it would exempt organized labor once and for all from prosecution under antitrust statutes. A year later, Wilson signed the Seamen's Bill, which provided basic protection for those abused workers; in 1916 the Adamson Act became law and guaranteed the eight-hour day for railroad employees. Overall, Gompers was quite pleased with both his relationship with Wilson and the fruits of his new policy. He now had easy access to the White House and in Wilson found an ally in the highest ranks of politics. Not surprisingly, Gompers supported Wilson with a public fervor unknown in past campaigns during the 1916 election and took great pleasure in the fact that Wilson won reelection with strong labor backing.

This political alliance deepened with the coming of war. After winning reelection on an antiwar platform, Wilson began preparing America to enter that conflict. For his part, Gompers had relinquished his lifelong pacifist sympathies and headed the American Alliance for Labor and Democracy to bring the message of preparedness to the American worker. Gompers's role in fashioning a national prowar consensus was critical, for the opponents of American involvement were vocal and numerous. American socialists, with an influence broader than their membership totals would suggest, were surprisingly firm in their opposition. In the vast regions of the West and Southwest, nonsocialist farmers, workers, and even small businessmen rejected prowar arguments. Organized workers as well, in the rank and file if not among the AFL leadership, strengthened this antiwar sentiment. Cynics suggested that, in leading the administration's counterattack, Gompers more than repaid Wilson for past favors. But that analysis misreads a central component of Gompers's thought. Especially in light of the persistent rumors that America's immigrant population provided a breeding ground for treasonous attitudes and actions, Gompers's presentation of his prowar position as but his patriotic duty indeed makes sense. To do otherwise would simply identify *his* American movement with *those* aliens and dissenters and, in his mind, prove to the public that organized labor was not a responsible partner in modern corporate America. In a manner perhaps unforeseen, Gompers's activities during the war actually did complete his own process of Americanization. The relentless attacks upon socialists in which Gompers asserted, without evidence, that Germany "controlled" that indigenous movement; his ignoring of the ferocious antilabor motivation of the preparedness movement nationwide; the blithe approval he gave to the curtailment of the civil and political liberties of opponents in the name of defending "democracy"—these actions point to the presence of a nativist mentality in full bloom. In the past, Samuel Gompers had frequently exhibited a deeper and richer understanding of the variety within American culture. In many ways these war years were his least admirable.

Gompers himself understood these years in a different fashion. In the AFL's participation on the National War Labor Board Gompers perceived the culmination of his long search for organizational acceptance and respectability. The board consisted of representatives of management, labor, and the public and was charged with maintaining production through avoidance of work stoppages. To achieve industrial peace, the board formally acknowledged labor's right to organize and forced employers to negotiate with the unions representing workers. Gompers reveled in the presumed recognition of labor's institutional presence in American life and took great personal delight watching the business community squirm when forced to confer with labor as equals. This experience with the board, coupled with his participation in the Versailles Peace Conference after World War I, capped his career. He had achieved a central goal, he thought, by bringing organized labor inside the corridors of power.

As he prepared his memoirs, Samuel Gompers reviewed his career with a justifiable pride. He had presided over the labor movement since its early chaotic days and, through numerous crises, shepherded it to a level of institutional stability and cohesion. This achievement occurred in an environment intensely hostile to the very idea of a union. Gompers's sharp retorts to critics who forgot this fundamental fact were to the point. Although he could not foresee the future, Gompers could nonetheless feel confident that his legacy would continue beyond his lifetime. The principles he expounded—voluntarism, trade union autonomy, business unionism—were far more than merely personal maxims. Over more than fifty years Gompers, with others, had fashioned from these principles a pragmatic labor organization that had successfully held its position against all challenges.

There is more, however, than simply justifiable pride in *Seventy Years of Life and Labor*. An awkward self-congratulatory tone pervades the autobiography. Somewhat under control in discussions of his early years in the labor movement, where the tone is more authentic with the contemporary record, this tone noticeably increases as he recounts his battles with opponents in the Knights and socialist movement. As he turns to the twentieth century, and especially the years of the Wilson administration, this tone reaches a fever pitch. Opponents become straw figures; his insight is unerringly accurate; and the consequent benefits are obvious to all but the most obdurate. In part, this boastfulness reflects the manner in which the autobiography was written. The early sections clearly seem crafted by Gompers himself, and they remain a highly valuable account of the early movement. But as Gompers wrote his memoirs in the years immediately before his death, he was often sick and even more frequently without energy. Some of the congratulatory tone can be attributed to the work of his private secretary, who drafted and polished many of the later chapters. Gompers certainly reviewed and approved them, but it would be almost inhuman to ask a sick and aging public man to resist such fulsome praise and approval. But there is another, more substantive explanation of this boastfulness.

Had Gompers written his memoirs in late 1919 or early 1920, instead of a few years later, he might have felt less need to congratulate himself. At that earlier point, the victories wrought during the war period still appeared intact. Although his ally Woodrow Wilson was seriously ailing and the National War Labor Board was no longer in existence, Gompers had little cause to doubt labor's vitality. The Democratic party still perceived the AFL as a valued, if subordinate, ally, and Gompers himself retained his extensive corporate contacts. More to the point, AFL membership continued to grow. Between 1916 and 1919, in large part as a result of the wartime government support, the AFL ranks increased by some 57 percent. A year later, although the wartime structure was largely dismantled, membership still rose another 25 percent as the AFL represented more than four million members for the first time in its history. But that would be the federation's highest point until the eve of the next world war. A slight decline began in 1921, and by Gompers's death in 1924, membership had fallen some 30 percent from the 1920 level. Certain unions, especially in mining and the metal trades, feared for their existence.

The reasons for this decline in membership, and an even more dramatic decline in the standard of living for many skilled and nonskilled workers during the 1920s, are complex. Collectively, however, they call into question certain fundamental aspects of Gompers's principles. That long-sought acceptance from the corporate community now seemed a doubtful stragegy. Across the country employers, large and small, prepared to roll back labor's wartime gains, and Gompers himself, as he notes in his memoirs, could not even obtain a reply from his erstwhile NCF colleague, Judge Gary, to a request for a meeting during the great 1919 steel strike. By 1920 this business attitude formalized into a nationwide open shop drive. Presented to the public as the American Plan, it was more than simply another antiunion campaign. At the heart of the American Plan was a political and cultural attack on the very idea of labor unions couched in the argument, alternatively subtle or blunt, that workers' organizations were by definition un-American. Not only were his corporate contacts distinctly unsupportive in this era, but the pride Gompers took in them appeared, at the least, misplaced. To seek an alliance with an opponent who would rather deny your right to exist was a dubious proposition.

The postwar years treated Gompers's political record with a similar harshness. With the end of the war, and Wilson's preoccupation with the peace treaty and his ensuing sickness, the AFL lost its most influential ally. Gompers still received a polite hearing in Democratic party councils, but at the national level at least, candidates after Wilson were anything but strong supporters of labor. Moreover, they did not win election. Recognizing this, in 1924 Gompers publicly committed his prestige and the credibility of organized labor to the independent presidential campaign of Wisconsin senator Robert La Follette. As the returns came in a month before he died, they were depressing. That La Follette did not win was not surprising, but it was disheartening that in working class wards nationwide a clear majority of the votes went to one of the major party candidates. After decades of proclaiming a policy of extreme caution in politics, Gompers found his own membership unprepared for change.

From the perspective of his career in the 1870s and 1880s, Gompers rejected certain understandings in the years after 1900, and that severely limited his ability to educate his membership. He no longer discussed the interrelationship between political and economic activity, and consequently he lost the breadth and vitality that had marked his earlier analyses of labor in America. In the mutual and bitter antagonisms between the AFL leader and the nation's varied populists and socialists, moreover, an opportunity was squandered to more forcibly present an alternative program for national debate. His earlier insistence on the necessity of developing workers' economic power before entering the political arena had also changed in practice. Elated over the passage of the Clayton Anti-Trust Act in 1914, Gompers could only listen in anger as the 1917 *Hitchman* decision once again exposed labor to antitrust litigation. Even more pointed was the wartime experience. In less than two years the AFL went from a period of high, government-aided growth to the start of a decade-long decline. As Gompers had earlier stated so frequently, it was folly to rely on government if workers themselves were neither fully organized nor self-conscious.

This narrowing of vision was the Achilles' heel in Gompers's often admirable career. In a certain way, Gompers became trapped by the very forces he helped set in motion. His struggles against the self-destructive jurisdictional claims by the national craft unions is a case in point. But Gompers was also a victim of his own insecurities and desires. He exhibited a fatal attraction to the powerful and respectable in society and placed a disproportionate emphasis on the value of their approval. Conscious of his status as an outsider, despite his protestations to the contrary, he sought acceptance even at the expense of the "less respectable" segment of the work force. His attitude toward the newer immigrants suggests the dimensions of this tension. In demanding their Americanization as a precondition to his acceptance of them into the community of American labor, Gompers added his voice to the chorus from the business community that insisted there was but one acceptable definition of American citizenship. It also allowed him to insist, as he does in his autobiography, that the path he took in labor organizing was the "natural" way in contrast with the proposals of his critics. The exciting atmosphere that had marked the meetings of *Die Zehn Philosophen*, where ideas were alive and every proposal scrutinized, had thinned considerably.

Samuel Gompers remains a central figure in American history during the society's most intense capital development. The choices he made from the possibilities he perceived were of great importance at the time and still influence the organization he founded. Despite his many achievements, however, the larger aspects of the qualities of his leadership remained weak. In his search for acceptance, he jettisoned the vision of working class unity that had motivated him in the 1870s and

1880s. The K of L slogan, that "an injury to one is the concern of all," Gompers dismissed, a casualty of the polemics of the 1880s. But he might have listened to the words of a personal hero, Abraham Lincoln, who once commented that "the strongest bond of human sympathy, outside of the family relation, should be one uniting all working people, of all nations, and tongues, and kindreds." Had Samuel Gompers been able to discover the power and vitality of that American tradition, and joined to it his exemplary abilities as an organizer and administrator, his achievements and his legacy to succeeding generations might have been even more impressive.

SEVENTY YEARS OF
LIFE AND LABOR

1

A YOUNG WORKER

1850–70

From East Side London to East Side New York

THE FIRST HOME that I remember was in a three-story brick house at No. 2 Fort Street, in East Side, London. I believed I was born in that house until my trip to London in 1919 when a painstaking reporter consulted the London birth registry and announced that I was born in No. 11 Tentor Street and that my parents soon afterwards moved to Fort Street. I accepted the revision philosophically, for many years of contact with reporters had accustomed me to receiving from them much novel and sometimes interesting information about myself. Like all the other houses in the neighborhood, ours had worn gray with the passing years. My father and mother lived on the ground floor. My paternal grandparents lived in the second story with their four girls and one boy just ten months older than I. On the top floor lived Mr. Lellyveld, who had two sons, Ascher and Barnett.

Just across the street from our house was a silk factory. That sec-

1

tion of London is known as Spitalfields, then about a mile from the London Ghetto. Our apartment consisted of one large front room and a little back room, which we used in the winter for storage and for things which had to be kept cool. In the summertime father constructed bunks in the little room and we children slept there. In the wintertime we all slept in the big room—father and mother in the big bed that had a curtain around it and we children on the floor in a trundle bed that was rolled under the big bed in the daytime. I was the oldest. Besides me there were Henry, Alexander, Lewis, and Jack. That front room was sitting-room, bedroom, dining-room, and kitchen—the center of our busy little lives as we learned the ways of childhood in East Side, London. Like all children of the poor, we early found our way to the city streets—the place where we began contacts and struggles with our fellows. It is the education of the street that produces that early shrewdness in the children of those "have not" that often leaves an ineradicable difference between them and the children of those "who have." Life in the streets had manifold fascinations, but we were required to be home for meals and at other definite times.

My parents were both Hollanders born in Amsterdam. On the paternal side the family name, Gompers, came originally and many years before, from Austrian origin where it was spelled Gompertz and, in some instances, Gomperz. On the maternal side the family name was Rood. During the Napoleonic rule in Holland, a French soldier fell in love with a Dutch girl. They were married, lived and died in Holland, surrounded by a large family. That was the beginning of our Dutch branch of Roods.

My father and mother were unacquainted with each other in Holland, although they lived only a few streets apart. After my father went to England, his father established a profitable business between the two countries, traveling back and forth five or six times a year. On one of these trips he became acquainted with my maternal grandfather and his family, the Roods, who were well-to-do tradesmen. My mother listened to grandfather's glowing accounts of Old England and became very anxious to go there. She accompanied grandfather to London where she lived with the family about two years, and there she and father married.

Our home preserved many of the customs of the Dutch community from which mother and father came. In our big room was a large fireplace in which mother had a Dutch oven that produced what seemed to us children marvelously delicious things to eat. All mother's cooking utensils were of the squat, substantial Dutch make, necessary for the old-fashioned Dutch cooking that nourished us youngsters three times a day. Our bread came from a neighboring bakery. I was always glad to be sent to purchase the loaf. We bought a "quarten"—a four-pound loaf. In those days the bakers were required to weigh each loaf as they sold it, and if the big round loaf was a bit under weight, an extra slice was cut from another loaf. That extra slice never reached home—the fresh, warm bread was irresistible to my sturdy appetite.

Our water came from a big barrel in the back-yard. Our neighborhood, like all others, had a water man who came around at regular intervals and turned on the plug so that all water barrels in the neighborhood could be filled. It was a serious matter to locate that water man to secure extra water for emergency needs. Our floor was scrubbed regularly and covered with sand.

In the evening we burned eight-penny rush lights or large candles which stood in old-fashioned brass candlesticks. These made a fairly good light for that time. On special occasions we used a paraffin lamp, which was considered a great discovery. Kerosene was too high for daily use. Every hour of the night the beadle made his round.

At regular intervals our "sitting-room, bedroom, dining-room, and kitchen" was converted into a bathroom. Mother brought in the wash-tub and, with thorough-going Dutch cleanliness, scrubbed us youngsters or superintended the process.

In those days they called me the sleepy-head. Mother couldn't get me up in the morning and couldn't keep me out of bed in the evening—a distinct inconvenience in that room that served all the needs of the whole family. Perhaps I was stowing up sleep for later years when I slept when there was nothing else to do.

Many of our neighbors were descendants of French Huguenots who fled from France after the revocation of the Edict of Nantes and built their characteristic houses with little leaded window-panes and in that new home plied their wonderful skill in silk weaving that brought fame and wealth to Spitalfields. But the passing of time had brought shadows to the buildings and changes to the industry. One of my most vivid early recollections is the great trouble that came to the silk weavers when machinery was invented to replace their skill and take their jobs.

No thought was given those men whose trade was gone. Misery and suspense filled the neighborhood with a depressing air of dread. The narrow street echoed with the tramp of men walking the street in groups with no work to do. Burned into my mind was the indescribable effect of the cry of these men, "God, I've no work to do. Lord strike me dead—my wife, my kids want bread and I've no work to do." Child that I was, that cry taught me the worldwide feeling that has ever bound the oppressed together in a struggle against those who hold control over the lives and opportunities of those who work for wages. That feeling became a subconscious guiding impulse that in later years developed into the dominating influence in shaping my life.

When six years of age I was sent to the Jewish Free School in Bell Lane and learned rapidly all that was taught there—reading, writing, arithmetic, geography, and history. The school was an old institution when I attended it. It provided instructions for both boys and girls, as well as for select students known as the Talmud boys—twenty-one in number. Mr. Moses Angel was head teacher. My immediate teacher was Mr. Speyer. When I was ten years and three months I had to go to work. When I left school I stood third to the highest in my classes. As I made rapid progress in my studies, the teacher told Father that it was wrong to rob me of an education, particularly as I showed ability. But Father could not do otherwise. Though I left school at an early age to help earn a living, I did not then realize the wrong society had done me. I was eager to learn more and found opportunity in the Night Free School where I added to my meager equipment. French and music were among my studies there. Though I could never speak French, the rudiments and rules of grammar and fair pronuncication I never forgot. Years later they helped me during my trips to France and in those important international gatherings that began with the Paris Peace Conference. Of almost equal value has been my knowledge of Dutch, which, without formal study, I somehow assimilated from Dutch friends and neighbors. My knowledge of this language enabled me to write Grandfather's letters for him as well as to keep his accounts. My ear had become attuned to both French and Dutch, so that it was easy for me to manage to make myself understood in these languages in later years.

At night school I learned something of the Talmud. I was taught Hebrew—not the mongrel language spoken and written by many Jews of the present age—but that honorable language that unlocked a literature of wonderful beauty and wisdom. The discipline gained from studying the Talmud is essentially the same as resulting from any legal study. It develops the more subtle qualities of mind; the student learns to deal with abstract problems, to make careful discriminations, to follow a line of reasoning from premise to conclusion. This legal training given to Jewish boys is fundamental in explaining the intellectual quality of many of the Jewish people. Again and again in after years I was told that I missed my career in not studying law.

My paternal grandfather, for whom I was named, had come to London from Amsterdam in 1845. His people had lived in Holland for several generations. They were working people. My grandfather was then a dealer in antiques. He was a calico printer by trade. One time he had trouble in the shop, and he declared that he would never again work for a boss; so he left his trade and became a dealer in merchandise. He traveled much between England, Holland, France, Belgium and Switzerland, Germany, and Austria, and his trips sometimes lasted for months.

With his philosophy and his kindly generosity, Grandfather was the most potential influence in my early life. He would illustrate his philosophy by story or incident.

Our grandfather was scrupulously clean as was shown in one peculiarity which used to afford us fun. He disliked paper money as being dirty, and whenever in later years he got a dollar bill he would at once exchange it for coin. He was generous and kind, and yet at times, though not often, he would be seized by manifestations of savage outbursts of uncontrollable rage which lasted but a moment. Afterwards he would not only express regret but would make more than ample amends. These outbursts of temper, I afterwards learned, are a family characteristic which I too possessed. But they grew in frequency as Grandfather became older. Afterwards when we came to the United States, and Grandfather followed us in 1868, I witnessed a terrible paroxysm of temper on his part—absolutely without justification. Then I seemed to see myself in the same rage. I said to myself, "Sam, that's you and that ain't good." I accused myself and for days was very unhappy. It had its influence upon me and my whole conduct. From that time I determined to become master of myself.

[Grandfather] was extremely neat in person and dress, even fastidious. When going out he carefully brushed and buttoned his tailored frock coat and precisely adjusted his silk hat. He was very fond of music. Some nights he would take me with him to some London concert hall. In those happy hours I lived in another world and quivered with the beauty of tone and melody or grew tense when the music dropped in minor or developed in some grand effect. Grandfather introduced me to a world that brought a lifetime pleasure. Music appeals to my whole nature as does nothing else. Many a time to find relief from the strain of struggle of the labor movement I have sought music. The beauty of wonderful music would hold me speechless, motionless—only waking at the end to gasp to myself, "God, how beautiful!"

I early found in the theater a source of very keen delight. Though only the poorer kind, where the tickets were but sixpence, it was my entrance to a wider world. As I watched the actors I lived with them the scenes of the play. My emotions are naturally strong, and fortunately no one ever attempted to teach me self-repression. On the contrary, my life has practically forced me to develop all of the various phases of my nature, which helped me to understand all kinds of men and to enter into their hopes and plans. My love of the theater gave me my first experience in the business world. We boys used to pool our pennies and buy matches—fuses we called them—which we sold on the street for an "a-penny" (half-penny) a box. If we had good luck and made enough money, we went to the theater for a long evening of delight. If we didn't sell the fuses in time for the play to begin, we would go home and play theater.

There were many of our relations in London whom we saw occasionally. There were members of the Gompers family in Holland, one or two of whom came across to see us, staying with us in our consolidated one-room house. Others were scattered in other European countries, though we had no definite knowledge of them. Another branch of the family was in London in one of the well-to-do sections. We had no intercourse with them. It was not until we had been in the United States many years that we had any idea of the ramifications and activities of the Gompers family in Europe. Not infrequently letters came from various people of our name, asking help in tracing family connections. After I had been living in Washington about ten years, a letter came from Madame Rosa Gomperz of Budapest. The tone of the letter showed the writer to be an unusually high-minded person, full of idealism and tenderness for humanity. Madame Gomperz asked for information of our branch of the family, stating that at her request her son-in-law David

Kaufmann was gathering data for the compilation of the history of the Gomperz family. As he died before finishing this work, the material was put into manuscript form by Dr. Max Freudenthal, husband of Irma, daughter of Madame Gomperz.

I greatly prize my copies of the *Die Familie Gomperz*, which gives the history from Solomon and his wife Jacket (1600) from whom the lineage is traced and who laid the foundation for great wealth and scholarships which were to follow through the various generations. Their home was a place of hospitality and the source of benevolent deeds for the poor. Various members of the family occupied official positions in the Prussian government. Others were rabbis, one of whom founded a public institute for instruction in the Talmud. Elias Gomperz founded one of the largest banks in the Prussian state and performed responsible offices under the Great Elector. A highly educated member of this family moved to Amsterdam to have the advantage of opportunities for study afforded by the Dutch universities. There he founded another branch of the Gompers family. His descendants showed the same traits that achieved distinction for the Cleaves-Julich branch. Various members became renowned statesmen, rabbis, merchants, brokers, publishers, dramatic critics. Descendants of the Gompers family in Nymwegen found their way to the New World. Some members of the family had business reverses. Members of both the prosperous and the poorer branches moved to London. Representatives of the more prosperous branch became prominent in educational and literary circles. My father came from the Gompers family in Amsterdam, Holland, who were poor and belonged to the working class.

Our Gompers family in East London was widely separated from the distinction and wealth gained by some of the other branches. Our home was among the poor, and our lives were limited by all the obstacles that poverty entails. We had little of the comforts or the beauty of life. Where we lived there were endless rows of shabby houses bordered by pavements—nothing else, no trees, no green grass, no flowers. Sometimes on holidays, our elders could find time to take us children out to Victoria Park where there were grass and trees and water and swans. I never knew the pleasure and sense of individuality of living in a separate house, with four walls of its own, until I bought my present home in 1917. All my life I had wanted a home surrounded by grass and trees, where I could hear the birds night and morning.

On the holiday that all England celebrates, Guy Fawkes' Day, we boys were on the streets as was all London. It was part of the holiday custom to beg. Henry, Simon, and I were little shavers, but we joined in the spirit and custom. On that day each group of boys constructed a little dome-like grotto of oyster shells. We got our shells from a place near by on our street. In the grotto we built a red fire and then we stood by it with oyster shell in hand, accosting each person who passed with, "Please remember the Grotto once a year." When we got enough money, we went to the theater. Truly, life in the London streets, though precarious, was adventurous, wonderfully interesting and happy.

Our family, though not scrupulously orthodox, observed fast days and the important ceremonials in those London days. Although educated—if the term might be applied to the slight school I was permitted—in a sectarian school, my nature has been in conflict with the restrictions of sects, against conformity to ritual or the idea of authority vested in superiors. Fast days invariably came at a time when I wanted to eat—and I early felt that natural instinct was of greater importance than blind obedience. By nature I am a non-conformist. I believe that restrictions dwarf personality and that largest usefulness comes through greatest personal freedom. Somehow I have never been able to separate an act of worship or service, as I prefer to call it, from some concrete human need. My mind has ever hungrily grasped ideals, and I have followed them with unflagging devotion under the inspiration of service to my fellows. Service has been to me the great spiritual purpose that illumines life.

My father found it extremely difficult to support a family of six children on his scanty wages earned at the cigarmaking trade, so at the age of ten years and three months I was placed to learn the trade of shoemaking. After I had been at work for eight weeks the boss gave me three pence (six cents) a week as wages. But there was something about the noise of the shop that repelled me, and I was glad when one Sunday morning soon after, my father put the "choice" to me of continuing in the shoemaking trade or becoming an apprentice to that of cigarmaking. I chose the latter with the remark—evidently suggested by my father's activity in the Cigarmakers' Society—that I would prefer to learn cigarmaking because there was a society among the cigarmakers but none among the shoemakers. I was accordingly legally indentured to David Schwab, a cigarmaker at Bishopsgate Street, a most eccentric individual. I was to receive one shilling (12 cents) a week for the first year and two shillings a week for the second year. Schwab lived on the floor above his shop. Not infrequently would he appear downstairs in his nightie or underwear—scolding or giving directions about some matter that had just occurred to his mind. Even though now a workman, boyish instincts often prevailed. If I worked until the close of the work-day, it was too late for me to enjoy my favorite diversion—the theater. Henry and Simon occasionally came to my rescue. One or the other would gravely come to the shop and tell the boss that mother was very ill and I must go home. Only thus could I secure the opportunity for pleasure.*

It became harder and harder to get along as our family increased and expenses grew. London seemed to offer no response to our efforts toward betterment. About this time we began to hear more and more about the United States. The great struggle against human slavery which was convulsing America was of vital interest to wage-earners who were everywhere struggling for industrial opportunity and freedom. My work in the cigar factory gave me a chance to hear the men discuss this issue. Youngster that I was, I was absorbed in listening to this talk.

The sympathy of English wage-earners was with the cause of Union which was bound up with the anti-slavery struggle. We heard the story from the Abolitionists. This was true of all the workers of Great Britain even though their own industrial welfare was menaced as was that of the textile workers who were dependent upon cotton shipped from our southern ports. Even against their own economic interests the British textile workers were opposed to the Palmerston diplomatic policy of recognition for the Confederacy and the plan of the British and French governments to raise the blockade of the cotton ports. The spirit of the Chartists was still dominant in British labor.

But my little contribution to the family budget was not enough to solve the difficult problem of feeding and clothing a large family on the restricted income earned at the cigarmaking trade. Emigration to America promised relief.

The Cigarmakers' Society (Union) of England, whose members were frequently unemployed and suffering, established an emigration

*A practice that prevailed in our shop as in all the others of the time makes me seethe with indignation even today as I recall the daily scene. English cigarmakers did not have the privilege of what in American cigar shops are called smokers, or the right to a definite number of cigars to smoke. Every night the working force was lined up at the door and the foreman ran his hands expertly over the body of each to make sure no cigars were being carried away. It was treatment no one could endure with dignity.

fund—that is, instead of paying the members unemployment benefits, a sum of money was granted to help passage from England to the United States. The sum was not large, between five and ten pounds. This was a very practical method which benefited both the emigrants and those who remained by decreasing the number seeking work in their trade. After much discussion and consultation father decided to go to the New World. He had friends in New York City and a brother-in-law who preceded us by six months to whom father wrote we were coming.

There came busy days in which my mother gathered together and packed our household belongings. Father secured passage on the *City of London*, a sailing vessel which left Chadwick Basin, June 10, 1863, and reached Castle Garden, July 29, 1863, after seven weeks and one day. Our ship was the old type of sailing vessel. We were nine days in the British Channel. Someone asked the captain how long it would take us to reach New York. He replied that at our present rate we would reach London in three days. While we were in the Channel we sighted a vessel which the captain thought at first was the *Alabama*, but a closer view revealed a French man-of-war. The famous Confederate cruiser did not cross our path. At last our old tub finally got under motion, and we steadily moved westward. We boys found the boat a bit restrictive. However, we found amusement in games—chiefly playing top. We had none of the modern comforts of travel. The sleeping quarters were cramped, and we had to do our own cooking in the galley of the boat. Mother had provided salt beef and other preserved meats and fish, dried vegetables, and red pickled cabbage which I remember most vividly. We were all seasick except Father, Mother the longest of all. Father had to do the cooking in the meanwhile and take care of the sick. There was a Negro man employed on the boat who was very kind in many ways to help Father. Father didn't know much about cooking.

When July Fourth dawned we were still in mid-ocean. Though this was our first experience with the celebration of the anniversary of the American Republic, we responded with good will when the captain ordered all on deck to participate. Of course, the festivities ended in which all saluted the Stars and Stripes—the beautiful emblem of America that was then in a mighty contest for human freedom. In the years that followed there grew in me a feeling of pride and ownership in the Red, White, and Blue, until the time came when I looked up at it under foreign skies, from the ramparts of a great world-war, and felt it in my heart to say: "America is more than a name, America is an ideal. America is the apotheosis of all that is right."

When we reached New York we landed at the old Castle Garden of lower Manhattan, now the Aquarium, where we were met by relatives and friends. As we were standing in a little group, the Negro who had befriended Father on the trip over came off the boat. Father was grateful and, as a matter of courtesy, shook hands with him and gave him his blessing. Now it happened that the draft and Negro riots were convulsing New York City. Only that very day Negroes had been chased and hanged by mobs. The onlookers, not understanding, grew very much excited over Father's shaking hands with this Negro. A crowd gathered round and threatened to hang both Father and the Negro to the lamp-post. Father's natural independence and dignity then asserted themselves. He turned to the crowd and explained to them why he shook hands with the Negro and thanked him as he had done, and he ended: "Any one of you would have done the same."

On the first day, we found a home in Houston and Attorney Streets. Those four rooms signified progress from the little London home. Our neighbors were chiefly American, English, and Holland Dutch. I was then thirteen years, six months, and two days old.

Father began making cigars at home, and I helped him. Our house was just opposite a slaughter house. All day long we could see the animals being driven into the slaughter-pens and could hear the turmoil and the cries of the animals. The neighborhood was filled with the penetrating, sickening odor. The suffering of the animals and the nauseating odor made it physically impossible for me to eat meat for many months—after we had moved to another neighborhood.

Back of our house was a brewery which was in continuous operation, and this necessitated the practice of living-in for the brewery workers. Conditions were dreadful in the breweries of those days, and I became very familiar with them from our back door.

Our little home was not far from the shipyards of John Roach. Every morning at eight o'clock a bell rang the beginning of the workday. I remember the incident vividly for the great majority of workmen had been at work at least an hour. John Roach was one of the first employers to establish the eight-hour day. He was an extraordinary man of the type of employer who knew his employes personally. His successful development in the shipbulding industry was due to his personal initiative and ability.

New York in those days had no skyscrapers. Horse tram cars ran across town. The buildings were generally small and unpretentious. Then, as now, the East Side was the home of the latest immigrants who settled in colonies making the Irish, the German, the English and Dutch, and the Ghetto districts. The thousands from Eastern Europe had not then begun their great immigration. At first I did not feel much curiosity about the new country, nor did I sense the new life in which I had come. The work in Father's shop seemed no different from the work I had done for three years in London, but gradually experience and outside contacts made me feel the freedom of opportunity and the bigness of the ideal on which American conditions and institutions were founded. Unwittingly, I was reborn to become spiritually a child and citizen of the United States, and after I reached my majority I secured the privilege and obligation of citizenship on October 4, 1872.

Always of a gregarious nature, I soon found boy friends in New York. When I was fourteen, judge and jury clubs were popular among young men in New York. A number of my boy companions formed an organization for pleasure and mental advancement, and named it the Arion Base Ball and Social Club. As president of the club, I was intensely interested in all its activities—as a debater, attorney, and judge. By reason of my activity in the debating club which I helped to organize, I cannot say whether I was attracted by or drifted to the debating club in Room 24, Cooper Union, the institute founded by Peter Cooper. In any event, I came in contact with young men, many of whom were striving to learn. One of these was Peter J. McGuire, then an alert attractive young Irish-American hungry for information and opportunities to discuss current problems.

I attended these lectures and study classes over a period of twenty years. Classes were organized in the fall, spring, and winter. Among the courses for which I registered were history, biography, music, mechanics, measurement of speed, elocution, economics, electric power, geography, astronomy, and travels.

It was in the early years that I found the fraternal movement which appealed to me very strongly. We changed the name of the Arion Club to the Rising Star Social and Debating Club, the members of which generally joined the Court Empire City of the Ancient Order of Foresters, and the club was maintained until its members had all attained the age of twenty-one, when we organized the Rising Star Lodge of the Independent Order of Odd Fellows and later the Stephen A. Douglas Lodge 357 of the Odd Fellows of which I was the first chief executive officer, Noble Grand. Then I became Deputy Grand Master of the District. In 1873 after I had been the Chief Ranger of the Court Empire City of the Ancient Order of Foresters, 5345, I was presented with a gold diamond-studded medal for service to the fraternity, and I have that medal yet. While I was Chief Ranger I proposed for membership Alonzo B. Caldwell, then Sunday editor of the *New York Evening News*. There was a deep friendship between us. It was he, I, and a few others who resented attempts at unnecessary domination exercised by the High Court officials of England. When no redress could be had, we established the Independent Order of Foresters. That was founded in Newark, New Jersey. The spirit of fraternity, helpfulness, and friendship developed by such organizations was not only a help to the members, but to all with whom they came in contact.

In 1864 I joined the Cigarmakers' Local Union No. 15 which was the English-speaking union of New York City. This organization was not strong. There was also Union No. 90 of German-speaking cigarmakers which was affiliated to the German Labor Union that met in the Tenth Ward Hotel. All my life I had been accustomed to the labor movement and accepted as a matter of course that every wage-earner should belong to the union of his trade. I did not yet have a conscious appreciation of the labor movement. My awakening was to come later. However, I attended union meetings and observed union regulations.

For the first year and a half after we came to New York I worked with my father at home. Father paid a deposit for materials and worked at his bench at home instead of in a shop. My first job as a journeyman was at M. Stachelberg's on Pearl Street. I was then between sixteen and seventeen. There was much unrest in the shop. The men were discontented. They asked me to present to the employer their grievances and the new conditions they wanted. When I did so, Mr. Stachelberg told me that I, a mere boy, ought to be ashamed to be representing men old enough to be my father and that I ought to be at home where my mother could "dry me one behind the ear." I told him that the men were entitled to have whoever they chose. When Stachelberg found that

I couldn't be intimidated, he tried to bribe me. He sought me out in conversation, offered to treat me to beer, and to do everything to alienate me from the men. However, I stuck by the men and finally succeeded in winning the case. This was about 1866.

Though but a boy in years, I was living the absorbing, eager life of a young man. My sturdy physique gave me the strength of an ox. My mind was tireless in effort and ambition. At the drop of a hat, I was ready to fight physically or mentally for anything to which I had given adherence. One day Jack Polak, a very dear friend of mine, said to me: "Sam, I've got to go away for the summer. Will you look after my girl for me?"

I carelessly promised and in a few days hunted up Sophia Julian. Sophia was a stripper girl who worked in the same shop that I did. She was very pretty, with a clear olive complexion and a glowing color like peach-blow, soft musical voice, and black curls that she arranged most attractively. Sophia had been born in London and when only a young child came to America where she lived with her father and stepmother, her own sister and brother and two half-brothers and sisters. We drifted along all summer. There were Sophia Julian and Mary Ancona who were chums, and Jack Davis and I who were chums. Sophia and Mary Ancona lived in Brooklyn as did Jack Davis. Two or three times every week I went in the evening to Brooklyn, and it was a journey in those days, before the subways were constructed. I took a stage coach to the ferry, the ferry from the Battery to Hamilton Avenue. By the time I returned the stage coach was not running, and there was then no street car north from the Battery. I established relations of reciprocity with the driver of a milk wagon whereby I exchanged cigars for a seat on the tail-end of his wagon as far as the old Barnum Museum at Ann and Broadway. From there the street car ran over to East Broadway and Clinton Street to Houston. But sometimes I was too late for my milk wagon driver or the last car had left Ann Street—sometimes I missed both and that five-mile walk after midnight through an unilluminated, badly paved section of New York noted for its hold-ups and rough work was a tax on loyalty.

On my birthday, January 27, 1867, we discussed how best to celebrate the day, and someone suggested that we get married. Sophia did not show any disposition to oppose. It was too late to carry out the plan that night, so we determined on the following day. On January 28, without consultation or announcement of plans, we simply went to the Justice of the Peace at the City Hall of Brooklyn, and we were married. Jack and Mary stood up for us as witnesses, and we stood up for them, and so both couples were married. We went to a cheap restaurant and got a bite to eat as our wedding supper, and then we went to the theater to see the play "La Poveretta" or "Under the Snow." Then I took my new wife to her home, and I went over to my home. I was seventeen years and one day old when I married Sophia Julian, and she was sixteen years and six months. When the marriage license was published, there was a sort of a hullabaloo about it, and then it was simply all right and my wife came over to our house and lived with us. She was working, and so was I. We paid board and saved whatever we could until finally we concluded to put up our own little nest and bought some furniture for which we paid cash—not on time—and made our home in which we then gathered our children, one after the other.

After we had been married for a short time I was out of a job and had to find a position outside of New York. I found work over in Hackensack with George Edmonson and moved my family over there. We stayed for about a year. It was while living in Hackensack that our first-born came to us. Just before that birth I took Mrs. Gompers over to my mother's home so that she would have the proper attention. It was in New York City on September 4, 1868, my first son, Samuel J., was born. My wife never returned to Hackensack for Edmonson moved to Lambertsville, New Jersey, and we cigarmakers followed him there. I left my wife and child at my father's in New York until I could determine whether it would be wise to move to Lambertsville. My stay there was during the summer months. I lived in a boarding house with a number of other workmen. In the fall I returned to New York where I again found work.

As an Onlooker

In those early years the fraternal or lodge movement absorbed practically all my leisure. It was its human side that drew me. I saw in it a chance for men to develop and to lend a helping hand when most needed. The lodge was to me a form of education extension. In time its limitations became evident, for I had been making ready to reach out for something bigger and more fundamental. I was a member of the union in my trade for practical reasons, while my idealism and sentiment found expression in fraternalism. As yet I did not understand that the philosophy and scope of the trade union movement could be made broad and deep enough to include all the aspirations and needs of the wage-earner.

I attended union meetings rather casually in the sixties. Local Cigarmakers' Union No. 15 met in a room over the saloon of Garrett Berlyn, 46 East Broadway. He was the father of Barney Berlyn who was one of our members and was elected corresponding secretary in 1870. Barney afterwards became an ardent Socialist. Our union was not very strong. It was affiliated to the old National Union of Cigarmakers organzied in 1864 and later to the Cigarmakers' International Union of America, as the movement was called after the reorganization in 1867. John J. Junio of Syracuse was president. At that time the cigarmakers of this country were as a rule Armenians, Englishmen, and Hollanders. There were a few Germans who had come to the United States from 1855 to 1867. After the Civil War, when cigarmaking began to develop from a house trade into a factory industry, the proportion of German workmen was largely increased.

There was a vast difference between those early unions and the unions of today. Then there was no law or order. A union was a more or less definite group of people employed in the same trade who might help each other out in special difficulties with the employer. There was no sustained effort to secure fair wages through collective bargaining. The employer fixed wages until he shoved them down to a point where human endurance revolted. Often the revolt started by an individual whose personal grievance was sore, who rose and declared: "I am going on strike. All who remain at work are scabs." Usually the workers went out with him.

The union was generally in a precarious condition financially. Strike funds were never assured, and there were no other benefits. The union represented a feeling of community of burdens of those working in the same industry. It had to acquire a new meaning before it became an industrial agency. It had to strengthen its defensive resources and develop cohesive forces. But that was not only the embryonic stage of unionism; it was the fledgling period of industry. Industrial production was uncouth, unscientific, just about as planless as unionism.

Any kind of an old loft served as a cigar shop. The tobacco leaf was prepared by strippers, who drew the leaves from the heavy stem and put them in pads of about fifty. The leaves had to be handled carefully to prevent tearing. The craftsmanship of the cigarmaker was shown in his ability to utilize wrappers to the best advantage to shave off the unusable to a hairbreadth, to roll so as to cover holes in the leaf, and to use both hands so as to make a perfectly shaped and rolled product. These things a good cigarmaker learned to do more or less mechanically, which left us free to think, talk, listen, or sing. I loved the freedom of that work, for I had earned the mind-freedom that accompanied skill as a craftsman. I was eager to learn from discussion and reading or to pour out my feeling in song. Often we chose someone to read to us who was a particularly good reader, and in payment the rest of us gave him sufficient of our cigars so he was not the loser. The reading was always followed by discussion, so we learned to know each other pretty thoroughly.

It was in 1869 that the convention of the cigarmakers which met that year in Chicago issued a general amnesty proclamation to all unfair cigarmakers offering to take them into unions without payment of initiation fees and unpaid obligations. The declaration temporarily made considerable stir in New York. A number of workers drifted in, but they just as easily drifted out—no permanent growth came from offering union membership at a bargain sale. The organization was then making its fight against the introduction of molds and methods that seemed destined to destroy individual skill. In old Turner Hall, Orchard Street, New York City, our members divided into those favoring a strike against the introduction of molds and those opposed. The crowd of boys with whom I was associated voted for a strike, and I followed along. The strike came. It was a hard struggle. From that time I began to realize the futility of opposing progress. The organization lost that fight as molds and bunch-breaking machines enabled immigrant workers to become rapidly adept in producing cheaper grades of cigars. Bohemian cigarmakers began to come in appreciable numbers. In Bohemia cigarmaking was a government monopoly, and practically all the work was done by women. This class of workers made the elimination or even the control of mold usage impossible. A prolonged strike against molds in Straiton and Storm's shop ended disastrously. Fred Blend, president of the International at the time, tried to help us, but the International had no money. Members left, and union disintegration went on.

This condition of depression extended to the whole labor movement in New York. William Jessup, one of the prominent labor men of New York at that time, was making a heroic but discouraging effort to build up the carpenters' organization. Jessup was also president of the Workingmen's Council—then the English-speaking central body of New York City. The *Arbeiter Union*, the central body for the German workers, was the more virile and resourceful organization. Its members were educated and disciplined in European labor movements and were generally associated with the International Workingmen's Association. It was an aggressive, rational body.

A very distinct type of American workingman was that to which Alexander Troup, then of New York, A. C. Cameron of Chicago, Martin A. Foran of Cleveland, Thompson Murch of Maine, and William H. Sylvis of Troy belonged. There was an intellectual quality that kept them from feeling the barriers of a wage-earning class. They looked at industrial problems from the point of view of American citizens and turned instinctively to political activity for reform. One of the men who made a most vivid impression on me was William H. Sylvis, who became president of the National Labor Union after J. C. C. Whaley. Sylvis was an iron molder who gave the best of his life to building up the Iron Molders' Union. He was a trade unionist, but he also had a political slant. He came to New York frequently in the course of his work, and I had many long talks with him that helped me greatly.

These men were prominent in the National Labor Union and approved its venture into the political field. Troup directed the New York State movement that was part of the larger plan. Neither survived the political venture into the presidential campaign of 1872. This policy of condemning existing political parties and building up a labor political machine did not appeal to me, and although I cast my first presidential vote in 1872, it was for General U. S. Grant.

It was late in the fall of 1870 my attention was called to a Cooper Union meeting at which the two Englishmen, Mr. Mundella and Thomas Hughes, M.P., were to speak on the scope and influence of trade unions. Mundella made the mistake of attempting to instruct the American workingmen and advised co-operation and arbitration in the place of strikes. The incident started me to pondering the character and the functions of trade unions. In my own trade, the workmen were powerless against substitution of machines for human skill. Regularly we suffered annual reductions in wages. We had no chance to try either co-operation or arbitration, the remedies recommended by the English speakers, yet we needed protection desperately. In the labor meetings of the early seventies I found passionate feeling, idealism, but little practical aid.

In those days New York was the haven for the overzealous soldiers in the European struggle for freedom. Their talk stirred me deeply. I began to watch their gatherings. Back of their activity was an organization called the International Workingmen's Association whose headquarters were established at London in 1864 and whose presiding genius was Karl Marx. The organization was trade union in inception. It had subsidiary organizations in the various European countries and was controlled by a central General Council. It sought to build up trade unions and held that national trade union movements must act collectively for proper regulation of immigration so that the workingmen of one country could not be used against the workingmen of other countries.

Marx was not consistent in all his writings, but his influence contributed to emphasize the necessity for organization of wage-earners in trade unions and the development of economic power prior to efforts to establish labor government through political methods. The International tried either to establish divisions in the various countries or to secure the co-operation of the national labor organization. In the United States a somewhat loose relationship was established with the National Labor Union, but American workingmen did not feel the same identity of international interests that naturally developed between men of smaller, contiguous countries. Although the International was to concern itself wholly with the affairs of wage-earners, it speedily acquired the reputation of being a powerful revolutionary agency. Our American press seized upon the custom of addressing its members as "citizen" as proof of their identification with the French Commune. Later, a more real basis for disfavor developed through the domination gained by a group of intellectuals who were more interested in the thrills of propaganda than in achieving practical industrial betterment. I watched the period not fully understanding and certainly not appreciating how the mistakes of those years were to help me in developing effective policies in later years.

Early in [1871] New York labor inaugurated an eight-hour move-

ment for the enforcement of the eight-hour law and the establishment of
that standard in all industries. The movement aroused intense enthusiasm. Sections of the International then organized in New York City
joined whole-heartedly. Early in September came the great eight-hour
parade, intended to visualize the purpose and scope of that movement.
The cigarmakers organization was too weak to make a fight for eight
hours at that time, but we joined the parade. We marched down Fourteenth Street to Fourth Avenue along the Bowery to Chatham, from
there to the City Hall, then up Broadway to Eighth Street and over to
Cooper Union. There were about 25,000 men in line. Two sections of
the International and a group of Negro workers attracted the most attention. The Internationals carried the red flag and a banner with the
French slogan, "Liberty, Equality and Fraternity." Eight-hour banners
appeared all along the line of march.

The parade ended with a monster mass meeting in Cooper Union
under the joint auspices of the Workingmen's Unions and the Arbeiter
Union. At that meeting it was resolved to continue the agitation until
the eight-hour day should generally prevail. It was evident then that the
building trades would probably succeed first.

Meanwhile, trouble was brewing in the International. Section 12
of the American group was dominated by a brilliant group of faddists,
reformers, and sensation-loving spirits. They were not working people
and treated their relationship to the labor movement as a means to a
"career." They did not realize that labor issues were tied up with the
lives of men, women, and children—issues not to be risked lightly.
Those pseudo-Communists played with the labor movement. This experience burned itself into my memory so that I never forgot the principle
in after years.

Victoria Woodhull was then dazzling New York by the brilliancy
of her oratory. She was a passionate advocate of woman's suffrage and
human freedom even to the length of irresponsible action. An unhappy
marriage experience in addition to her philosophical anarchy made her
an advocate of free-love as a part of her program of human freedom.
Mrs. Woodhull and her sister, Tenny C. Claflin, published the Woodhull and Claflin *Weekly* which with good reason was dreaded by many a
person whose private life did not conform to the conventional moral
code and which added no luster to the movement.

In the fall of 1871, No. 12, to which this group belonged, issued a circular in which they made the International responsible for free-love, anarchy, and every extreme doctrine that appealed to their speculative fancy. The labor movement was appalled. Its enemies rejoiced and hastened to profit. The daily papers utilized the opportunity for a campaign of ridicule and calumny. They classified all labor purposes as Communism.

The bona-fide trade unionists in the International repudiated the circular and tried to purge the movement of the reformers and "intellectuals." Men like Fred Bolte of the cigarpackers, Konrad Carl the tailor, Edward Grosse the printer, Fred Bloete the cigarmaker, F. A. Sorge the music teacher took the situation before the General Council in London in order that the administrative body should have the necessary information for disciplinary action. The final result was the expulsion of the "radicals" who then set up dual offices in Spring Street and continued to speak in the name of the International. I was coming to an appreciation of the difference between revolutionary ideals and revolutionary tactics for securing them. But the slow, less spectacular methods of constructive progress were more difficult than the dashing, spotlight tactics of the smaller group.

Winter unemployment was a regular recurring evil in those times. Unemployment hardships were unusually pressing in February and March of 1872. The administrative council of the International Workingmen's Association tried to get the city authorities to take action or at least to secure the use of police and court halls for the discussion of questions affecting public welfare. The Board of Aldermen concurred in the request, but were vetoed by the Comptroller. The papers began gravely to record evidences of the existence of a New York Commune. More definite "proof" was found in the grand mass meeting for the unemployed held in Tompkins Square, March 14, 1872. As the Spring Street faction managed the demonstration, the red flag was in evidence everywhere. For days carts and wagons had been driven over town bearing white canvas announcements of the assemblage. If that Spring Street crowd had only had the same keen appreciation of constructive policies that they had of advertising and propaganda they would have done wonders.

Early in 1872 the agitation for eight hours was resumed. The building trades and several of the German organizations were most active. The directing spirits in the Eight-Hour League were George E.

McNeill, Ira Stewart, and George Gunter. These men saw the shorter work-day as the first step necessary in industrial betterment. Working-men must be able to divide their time so as to best conserve their efficiency as men and consequently as workers. The activity of the League paralleled the revival of trade unionism after the Civil War.

Despite all our difficulties, several organizations established the eight-hour day in their trades, but only one, the stone-cutters, maintained that gain through the panic and the industrial depression of the following years.

Unquestionably, in these early days of the seventies the International dominated the labor movement in New York City. The older type of labor organization in the United States had been transplanted from England and was of the fraternal benevolent character. The American trade union, the militant economic force, was yet to come. New York City was the cradle of the modern American labor movement. The United States was then preponderantly an agricultural nation, and industry was in its infancy. The factory system was so new that in comparatively few places had it produced its necessary reflex—the organization of labor. Through the gates of Castle Garden were sifting industrial workers from Europe, welcomed by employers who exploited their need and ignorance. The situation produced its own antidote—the workers from the old countries had had more or less experience in the labor movement, and they began building their defenses. As the early immigration was dominated by English, Irish, and Scotch, so the early labor movement bore the imprint of British organization and methods. The majority of the immigrants who came from the working class or were forced into it by reversals of fortune found homes and work in New York City from whence they filtered to other industrial communities. But New York was the receiving ground. As the tide of reaction swept down over the movement for democracy in Germany, in Hungary, in Italy, in France, New York gave refuge to those whose only safety lay in flight. New York was vividly cosmopolitan with depths in its life that few understood.

These were some of the elements that found their way into the industrial life of New York from which an Americal labor movement was to be developed. Somehow that movement safely combined the fervor of the revolutionists with the systematic orderliness of constructive minds. This was the great contribution of New York. From that industrial center came the first constructive, efficient American trade union organization, that of the cigarmakers, followed by the furniture workers, the printers, the tailors, the plasterers, and others.

Finding the Labor Movement

After I went back to New York from Lambertsville, it was frequently necessary to hunt a new job. This necessity was due to fluctuations in the industry, at that time anything but stable; to lockouts, then much more common than strikes; and to resistance to wage reductions which recurred regularly with the changing seasons. I usually found employment with little difficulty. I took pride in my workmanship and used my materials with scrupulous economy, partly because that accorded with my standard of workmanship and partly because waste was extremely distasteful to me. At one time Stachelberg [an employer], when taking friends through the shop, pointed me out and said, "That is Mr. Gompers, president of the Cigarmakers' Union. He is an agitator, but I don't give a damn, for he makes me good cigars." In each place I worked I had the respect of employers and fellow-workers.

When my father was made foreman of the Eagle Cigar Company, 32 Platt Street, while I was working there, although my home was but a block and a half away from where he with my mother and the younger children were living, in all the ten months of my father's foremanship, I never entered his house. While always courteous to my employers and their representatives, I never permitted any relationship that might be misconstrued by my fellow-workers.

One of the men was named Cohen. He was a small man, a weakling about forty-five years or so, whose sight was considerably impaired. The loft was lighted by windows in front. I had a seat in the first row as did Cohen or "Conchy" as we all called him. Of course, the light was much better nearer the windows than in the back row. One Monday morning, I came into the shop and found that some fellow, who had been a strike breaker in one of the lockouts, was seated at the front bench against the window, in Conchy's seat. Conchy had been removed to one of the seats or benches in the rear. I went up to Conchy and asked, "What did they want to do that for?" Conchy replied, "I don't know."

I left him, went back to my seat, and called one of the call boys (a call boy was provided for each factory to supply the workers with material, etc.), and told him to go down to Mr. Smith, the new foreman, and tell him I wanted to see him. He went down and then came back up and said that Mr. Smith was busy and couldn't come up. I said to the call boy: "Will you please tell him I want to see him on a very important matter?" Finally, Mr. Smith came up. I called his attention to what I thought was an injustice to remove one of the old employes whose sight was getting dull to a dark seat and give this young fellow a preferred seat. He said: "That is my business and I will do just as I please." "Do you mean to say that you are going to let this young fellow keep that front seat and make Conchy stay back there?" "Yes, I am. What are you going to do about it?" Smith replied. I began gathering up my tools as I replied, "Not much except that he can have this seat too." Then as if an explosion had occurred, every man in that shop—there were about fifty of us—rose and reiterated one after another. "Yes, and he can have this seat too." "And this seat," "And this seat," etc. Conchy got his old seat, and then we went to work.

In 1873 came one of the most important changes in my life. I left my old job and found employment with David Hirsch & Company at 122 Chambers Street, then the only union shop in the city. It was also a high-class shop where only the most skilled workmen were employed. David Hirsch was a German "exile." He had learned the cigarmaking trade in Hamburg when he worked with Karl Laurrell, Louis Baer, and a few others whom I met in his shop. Because he was an active Socialist he was directed to move from Hamburg. Of course, he was at liberty to move to another German city, but for propaganda purposes the Germans chose to interpret such orders as "exile." Hirsch came to New York where he started a shop of his own. Soon he was giving employment to some of his fellow-Socialist "exiles." When I went to the shop, Hirsch was employing between fifty and sixty men. He was a bit autocratic, but on the whole very fair. Some of the employes were members of No. 15. Others belonged to No. 90, which was a German-speaking body. There a new world opened to me. The cigarmakers employed at Hirsch's were practically all Germans—men of keener mentality and wider thought than any I had met before. They talked and read in German, but there was enough English spoken to enable me to understand that the trade union movement meant to those men something vastly bigger than anything I had ever conceived. Many of them were men who had learned the labor movement in Europe and who were refugees because they were active for the struggle for political as well as economic freedom.

With all the energy and confidence born of my young strength, I talked from my limited experiences—fraternal idealism, the Odd Fellows Order, etc. On labor matters my thought was wild. I had been feeling profoundly the injustice that society meted out to wage-earners. I was familiar with the vocabulary of revolutionists, but I had not yet attained a practical understanding of the scope and the power of economic organization. In truth, neither had the others. We were all groping our way, trying to develop the language, the methods, and the fundamentals of trade unionism. Some had a better understanding—fortunately they were to become my teachers. They are with me in lifelike vividness as I think back over those early days.

The man whom I loved most and for whose brain, heart, and character I have always had boundless admiration was Karl Malcolm Ferdinand Laurrell. He was so gentle and yet so able. I heard much of him about the shop before I met him—his was the dominating mind. Laurrel spoke with a distinct Teutonic accent and very tersely—especially when not pleased. He didn't seem to think much of me at first. But that was probably due to my enthusiasm for the fraternal orders. Karl, Pher-kopf (*Pherd Kopf*—horse head) as he was generally called, had passed through that stage of thought and had been convinced that the trade union was the fundamental agency to which working people must trust. At first he regarded me as "fresh," but soon he began talking to me, explaining a bit now and then as though he would teach me. He afterwards explained he thought he saw ability in me, and he wanted to save me from mistakes. His kindly talks and warnings did more to shape my mind upon the labor movement than any other single influence. The principles of trade unionism that I learned then remained the basis upon which my policies and methods were determined in the years to come. I have always felt that he watched over me with chastening criticism, for he wanted to save me from allowing my sentiment and emotion to be perverted into the channel of "radicalism."

Laurrell was a Swede by birth—a bit wild as a lad, his mother put him under a sea captain, and for two years he learned discipline in the stern school of seafaring life. After he came on shore he went to

Copenhagen where he learned the cigarmaker's trade. There he came in contact with German thought and the continental labor movement—political and economic. Strong and vigorous, mentally and physically, he forged to the head of both the revolutionary and labor movements. He was elected secretary for the section of the International Workingmen's Association comprising Denmark, Norway, and Sweden. Through this work he came into correspondence with German leaders. When the revolution was stirring all of Europe in the seventies, Laurrell was in the crowd that made a demonstration before the royal palace in Copenhagen. For days he hid from the soldiers, and when his bruises had healed, made his escape to the Navy yard where he had friends and from there found passage to Hamburg where he worked for several years. Then he came to New York. Laurrell knew from experience the revolutionists, the Socialists, the anarchists, and the trade unionists.

Those early Germans were good organization men. Trained in the continental movement, they brought to this country practical methods and lost little time in forming trade unions of fellow-countrymen or in joining existing unions. They were very different from the later immigrants—the "martyrs" of the repressive Bismarckian laws. The latter were zealots and impractical visionaries.

After I had known Laurrell but a short time, I remember going to him one day and enthusiastically telling him some wild plans I had for human betterment. When I had finished, convinced that I had talked well, I sat back with manifest satisfaction to let Laurrell reply. He had been working silently, but had not missed a point, and point by point he replied. Soon my self-confidence began to ebb, and I began to feel physically smaller as Laurrell systematically and ruthlessly demolished my every statement. By the time he had finished I vowed to myself, "Never again will I talk that stuff—but I will find principles that will stand the test."

I remember asking Laurrell whether in his opinion I ought to keep in touch with the Socialist movement. He replied, "Go to their meetings by all means, listen to what they have to say and understand them, but do not join the Party." I never did, though it was my habit to attend their Saturday evening meetings. There were often good speakers present, and the discussions were stimulating.

As the days went by, my mind was groping for something fundamental, something upon which one could base a constructive program. I spoke to Laurrell of my need. He replied, "If you wish to know, I will give you something tangible, something that will give you a background philosophy." He placed in my hands a copy of the Communist Manifesto. As it was in German and my knowledge of the language was still inadequate, he translated and interpreted it for me paragraph by paragraph. That document brought me an interpretation of much that before had been only inarticulate feeling.

This insight into a hidden world of thought aroused me to master the German language in order that I might read for myself. I buckled down to hard work and for months read not one word of English in papers or books. I read all the German economic literature that I could lay hands on—Marx, Engels, Lassalle, and the others. Time and again, under the lure of new ideas, I went to Laurrell with glowing enthusiasm. Laurrell would gently say, "Study your union card, Sam, and if the idea doesn't square with that, it ain't true." My trade union card came to be my standard in all new problems.

Gradually, but inevitably, my interest began to center on the problems I found in the shop—the problems of daily life and the workplace where we spent the greater number of our waking hours. I began to see that the fundamental things had to do with the relations between those associated together in making things, and proper compensation for such service. Life was becoming more real and more serious.

While working at Hirsch's, I made an affiliation which did not at the time make much impression upon me. Our cigar factory was located in the rear part of the loft and the rear of a shoe factory opposite was not more than eight or ten feet away. When one of the shoemakers became friendly with me, we had many talks together, and he expressed appreciation of my leadership. One noon he asked me to meet him when we quit work, about 5:30 or 6 P.M. I agreed and met him that evening, when he asked me whether I would consent to become a member of a secret organization of great importance to labor. I consented, and he took me into the building where I waited below. In about half an hour I was invited up two flights of stairs, and then I was conducted into a room and there obligated, and a great lecture ensued.

I am unwilling to give the nature of the obligation or of the lectures, for since I assumed the obligation I have never violated it. I have no intention of so doing now, but there is one thing of which I may speak. It is that the sum total of the lecture, apart from certain philosophical or theoretical declarations, was hostile to trade unions and the trade union movement. I never again attended the meeting of that local assembly, which was a member of District Assembly 49 [Knights of Labor].

It was the custom of the cigarmakers to chip in to create a fund for purchasing papers, magazines, and books. Then while the rest worked, one of our members would read to us perhaps for an hour at a time, sometimes longer. This practice had a great deal to do with developing the interest of cigarmakers in leading economic questions. We subscribed to several labor papers for the shop. In those early days our unions did not have funds enough to publish trade journals, so it was the custom to make some labor paper the official organ in which to publish convention proceedings, official communications, and the union directory. The *Workingmen's Advocate*, published in Chicago by A. C. Cameron, contained the official news of the cigarmakers' union. Cameron was an able writer and active labor man whom I afterwards came to know very well. He was more interested in inducing labor to organize politically than in developing trade union power. He represented the old idea of the labor movement which was replaced by the trade union as developed in New York City. As the *Workingmen's Advocate* was also the official organ of the National Labor Union, the Chicago Trades Assembly, and for some years, of the Miners, it kept us in touch with the general labor movement. We had also the *National Labor Tribune* then published by John M. Davis in Pittsburgh which was the official organ of the Amalgamated Iron and Steel Workers and later became an advocate of the Knights of Labor.

There were at that time many pamphlet publications of interest to labor, and cheap paper-covered editions of books. Henry George's *Progress and Poverty* was first published in pamphlet form. Additional chapters were published from time to time as separate articles until finally the material had grown to book size. If my memory serves me, the George articles read in our shop were published by the *Irish World*.

From my fellow-workers at Hirsch's I came to know more of the International Workingmen's Association. Many of them had been members abroad and deposited their cards with the local headquarters at Broome and Forsythe. Laurrell was a member of the local executive as was Fred Bloete, another cigarmaker, a magnificent man, kindly and big-hearted. He afterwards committed suicide. Karl Marx, the president, was then living in London, a refugee from Germany. His writings were a terrific indictment of society, couched in the terms in general usage in that chaotic period of the labor movement. Terms as Marx used them often had a very different meaning from what became fixed in later years. To understand Marx one must read him with an understanding of the struggle from the fifties to the seventies. Marx did not beguile himself into thinking the ballot was all powerful.

Perhaps the severest critic of Socialism was Karl Marx, and his denunciations of the Socialists in attacking trade unions has no superior even in our own time. He grasped the principle that the trade union was the immediate and practical agency which could bring wage-earners a better life. Whatever modifications Marx may have taught in his philosophical writings, as a practical policy he urged the formation of trade unions and the use of them to deal with the problems of the labor movement. Engels followed Marx's thought and urged those active in the International in New York to secure the co-operation of the trade unions at all hazards.

But the Lassallean program for political party action won over the militant economic program of Marx both in Germany and France. Then there developed another menace to the labor movement—the anarchists led by Bakounine [Michael Bakunin], who was aggressive and had been concerned in practically all continental revolutions since 1848. Marx realized that the anarchist group were about to control the International and succeeded in having headquarters moved from London to New York, preferring that the organization die on the Western continent rather than that it should become the instrumentality of anarchism. This transfer was made in 1873 when F. A. Sorge became the executive in charge of the disintegration that followed.

The International, in harmony with the Marxian fundamental of labor's solidarity, in 1873 adopted a resolution to further the formation of international trade unions. The furniture workers organized on this basis, and the National Labor Union was considering affiliation when the movement collapsed. I became much interested in the International, for its principles appealed to me as solid and practical—but I never joined, due to the influence of Laurrell who kept holding me back from alliance with any movement that had been associated with radicalism. Laurrell had been in the inner European circles of the International and knew more of its connections with European revolutions than was generally known. The injection of European quarrels into the I. W. A. demonstrated the necessity for an American movement under American control. His keen mind seemed to have grasped the fact that a new movement must be born out of the experiences of the old and that there must be leaders unhampered by past affiliations. So repeatedly he advised me: "Go to the meetings. Learn all they have to give, read all that they publish, but don't join."

At the meetings I met a group of the finest men it has ever been my good fortune to meet in any circle of life. Brainy men who reveled in life as a test of ability, men who dared as a matter of course. In that group was Fred Bolte of the cigarpackers—for years an executive of the American branch of the International. There was Conrad Carl the tailor, who had watched the transition of the tailor business from a skilled hand trade to a sweated industry, practically all machine work. One man who avoided public speaking, but who dominated every small-room conference, was David Kronburg. Kronburg was easily the master mind. I was attracted to him strongly, and we came to be fast friends. Kronburg had little patience with the Socialists who criticized the trade unions and urged radical action and political methods.

After a while I discovered meetings that were far more interesting than the open meetings of the International. These were the meetings or conferences of an inner circle which met also at the Tenth Ward Hotel. Out of the chaos of radicalism and revolutionary phraseology we were seeking principles that would bring opportunities for better living to fellow-workers. After a very busy and very serious discussion that lasted into the early hours of the next morning, Kronburg christened our group, *Die Zehn Philosophen* (The Ten Philosophers). But our interest went much deeper than academic discussions. It was a heart impulse that was a call to service. In a sort of mutual pledge, we dedicated ourselves to the trade union cause. From this little group came the purpose and the initiative that finally resulted in the present American labor movement—the most effective economic organization in the world. We did not create the American trade union—that is a product of forces and conditions. But we did create the technique and formulate the fundamentals that guided trade unions to constructive policies and achievements.

At these meetings in the Tenth Ward Hotel I often saw J. P. McDonnell—an ardent worker for Irish freedom who had spent several years in London in the office of Karl Marx.

P. J. McGuire, my old schoolmate at Cooper Union, was also a member of the International and a regular attendant of the meetings in the Tenth Ward Hotel. Pete was a fiery young orator with a big heart and as yet immature judgment. Others in the group were Fred Bloete, J. S. and Carl Speyer, Louis and Henry Baer.

From these men who were genuine revolutionaries in thought and in deed, men to whom principles meant something, I learned the fundamentals of the labor movement. They were men who did not hesitate to risk something to accomplish a purpose. They were alive in minds and bodies, and they did not find life dull or uninteresting. They were eagerly seeking new thought and new opportunity to bring about the betterment of their fellows. It is difficult for me to describe adequately what the New York labor movement during the seventies meant to me. There was a strikingly unusual group of brainy men of strong individuality—men not afraid to think and do even at a risk. They were eager seeking for truth. No idea, no suggestion was denied consideration. We were groping for principles with which to lay a foundation. Our minds were open, unhampered by dogmatism. In our hearts was courage for any effort. We were groping and crusading like the knights of old.

I Learn the Weakness of Radical Tactics

In 1873 began my experience with financial crises. The one that followed the Civil War occurred before I was old enough to watch with understanding. As a New York workman in 1873, I first watched the crisis and depression of what we now call the business cycle. During the summer of that year we heard rumors of pending financial troubles. The goldbugs were getting a tight clutch on the gold supply—and this the cigar manufacturers gave as their reason for dismissing the workers and reducing wages. The crash came in September when the Jay Cooke Company and Fiske and Hatch announced failure. The scenes downtown were wild on that rainy day.

Probably [labor's] first move came from the Arbeiter Union, or its official paper the *Arbeiter Zeitung*, suggested perhaps by the International or at least by members of the International. The Workingmen's Council followed quickly and these two organizations jointly worked out a plan including a mass meeting in Cooper Union December 11. Then the Spring Street Council pounced upon the dramatic possibilities of the situation [and] issued a circular.

Meanwhile the Tenth Ward, according to the plan of the *Arbeiter Zeitung*, had been divided into four sections and men sent out to take the census of unemployment. The same plan was followed in other wards. The result gave a definite basis upon which to form a plan for relief. The following fundamentals were endorsed by ward meetings and were urged upon the public: (1) employment for the unemployed on public works; (2) maintenance or money for at least one week for the needy while out of work; (3) Mayor and Governor to prevent evictions of unemployed because of failure to pay rent. This was frankly an emergency program—a prototype followed in practically every succeeding crisis until an effort was made to develop a constructive program in 1921.

The mass meeting authorized the appointment of a Committee of Safety—a name borrowed from the dreaded specter-conjuring agency of the French Revolution. Many street meetings followed to burn into the hearts of all tragic demonstrations of human need. The unemployed filled the city's streets and squares and marched to conferences with Aldermen and Mayor at the City Hall. It was a folk-movement born of primitive need—so compelling that even politicians dared not ignore. There is something about a marching folk-group that rouses dread. Those in authority did not rest comfortably. The press began hinting at the "Commune."

Meanwhile, plans were moving forward for a big out-of-door mass meeting in Tompkins Square on January 13, 1874. Mayor Havemeyer had promised to be present and to address the meeting.

Several times before that day groups of unemployed ranging from hundreds to thousands in numbers accompanied their spokesman to the City Hall. They remained outside listening to speakers, while suggestions were submitted to city authorities. Their physical presence gave urgency to their needs and demand for relief. The Police Commissioner granted a permit for the mass meeting and parade as far as Canal Street, thus protecting the City Hall from unpleasant personal contacts. This restriction blunted the effectiveness of the plan for the demonstration. Banks and McGuire protested but without avail. Elliott telegraphed to Governor Dix who declared he had no authority to intercede and referred the whole matter to the Mayor. The Mayor left all to the Police

Commission, which was controlled by a former associate of Boss Tweed. Dissension developed within the ranks of workingmen. The group of radicals, so-called Communists, saw in the situation an opportunity for propaganda. Propaganda was for them the chief end of life. They were prefectly willing to use human necessity as propaganda material. Practical results meant nothing in their program. This group got control by self-appointment to a provisional committee of the Safety Committee. They got money for their campaign from Mr. Kayser, ex-member of the Tammany ring. They issued circulars that had artistic and literary merit. They made speeches that contained good headline stuff. They painted the skies with "true" revolutionary plans and extravagant ideals.

Another group, representing the workingmen's unions, protested against demagogic methods and urged that relief for human beings was the real thing. The daily press played up the picturesque and made the city feel that Communists were in control and that they were on the verge of a revolutionary uprising. On the day before that set for the Tompkins Square demonstration, the Park Commissioners sent an order to the Police Commissioner forbidding the gathering because it "threatened public peace." The Police Commissioner sent an order to the Safety Committee demanding the return of the permit. But the Safety Committee was not to be found—none of them went to their homes that night.

But some of the labor men not on the Safety Committee, who learned of the situation, feared the results for those who would go to Tompkins Square the next morning. Laurrell was among this number. On the night of the twelfth he went to union meetings and, wherever he knew that working people would be gathered together, told them of the withdrawal of the permit and warned them against going to the Square on the morrow. That was not a pleasant task and required courage of a very real sort. As it was not generally known that the permit had been withdrawn, Laurrell was unjustly derided as a renegade.

Next morning people began assembling early in the Square. I reached the Square a little after ten. Soon the park was packed and all the avenues leading to it crowded. The people were quiet. There was nothing out of harmony with the spirit of friendly conferences between the chief public official and workless and breadless citizens. The gathering was planned as visible proof of suffering and destitution among New York unemployed. It was about 10:30 when a detachment of police surrounded the park. Hardly had they taken position before a group of workers marched into the park from Avenue A. They carried a banner bearing the words "TENTH WARD UNION LABOR." Just after they entered the park the police sergeant led an attack on them. He was followed by police mounted and on foot with drawn night-sticks. Without a word of warning they swept down the defenseless workers, striking down the standard-bearer and using their clubs right and left indiscriminately on the heads of all they could reach.

Shortly afterwards the mounted police charged the crowd on Eighth Street, riding them down and attacking men, women, and children without discrimination. It was an orgy of brutality. I was caught in the crowd on the street and barely saved my head from being cracked by jumping down a cellarway. The attacks of the police kept up all day long—wherever the police saw a group of poorly dressed persons standing or moving together. Laurrell went to Tompkins Square and received a blow from the police across his back, the effect of which remained with him for several months.

The next few days disclosed revolting stories of police brutality inflicted on the sick, the lame, the innocent bystander. Mounted police and guards had repeatedly charged down crowded avenues and streets. A reign of terror gripped that section of the city. They justified their policy by the charge that Communism was rearing its head.

The Tompkins Square outrage was followed by a period of extreme repression. The New York police borrowed continental methods of espionage. Private indoor meetings were invaded and summarily ended by the ejection of those present. The police frustrated several meetings held to protest against police brutality and in defense of the right of free assemblage for a lawful purpose.

I was in no way connected with the arrangement of this demonstration and was present as an intensely interested workingman and the import of the situation bore in upon me. As the fundamentals came to me, they became guide-posts for my understanding of the labor movement for years to come. I saw how professions of radicalism and sensationalism concentrated all the forces of organized society against a labor movement and nullified in advance normal, necessary activity. I saw that leadership in the labor movement could be safely entrusted only to those into whose hearts and minds had been woven the experiences of earning their bread by daily labor. I saw that betterment for working-

men must come primarily through workingmen. I saw the danger of en-
tangling alliances with intellectuals who did not understand that to experiment with the labor movement was to experiment with human life.
I realized too that many of those of the radical, revolutionary impatient
group were of the labor movement and just as sincere as many of those
whose judgment was more dependable. The labor movement is made
up of men and women of all sorts of natures and experiences. Their welfare depends on solidarity—one group cannot sit in judgment upon others or condemn publicly, but all must do what they can for mutural protection. Division is the great hazard of the labor movement.

Theodore Banks and P. J. McGuire followed a course in 1873 and
1874 that was not approved by constructive labor men—but they afterwards revised their understanding or concepts.

Conditions which in part shaped the happenings of January 13
were urging men in the various labor organizations in New York to unflagging search for something constructive. Within the International
were staunch trade unionists who wanted to start an American labor organization. Among these men were my friends Ferdinand Laurrell, David Kronburg, J. H. Monckton, M. J. McCloskey, George H. Forde, J.
Harvey, Joseph Allen, J. P. McDonnell, Fred Bolte, Karl Bertrand,
Robert Blissert. This group formed the Association of United Workers of
America which intended to further and promote trade unions. Laurrell
was a member of the first Federal Council of the Association.

The fundamentals which this organization endorsed were: "The
emancipation of the working class can be achieved through their own efforts and that emancipation will not bring class rule and class privileges
for them but equal rights and duties for all members of society. Economic betterment is the first step to the desired end; to its achievement
all political effort must be subordinated. Political action can be effective
only by constituting the labor class a separate political party. The emancipation of labor is not merely local or national, but is international."

Another group worked along a different line. They formed the
Social Democratic Party. The leaders were an insurgent group within
the old International, who rebelled against the domination of Section 1
which was almost wholly European in personnel and point of view. The
insurgents felt that an effort ought to be made to deal with specifically
American problems in ways devised to meet American needs. The
leader of this group was Adolph Strasser. Others were Hugh McGregor,

J. G. Speyer, and P. J. McGuire. In trying to unify the working people through a political party, Strasser and McGregor were experimenting with the Lassallean theory which they afterwards rejected. The experiment failed because the old dispute between the dogmatic Lassalleans and the Marxian trade unionists prevented the Social Democratic Party either from unifying the labor groups or from developing an agency that would serve the exigencies of American workingmen. It was not long before both Strasser and McGregor withdrew from the movement.

2

IN THE UNION CAUSE

1870–84

Building the American Trade Union

IN THE EARLY SEVENTIES the cigarmakers' organization was at very low ebb—at times its life seemed suspended. Of the labor unions that had developed before the War the majority were destroyed either during the War or the financial crises that followed. Such unions as survived were not fitted to cope with the changes that came in industrial scope or organization. There were no models to guide our trade unions.

In those early days the cigarmakers' organization was officered largely by western men, under the influence of the Chicago labor center where the policy of political action dominated. The development of the cigarmakers' organization was typical. It was an evolution in response to developing needs. Previous to the Civil War, cigarmakers were, as a rule, independent workmen. In every community where the demand for cigars was sufficient to warrant, the cigarmaker worked and sold his own cigars direct to the consuming public. Rarely did he employ helpers and then not more than one or two journeymen. If the journeyman became dissatisfied for any reason, he needed but small capital to become his own employer. During the Civil War the government imposed an internal revenue tax on cigar work, granted permits to employer and employes, and the factory was bonded. Through this system the small shops were driven out of existence and the factories developed.

In the sixties and seventies it was the general practice in the cigar industry of New York City to furnish stock to the cigarmakers and to demand a deposit of almost double the value of the tobacco furnished. Cigarmakers carried their stock home, made cigars in their own rooms, and brought back to the storehouse the completed cigars. At the storehouse more often than not fault would be found with the work whether justifiably or not, and the manufacturers would refuse to take the cigars which would be left upon the hands of the cigarmaker who would have to dispose of them as best he could. The usual custom was to sell them to the grocer, the butcher, the baker, or saloon-keeper, or whoever could be induced to give in exchange money or commodities.

With more stringent internal revenue laws the "turn-in-jobs," as that system was called, were done away with and the employer had to have some sort of factory. As many manufacturers thought they had an advantage in the mold and filler system under which practically unskilled workers could produce cigars, soon they added the tenement feature which was an entirely different method from the old home work or factory work. The manufacturers bought or rented a block of tenements and subrented the apartments to cigarmakers who with their families lived and worked in three or four rooms. The cigarmakers paid rent to their employer for living room which was their work space, bought from him their supplies, furnished their own tools, received in return a small wage for completed work sometimes in script or in supplies from the company store on the ground floor. The whole family—old and young, had to work in order to earn a livelihood—work early and late, Sunday as well as Monday. The system was degrading to employer and workman. It killed craft skill and demoralized the industry. With this situation in New York City and the regulations of the International Cigarmakers' Union prohibiting a union member from working with bunch-breakers, union membership was a very small proportion of the total number of cigarmakers. The membership of No. 15 was about 46;

of No. 90, about 85; of the International, 3771 in 1873. Drastic admission requirements excluded the workers.

In 1872 there appeared among the ranks of the labor movement in New York a man destined to have a tremendous influence—Adolph Strasser, a cigarmaker by trade, a Hungarian by birth, an organizer for the Social Democratic Party, a member of the Cigarmakers' Union. Strasser was a man of extraordinary mentality. He came to America some months before, traveling considerably through the South before settling in New York City. He had been identified with the I.W.A. and became a leader in American Section 5. Then for a while he was exceedingly active in the work of the Social Democratic Party. He shifted all his energy to the trade union movement, when he came to understand the unsoundness and impracticability of Socialist Party policy and philosophy or, as Strasser called it, "sophistry." He came into prominence in the union movement during the strikes of 1872, which grew out of the increased activity stimulated by the eight-hour movement. Strasser had a keen practical mind and did not allow precedent to restrict his ability to utilize constructive agencies. He became a member of our little union No. 15.

Late in 1872, under the leadership of Strasser and others from the International group at the Tenth Ward Hotel, a new cigarmakers' organization was started. This new organization was intended for those who were excluded by the admission requirements of the International, and it was to conform with the plan of the Workingmen's Association that was then thought to be truly international—that is, consisting of national divisions under a Central Council. This organization was later merged with another started by members of our union. Our plan was to reach those who were otherwise ineligible, thus to supplement the International as well as build it up. We called shop meetings and mass meetings of cigarmakers and finally launched the United Cigarmakers. The doors of this organization were open to all, regardless of sex, method or place of work, or nationality. The two main sections were Hungarian and German. We expected to add others and to merge with No. 15, thus forming an English section, and to co-ordinate the work of the three sections through a representative Central Council.

We got our undertaking endorsed by the state convention of the cigarmakers which met in Syracuse, March 1873. John Junio was presi-

dent at the time. Our local could not afford a delegate. Strasser attended
as the representative of the United Cigarmakers' Union [and] presented
urgently the needs of the cigar workers of New York City and urged that
every local be authorized to prescribe its own regulations and standards.
Though we did not realize it at the time, we were starting the revival of
the trade union movement. In September we sent a strong group of
nine delegates to the Detroit convention of the International to make a
fight for liberal changes in the constitution and to abolish the restrictions
that were preventing growth and development. The Detroit convention
gave local unions authority to permit their members to work in the same
shop with bunch-breakers, but not jointly with them or admitting them
to membership.

Despite the money situation and the financial crashes of that fall,
our organization meetings continued. Early in 1874 came a letter from
our International president, William J. Cannon of Cleveland, advising
and recommending to all unions to cancel all records of fines and loans
against union members and to build up the union by this method. We
found that the bankruptcy principle was not a stable basis for organization. Men must earn things in order to appreciate their real value. We
had to learn that unions must be maintained on the same basis of equity
essential for other human relations.

In the early summer we decided to try the co-operative principle. We were willing to try any method that offered reasonable possibilities for betterment. We were thus groping for something through local,
state, and national agencies. Developing one effort after another, we
sought to find how we could improve conditions for workers. Though
our co-operative store was in existence many years, it didn't solve our
problem.

Our educational propaganda gave so much publicity to the health
hazards of workers and consumers arising from badly regulated conditions in tenements, that the Board of Health could not refuse to take notice. The Chief of the Board directed that an investigation be made. The
report of this investigation was made public in the fall of 1874. To the
amazement of everybody it was a whitewashing report which endeavored to create the impression that tenements were superior dwelling
places. In our indignation, all the unions of New York met in protest in
public meetings against the outrageous attempt to conceal conditions
and facts that were dangerous to the health of the workers and users of

cigars. That rousing meeting inaugurated a campaign against tenement cigar manufacturing which lasted for more than ten years.

Meanwhile, things were going pretty badly with No. 15 which had benefitted but little from the organization campaign. E. Saqui was our corresponding secretary for several years and conducted practically all business done. Strasser, Laurrell, and I with a few others talked the situation over and decided upon the only practical course until the convention of the International Cigarmakers could change the membership provisions that excluded such a preponderance of cigarmakers in New York City. Our few members were to constitute a sort of holding company to safeguard our charter. Meanwhile, we set about organizing English in addition to German and Bohemian sections of the United Cigarmakers. We retained our membership in No. 15 in addition to membership in the new local. Owing to the progress that came during the spring and summer of 1875, we decided to reorganize all the cigarmakers of New York City in one local union, to dissolve the United Cigarmakers and to apply to the International for a new charter. We drafted a constitution which stated: "We recognize the solidarity of the whole working class to work harmoniously against their common enemy—the capitalists. We pledge ourselves to support the unemployed because hunger will force the best workmen to work for low wages. United we are a power to be respected; divided we are the slaves of capitalists." Our notion of democracy required that we furnish every member of the union with a copy of the constitution.

In the next meeting of the English section we voted to apply for a charter from the International. As I was president of the local, I wrote to International headquarters reporting the condition of our union. The letter was published in the official journal which had been authorized by the Paterson convention. It was one of the first of my literary productions that appeared in print. In that letter I stated: "One of the main objects of our organization is the elevation of the lowest-paid worker to the standard of the highest, and in time we must secure for every person in the trade an existence worthy of human beings."

A charter was granted to the local with the number No. 144, dated November 24, 1875.

We then set about developing machinery whereby our union could administer the affairs of cigarmakers. We decided that local authority should be vested in shop and district organizations. In each shop

where there were more than seven members of the union, a shop organization was to be formed with a president, vice-president, recording
and financial secretaries, collector, and delegates. The shop group was
to meet weekly. Cigarmakers in shops in which there were less than
seven union workmen were to be grouped in district organizations not
to exceed two hundred members. Regulations for their officers and
meetings were identical to those of the shop organizations. Delegates
from shop and district organizations together with the officers of No. 144
and its delegates to the Amalgamated Trades and Labor Union, the central body organized in 1877, were to constitute a Board of Administration, which should meet weekly to transact general union business. If
there was any decision reached by the Board of Administration, a demand by one-third of the delegates to the Board would refer the subject
to a referendum vote of the membership. No appropriation of money
above $25 could be made by the Board unless referred to the member-
ship.

There were regulations to prescribe the necessary procedure for
strikes. The union or groups of members could call a shop meeting and
submit a strike application which would be decided by secret ballot that
had to be reported by the shop president to the president of the union
on the same day. The president of the union should call a meeting of the
Board of Administration within three days. The Board voted by ballot on
all strike questions. If the Board approved the strike, it appointed a
Strike Committee to direct the strike.

Our plan attempted to meet a need that our fellow-tradesmen had
felt very keenly—the problem of finding employment. We proposed a
labor bureau to which employers and workers might send information of
work opportunities. Our type of organization which made the shop organization the basis, appealed to me as both democratic and practical. It
provided a way to deal with local matters that relieved general officers
and satisfied the desire for individual initiative subject to union sanction
and supervision.

In the spring of 1879 for the first and only time in my life I was
arrested. The cigarmakers at Kimball & Gaullieur's struck in July [and]
put their pickets in front of the shop. The company had a big burly policeman detailed "to protect the property." At that time I was president
of No. 144, and on my way to work in the morning I stopped to ask Sam
Elkins, one of the pickets, how things were progressing. As I was qui-

Shows the bonds he created in the union & his leadership

etly talking on the sidewalk, the policeman arrested me and Max Derby, who was with me. Justice Flammer fined Derby and me $10 each or ten days' imprisonment, refusing to delay examination until we could secure counsel. I would not have paid that fine if my life had depended on it, and so the alternate penalty of ten days' imprisonment began at once; I was put in the Tombs. Fortunately for the effect upon me, there was only one day of it. Kaufman Nickelsberg, a fellow-workman, had seen the arrest and carried word to my shopmates. As soon as they could get away, they went to the police court, found out my sentence and paid the fine.

The [International Cigarmakers] union grew slowly and steadily. It was a genuinely American trade union. During the first ten years the union uniformly elected me to some office, usually president or secretary, and delegate to local, state, and international conventions. When Strasser was chosen to fill a vacancy in the vice-presidency of the International we planned to utilize that connection for getting the principles we had evolved carried over into the trade organization. Slowly but steadily the influence of No. 144 began to go out. One of the first encouraging indications that came to us was the organization of a Cigarmakers' local in New Haven on the same basis as No. 144. Michael Raphael, an English cigarmaker and a fine type of man, was the leader in the New Haven movement. He was made an international officer in the next four years.

We made another step forward in organization that served to promote our idea of an American trade union. As I said, some of us had been in the habit of gathering at 10 Stanton Street where the headquarters of the customs tailors were. There was a back room upstairs over a saloon where we talked over the possibility of organizing a federated body of representatives of bona fide trade unions in New York. This was, I think, the first federated labor body to make trade unionism a prerequisite to membership. We took this plan up with members of locals and found such response that we decided to make the effort. There were, of course, both English and German central bodies, but these admitted representatives of other than trade union organizations, and we had become convinced that the labor movement must consist of trade unionists and be controlled by them. We had faith in the democratic theory that wage-earners understood their problems and could deal with them better than outsiders. We preferred to rely upon ourselves, make mistakes perhaps, but we could profit by them and thus advance along the road to knowledge and progress free to follow our best judgment. So, after vainly trying to unite the English- and German-speaking bodies, we organized the Amalgamated Trade and Labor Assembly, elected Joseph Wilkinson president, and Carl Speyer secretary. The organizations that sent representatives were the Customs Tailors' Union, the Cabinet-makers' Union, Typographical Unions Nos. 6 and 7, Fresco Painters, Cigar Packers' Unions Nos. 1 and 2, the Wood Carvers, the Varnishers, the Bootmakers, the French and German Cabinet-makers, Cigarmakers No. 144, and the Upholsterers' Union. Our membership fluctuated, but uniformly contained the strong trade unions of the city. It is important to note that the leaders in these unions were almost invariably trained in the school of the International Workingmen's Association, which taught the primary importance of economic organization.

Our activity did much to counteract the movement toward secret organization upon the supposition that the trade union was a failure. We tried to give other local unions information of the principles that were making No. 144 a success even under adverse conditions. The New York State Workingmen's Assembly recommended to all central bodies to secure copies of the constitution of the Amalgamated Trade and Labor Union. The objects of that organization we defined under five heads: to organize trade and labor unions; to promote the consolidation of all unions; to secure labor legislation; to secure and maintain a fair rate of wages; and to secure the shortening of the hours of labor. The constitution established as a fundamental requirement: "This Union shall consist of delegates (who shall be working at their respective vocations) regularly elected by the several organizations." Thus, from two approaches our group was developing the principles of trade unionism upon which the first real American trade union movement was to be grounded.

Our next move was to get a labor paper to promote the cause of trade unionism. There was in New York a weekly paper printed in English called *The Socialist*. It was the result of a fusion movement initiated by certain members of the old I. W. A.—A. Strasser, P. J. McGuire, J. P. McDonnell. By capturing this organ we trade unionists hoped to accomplish two points—to secure a going concern and to retard Socialistic activity. Hugh McGregor was editor of *The Socialist*—so we had friends on the paper and among leaders in the movement. McGregor's relation to this paper indicates the groping for something practical in a chaos of thought and terminology. McGregor was never a Socialist, but always a consistent individualist. Our trade union group gained control of the paper and changed the name to *Labor Standard* and made J. P. McDonnell editor. McDonnell remained identified with the *Labor Standard* as long as he lived and made it the spokesman for the trade union movement. The Amalgamated Trade and Labor Union also made the paper its official organ.

The Great Strike

To appreciate why the great strike of 1877 marked an important turning point in the history of the Cigarmakers' Union, it will be necessary to sketch over conditions preceding it. In the fall of 1875 we reopened our campaign to organize cigarmakers with a mass meeting in Concordia Assembly Rooms. [Yet] the year 1876 found the ranks of the Cigarmakers' Unions of New York almost depleted. Our membership had fallen to 1200 by 1875, and the strike of that year brought the total down to 500. Our wages averaged about twelve dollars a week. However, our craft had not suffered as seriously as the building trades which were turning to secret organization as their only defense.

It was this serious industrial situation which gave the greenback its popularity as an issue. The government was trying to get away from cheap money conditions. But wage-earners generally saw in contraction an elimination of money that served our purposes. As the labor unions began to lose numbers and power, wage-earners turned to political propaganda, hoping for relief. The National Labor Union decided to cooperate with the Independent Party. Peter Cooper was nominated for the presidency on a platform which demanded the repeal of the Specie Payment Act. I cast my second presidential vote for Peter Cooper, as did practically all the wage-earners of New York. In the years that followed I learned that cheap money was not the answer to labor or financial problems.

Despite discouragements, our effort to organize the cigarmakers kept bravely on. We held mass meetings regularly and kept up educational work by means of talks and circulars which we had printed in German, Bohemian, and English. The slogans we raised for the guidance of all were: "Unions for all working people." "Reduce the hours of work." "Bring worst paid workers to the level of the highest."

To compare our work with that of those who advocated a political

party, I went around one evening to a mass meeting of the Social Democratic Workingmen's Party to hear my old friend P. J. McGuire. He was
a fiery, eloquent talker, but his promises for the co-operative commonwealth did not appeal to me as I thought over our urgent situation in
New York. In contrast with the glorious promises which McGuire held
out, I saw the New York Legislature considering drastic legislation to injure wage-earners—such as the repeal of the eight-hour law and a Convict Labor Bill that would have intensified existing evils. We appointed
a committee to visit Governor Tilden and Mayor Wickham to present
our position and needs. Such experiences strengthened my conviction in
the economic work of my union.

During the summer of 1876 the unemployment situation grew
steadily worse. The city authorities selected that time to suspend improvements on public works. The workingmen protested against this
course as a harmful, cruel policy. In the fall of 1876, the seemingly impossible happened. Wages were again reduced, and working forces de-
creased. In December about two-thirds of the shops closed entirely, to
remain closed until sometime in January. The others dismissed more
than half their men and reduced wages. There were between five and
six thousand cigarmakers idle in New York City. I had been made president of No. 144, an office I was to hold through the coming months
which held important developments.

Mass meetings for organization and as unemployment demonstrations continued. We tried to organize discontent for constructive purposes. The crash that broke the months of strain came in the revolt of
the railroad workers in July 1877. That was in the pioneer period of rail-
roading. The railway unions were but fledglings. In fierce competitive
fights, railroad managements cut passenger and freight rates far below
the maintenance level. They were preparing to shift the resulting losses
upon their employes by wage cuts. In 1873, wages of railroad workers
had been reduced ten per cent; a similar wage reduction was announced
for June 1, 1877. Railroad officials had organized and united upon a uniform policy. They did not even consider consultation with their employes. They handed down an order that meant another ten percent reduction in the standards of living of their employes. Made desperate by
this accumulation of miseries, without organizations strong enough to
conduct a successful strike, the railway workers rebelled. Their rebel-
lion was a declaration of protest in the name of American manhood

against conditions that nullified the rights of American citizens. The railroad strike of 1877 was the tocsin that sounded a ringing message of hope to us all.

In New York we were stirred deeply. While we had put our faith in constructive methods, yet the sky of Pittsburgh reddened by fires started by company agents and desperate men denied all other recourse, brought us the message that human aspiration had not been killed or cowed. John Fortune, then president, and Strasser, secretary of our Amalgamated Trades and Labor Union, arranged for a mass meeting in Cooper Union to express our sympathy for the railroad strikers. That meeting was held on the evening of July 26. Though the heat was intense, several thousand men gathered. Resolutions which we adopted declared: "That it is the imperative duty of all workingmen to organize in trade unions and to the aid in the establishment of a national federation of trades, so that combined capital can be successfully resisted and overcome."

Heartened by the courage of the railway workers' protest against injustice, our union inaugurated a strike in the De Barry factory with a demand for higher wages—$6 a thousand, minimum. This initial contest lasted five weeks and was the first successful strike in many years. It brought the first real improvement in our trade. The next step was the strike which followed in the factory of M. Stachelberg & Company and was also successful. The cigarmakers of the entire city and vicinity were elated over our unprecedended victories. The same tactics in other organized shops were equally encouraging. Members began flocking into our union.

While this splendid forward movement was in progress in New York, the time came for the eleventh convention of the International Cigarmakers which met that year in Rochester. I was one of seven delegates who represented 17 local unions with a joint membership of 1016. Our first work was to draft a new constitution. I made suggestions based on our experience in New York which made me feel that if members were to be held in our union they must be offered practical benefits and that if the cigarmakers risked their welfare to be true to union labels the union ought to aid them if victimized. Outside New York, Detroit, and Chicago, there were 217 union cigarmakers in the United States and Canada. I proposed to establish out-of-work, sick, and traveling benefits. In New York we were convinced that the organization could retain a stable membership by offering them benefits that would make it worth their while to pay dues regularly. Trade unionism had to be put upon a business basis in order to develop power adequate to secure better working conditions. My resolution proposed a sick benefit for the members in good standing. This was laid on the table. I then moved that we provide out-of-work benefits on the same basis. This was defeated. Although not successful in securing the adoption of these provisions in that convention, we had begun the campaign of education necessary for their final establishment. I succeeded in helping to elect John L. Derr as first vice-president; John Burke, second vice-president. On the twelfth ballot Strasser was elected president.

When I returned to New York, I found that under the elation of victories gained by organized workers, the tenement house workers, made desperate by wage reductions, determined to take a chance. They all went out on strike without organization or discipline.

We union men saw our hard-earned achievements likely to vanish because of this reckless precipitate action without consultation with our union. The majority of tenement workers had contributed nothing to the up-building of labor conditions. They not only had not helped themselves, but they impeded our progress. Nor could they justify jeopardizing our welfare on the ground that we had neglected them, for our union had not only insisted upon liberal membership requirements in our own organization, but had fought for a more liberal policy in the International.

Organized labor has often been criticized for not jeopardizing its whole organization to rescue the unorganized or the "unskilled" workers as our critical friends diplomatically term them. That which labor's adverse critics define as "unskilled labor" is really unorganized labor. There are now a large number of workers who formerly were regarded as unskilled but who have been organized. Standards of work, wages, and hours have been so far improved that these critics no longer refer to them as "unskilled."

As I look back over the years I have spent in the service of the labor movement and review the various groups of workers that have been designated as unorganizable because unskilled, lack of organization stands out clearly as due wholly to lack of courage, lack of persistence, lack of vision. Every occupation calls for skill. There may be a difference in degree, but that is largely individual. The more knowledge a man has, the more efficient he becomes as a workman—whether his occupation be that of ditch-digger or engineer. The so-called skilled trades had to go through the same struggle to secure organization as any other group. In truth, those of us who helped to build pioneer organizations fought a fight of intensity and desperation little dreamed of in this modern period when labor organizations have achieved standing and power.

No. 144 had only $4,000 in the treasury when the general strike broke upon us. Our Executive Committee urged that those still employed in the "better condition" factories and tenement houses remain at work and contribute ten per cent of their earnings to the support of those on strike and that if victory came there would be little or no difficulty in securing improvements for those who remained at work in the meantime. But despite all suggestions, men and women just scampered pell-mell out of the tenements and out of the workshops so that we had nearly all the workers on strike. After the precipitate beginning of the strike, we tried to inject organization by providing that cessation of work should be followed at once by shop meetings in which delegates should be elected to represent them in the central organziation which was to direct the strike. These delegates met in Concordia Hall and formed the Central Association of Cigarmakers under Strasser's general leadership. When our Committee met the next afternoon, we found the bosses had locked out hundreds of cigarmakers, so we voted a general strike in the trade and began to plan how to take care of the strike. Few had savings—wages were too low for that.

The plan upon which we conducted that campaign was used as a prototype for many another large scale struggle. After we pledged the funds of the union unreservedly in support of the strike, we sent a circular letter to all members of the craft. The response was unexpectedly good, and in many cities those to whom we addressed circulars called upon other members of the trade to meet with them so as to raise funds for transmittal to our strikers. The result of these men gathering together began a movement for the establishment of local unions of cigarmakers in many of these centers. This revival of organization activity spread to other trades.

We held almost continuous meetings of strikers in order to get them to join the union, to maintain morale, and to have centers from which to issue directions as to the conduct of the strike. In order to take care of the physical needs of the strikers we established provision kitchens or relief stores from which we distributed food and money—chiefly food, which we purchased wholesale. At first we attempted to supply medical assistance, but as the weeks of the strike increased in number, and the pinch of want became very keen, it finally became necessary to diminish and then discontinue even the provision kitchen. Meyer Dampf was chairman of the committee to deal with the rent problem. Day and night he was busy, for more than anything else the strikers were anxious to keep roofs over their heads. On October 24, the employers brought into action a terrible weapon when Straiton & Storm evicted workers from ten tenements. We had been trying to guard against this catastrophe by helping with rent payments, but our resources could not keep pace with the demands made on them. The union rented more than a hundred rooms for evicted strikers, but could not provide for all. Every few days the tenement house employers brought dispossession proceedings against new groups of employes. The distress that followed was appalling.

We worked out an extraordinarily effective picket system during the strike. The pickets were under the command of Walter Smith and were given directions exact as military orders and instructed to keep within the law. Each had his definite field where he stayed until relieved and was required to make report at the end of duty. By the middle of October there were about fifteen thousand men and women on strike. In shouldering responsibility for this movement of undisciplined workers our few hundred organized cigarmakers had to bear the brunt of it all. The Amalgamated Trade and Labor Union gave us support and co-operation. As a result of the strike, trade unionists began to see the need of a Central Trade Agency and several more unions joined the Amalgamated.

Another strategic factor in our campaign was the factory we undertook to operate. M. M. Smith was unable to operate his large factory on Vesey Street. Our Central Committee made overtures to the firm to take over the factory and place about seven hundred cigarmakers at work and pay for it a percentage of the workers' wages. When the proposition was submitted to the union the men accepted it upon one condition—that I act as the superintendent and foreman. They placed the salary at $12 a week. I had at that time what was regarded as a good job at Hirsch's. I had been earning about $18 per week, but I quit my job to take the position. We rented the two buildings adjoining Smith's, threw the three buildings together, and employed twenty-four hundred workers. This undertaking was not a co-operative one in the sense of profitsharing. It was a collective action to furnish employment and strike funds. The whole project was entered into as a strategic move to get a number of cigarmakers at work to help to contribute toward sustaining themselves and those who were still out on strike.

Just before Christmas came a new offensive—a staggering one. A number of firms locked out their workmen who had been the financial backbone of the strike. The strike slowly crumbled away. It was a wonderful fight. I shall never forget the heroic sacrifices made and the burdens borne by the men and women engaged in that struggle. Although we did not win, we learned the fundamentals and technique which assured success later. The strikers had to go back wherever they could find employment and were welcomed by employers who had learned the value of skilled workmen.

The Cigar Manufacturers' Association had declared that under no circumstances would any leaders of the strike be employed for at least six months. As a consequence, for nearly four months I was out of employment. Blacklisted, I desperately sought employment, going home at night where my brave wife prepared soup out of water, salt, pepper, and flour. One night when there was no food in the house and our little girl was very ill I returned home to find a fellow-worker, Jack Polak, had called and offered my wife $30 a week for three months if she would persuade me to give up the union and return to work. I turned to my wife and said, "Well, what did you tell him?" My wife, indignant at the question answered: "What do you suppose I said to him with one child dying and another coming? Of course I took the money." Stunned by the blow I fell in a chair. My wife, all tenderness and sympathy, seeing I didn't understand exclaimed: "Good God, Sam, how could you ask such a question? Don't you know I resented the insult?" Occasionally, my wife suggested the commissary—but I refused that help, for I wanted to fight my own way.

A job was found for me with Matthew Hutchinson on Greenwich Street. Hutchinson employed about twenty-five men, and he made it a practice to mingle among them and listen to their discussions. He heard the men telling a story of the victimized leaders and stating that there was a combination among the bosses. Hutchinson, who talked very emphatically, said to the men: "Who in hell says that the bosses have combined? I haven't combined and I will employ whom I please and to hell with the others if they combine. Tell Gompers to come here and I will give him a job."

In those young days I was full of fire and dreams and burning with sentiment, and I might have followed any course or associated myself with any movement that seemed to promise freedom for my pals and fellow-workers. It was the wise counsel of my friend Laurrell that saved me: "Never permit sentiment to lead you, but let intellect dominate action."

I was heavily in debt, and most of the valuable trinkets that I owned including the gold and diamond-studded medal presented to me by the Court Empire City of the Ancient Order of Foresters had been pawned. I continued my activity in the union and for my fellow-workers, but the responsibility of my family forced itself upon me, and after consultation we decided that we would move to Williamsburg (now Brooklyn) about three blocks from the Havermeyers' sugar refinery. Of course, it would have been impossible for me to leave the union, for the principles which had been ingrained in me could never have been taken out of my soul, but I believed that after the years that I had given to our cause it would be necessary for others to take on the burdens and responsibilities of active service. I could not wholly disregard the wife and six children who were dependent upon me, and so I imagined myself in part separated from the active work in the movement. Each morning I walked from the house to the Grand Street Ferry, crossed by ferry to New York, and walked to the factory and in the evening returned by the same way. I stayed away from one meeting of the Board of Administration of the union, and perhaps I never passed a more uncomfortable week. The second week I went to the union meeting. I could not go home to supper, and so I had to buy some sort of a meal in New York. I went to the meeting, a discussion arose, an important committee was to be appointed, and the president appointed me as chairman of the committee. I could not refuse. I reached home about two o'clock in the morning, and a few hours later I went to work. And so it continued until nearly every evening kept me away from home, involving the expense of eating in restaurants and unfitting me for the work in the factory. I saw that the situation was hopeless, went home one Sunday morning and concluded it was no use; we moved back to New York, and if possible, with more zest and energy re-entered the struggle which has continued ever since. That, in my opinion, was the turning point of my life.

Building an International Trade Union

The Cigarmakers' International Union is now one of the most democratically conducted bodies to be found anywhere. It was developed by men who really believed in democracy. The development of this democratic structure began with the presidency of Strasser in 1877 and is the result of the wider application of the principles of trade unionism developed by our New York local. We made of the International an organization controlled and conducted by the membership with the initiative and referendum, not only in all legislation of the organization, but the nomination and election of candidates for international offices by the members. The proposal of changes in the constitution and even resolutions adopted by conventions must be approved by our membership before they become effective.

When the great strike of 1877 ended in a compromise, manufacturers, worn out with poor workmanship, were glad to discharge strike breakers and hire skilled union workmen. Though we did not win the standards for which the strike of 1877 was made, yet we re-entered working relations with a sense of power that struggle develops. We were not the same men. Up to that time our cigarmakers' union was an organization in name only. There was no uniformity in dues or initiation fees. Strike benefits were paid if there chanced to be money. Strikes were inaugurated without authority or formality. Wages varied in the same town—in fact from shop to shop. There were no accepted methods and principles for trade unions. Our ideas were hazy. In truth, we had no trade union vocabulary.

Our union was a great deal more than a militant organization. As we studied our trade problems and tried out policies for bettering conditions for cigarmakers, we soon found that we had to understand our industry as a whole. Trade agreements were made early in the cigar industry. The procedure was very simple. Our union drew up a bill of prices and submitted it to the employer. If he accepted, the transaction was complete; if he refused, we undertook to negotiate an agreement. If we failed, a strike or lockout resulted.

A problem which demanded our thought from the beginning was how to stabilize the union and retain progress achieved. I saw clearly that we had to do something to make it worthwhile to maintain continuous membership, for a union that could hold members only during a strike period could not be a permanent constructive and conserving force in industrial life. The union must develop within itself cohesive forces that would make for continuous effort. I gathered all the information I could get on the benefits provided by the British trade unions. I saw that our problem was different from that with which the English had to deal, in that militancy must dominate until we established our right to represent the workers of our craft in making trade agreements. An out-of-work benefit, provisions for sickness and death appealed to me. Participation in such beneficent undertakings would undoubtedly hold members even when payment of dues might be a hardship.

As I have related, I proposed a system of benefits to the first cigarmakers' convention I attended. The next convention met in Buffalo in 1879. Again I was a delegate. There were only eleven delegates present, for our organization was still at low ebb. Developing financial strength was the foundation of stable unionism. Cheap unionism we were convinced did not contribute to stability or effectiveness. The British Engineers' Association had a method that served as a cohesive force throughout the organization. This practice provided a periodic equalization of funds. This was among the features included in the early plan I worked out and to which I finally converted Strasser. This plan together with the establishment of traveling, sick, and death benefits Strasser recommended to the convention, but they were not adopted until 1880.

I proposed that we consider providing for uniform dues and benefits for all members. These motions were referred to the Committee on Constitution of which I was the chairman. Our Committee recommended to the convention constitutional changes providing uniform dues of ten cents a week and initiation fee, traveling benefits, annual equalization of funds among all unions, a sinking fund on the basis of fifteen cents for each member and twenty-five cents for each newly initiated member, a traveling loan system. As protection to the benefits proposed we recommended that every union obtain permission from the Executive Board before inaugurating a strike.

The convention accepted our report, and the constitutional amendments then went to a referendum vote. Under the proposed equalization system the central office retained a fixed sum for operating expenses, and each local retained funds in proportion to membership. All in excess of these amounts was to be distributed among unions whose resources had been depleted by strikes or other unusual expenditures. The system provided mutual bearing of burdens. Because it was so fundamentally democratic, the proposal aroused opposition, but was finally adopted and is in effect at the present time.

Two other proposals which I submitted to the convention were adopted: that our International constitution be printed in German as well as English, and that our Executive Board be directed to communicate with other nationals and internationals to promote unity of organization and identity of purpose.

The convention re-elected Strasser as president, and we felt that we were starting on a period of splendid endeavor. There were substantial reasons for our belief. We had made a beginning in getting the trade union movement on a solid foundation; we had a publicity agency for that movement, and an effort was under way to unite the trades in a federated organization. We had found the way out of chaos of thought and method.

The loaning system under which journeymen traveling from one place to another could get an advance of money to buy railroad tickets, which had been abolished in the panic of 1873, was restored in 1879. The following year we succeeded in getting a sick and death benefit established. Amounts paid under these benefits were increased from time to time.

In September 1880, the Cigarmakers' International Union convention met in Chicago. The Buffalo Convention had adopted the rule of annual conventions—a custom too expensive to be maintained. I introduced a resolution which was adopted, asking the local unions to instruct their delegates to the next convention to vote upon biennial conventions.

The following proposal of mine that—"No local union shall permit the rejection of an applicant for membership on account of sex, color, or system of work"—held up the convention for three days, and at last to insure the declaration I felt myself compelled to agree to a compromise that the question of system of work be left to the discretion of local unions.

In the early history of our International union, any local union could go on strike of its own volition. It had the right to appeal to the Executive Board for approval, but that body had no power of disapproval. Under that old method, half or more than half of the members of the trade over the country might be on strike at one and the same time and thus prevent anything like financial support to those engaged in the dispute, thus inviting general defeat instead of securing general co-operation.

It was a sort of crusading spirit that sustained many of us in those early days. We placed the cause of labor before everything else—personal advancement, family, comfort, or anything. A fitting accompaniment to that adventurous period were the itinerant workers, tramp workmen or "hoboes" as they were called. The hoboes were really the early organizers of the International. Like the journeymen of the medieval guilds, they moved from place to place carrying the gospel of unionism throughout the industry. The International provided for the unemployed fifty cents and railroad fare, to the nearest town containing a union shop. Many hoboes would make the convention city a rendezvous. They knew that the delegates of necessity had some money, and they worked their game to the fullest. They always had their traveling cards and loan books, but these had been used to the limit. As they could get no additional loans, they would panhandle the delegates.

In September 1891, our Cigarmakers' Convention met in Indianapolis. Again I was serving Union No. 144 as delegate. The Indianapolis Convention was extremely well disciplined and hard working. One of the important decisions of the convention was the adoption of a constitutional amendment providing for the election of the officers by the initiative and referendum. The plan for electing International executives, with slight amendments to reduce expenses, has remained in force until the present time. Strasser at first opposed the proposal, but finally when an amendment was made that voting should be made compulsory declared himself in accord with the proposal.

It was in that convention that Strasser resigned. George W. Perkins was elected president and I, first vice-president, an office to which I have been re-elected ever since. Perkins was a tried and proven trade unionist, and the constructive work of the International continued without interruption.

Our organization held no convention from 1896 to 1912. Through

[handwritten annotation: Created a large beaurocray, thing go out of hand. Blamed Socialist]

the initiative and referendum the work of the organization went forward and officers were nominated and elected. Later, we began to find that the direct method of legislation had defects. We found that quite a number of local unions, particularly where Socialist Party organizations existed and influenced them, would vote upon a proposal, and then record the vote of the entire membership as if every member of the organization had voted one way. This was also true in the election of officers. This practice prevailed in the sixteen years elapsing between the conventions to which I have referred. Socialist publications, Socialist organizers and propagandists spread the poison of hatred and discontent, thus weakening confidence in the integrity of the officers of the International union. The Socialists in our organization formed an inner clique for the purpose of controlling elections and votes upon legislation. They were particularly industrious in discrediting trade unionists and in trying to tear down the reputations of those who were working hardest for the trade union movement.

When the Baltimore Convention opened in 1912, the minds of two-thirds of the delegates were so embittered against the officers that they would have been willing to disrupt the organization. After several days of the convention proceedings when the delegates observed the difference between the course pursued, the propositions made, the discussions of the real trade unionists, and the Socialists, the disaffected group changed their judgment and the convention came to a harmonious close. With the lack of opportunity for full and free discussion of union affairs under the initiative and referendum, and with other defects and the lack of proper machinery for the due observance of the rights of candidates, I am free to say that the confidence we had in the initiative and referendum within the unions became less pronounced than it was in the beginning.

In 1921, our convention was held in Cleveland. The interval of thirty years between the first and the second Cleveland Conventions afforded a basis for estimating progress. The results of my observation were gratifying as I tested the stability and constructiveness of our work. Our union had become a permanent factor in industrial organization. Our statistics showed that the average life of the cigarmakers had been materially lengthened.

I look back over the years of work for my trade, and I rejoice in the conviction that the bona fide trade union movement is the one great agency of the toiling masses to secure for them a better and higher standard of life and work.

Learning Something of Legislation

It was early in the seventies when we cigarmakers of New York City discovered the influence of tenement production. This was a problem of a different nature from those with which our union had been dealing. As the well-being not only of cigarmakers but cigar users was concerned, we felt that the problem involved public policy and hence should be dealt with by legislation.

First, as I have related, we tried to get Federal restriction under the taxing power of Congress. Several congressmen, including Abram S. Hewitt, thought Congress had power to place a prohibitive tax on tenement-made goods. Our first years of agitation were concerned with showing the harmful consequences of tenement manufacture. Industrial hygiene was then a new field. We had to teach the public the relation between sanitary work conditions, health of workers, and the spread of contagious diseases. When we began our agitation, even the Health Department thought we were fanatics.

We secured the introduction of an amendment to the Revenue Law to prohibit the manufacture of cigars in tenements. Strasser went to Washington to present the reasons for the amendment. He succeeded in getting its adoption in the House. Pinkney White of Maryland advocated the bill in the Senate, but that body voted to strike out our amendment. When the information reached us in New York, we quickly arranged an indignation meeting for Cooper Union. This setback to our purpose determined us to seek for another method. We then concentrated on securing state legislation.

After years of educational work, in 1881, our union inaugurated an intensive effort to get a state law. We persuaded a member of each house of the Legislature to act as sponsor for our bill, and at the same time kept labor men in Albany, not only to watch the legislative situation, but to advise the labor movement of developments so that the legislators might constantly be made aware that their constituents were interested in the tenement-house bill. As Strasser's office was still in New

York, our effort had the full backing of the International. In fact, we considered that we were taking the initiative for the International in a local effort which was of concern to all.

In order to inform the public I arranged with the *New Yorker Volkszeitung* for the preparation and publication of a survey of the tenements in which cigars were made. I made the survey. In order to gain admission to the apartments of the workers, I assumed the role of a book agent, providing myself with a set of Dickens. Knowing the financial and cultural conditions of the Bohemian tenements, I knew I would not be embarrassed by making many sales. None of them recognized me. Once inside an apartment I asked questions and quickly made observations. The ignorance of those Bohemians at that time was appalling. They had been isolated in life and work, rarely venturing outside the Bohemian colonies. In later years, when the cigarmakers' trade unions were able to break down the barriers that prevented Americanization of these Bohemians, they made magnificent American citizens and able trade unionists. Some of my questions led them to suspect me of being a Health Inspector, but despite suspicion, ignorance, and indifference I elicited facts, and prepared detailed reports on the various tenements, which were published serially in the *New Yorker Volkszeitung*, beginning October 31, 1881.

When the time for the election of Senators and Assemblymen came that fall, we realized the importance of seeing to it that men in sympathy with our tenement legislation were elected to office and that those who helped to prevent the passage of our bill were defeated. We knew that if we did not force home upon the "consciences" of politicians the importance of legislation to abolish tenements, our bill would never be enacted into law. We knew that the conscience of the law-makers resided in the ballot box. The way to arouse a politician's conscience lay in the organized use of ballots. We sent communications to all unions in the state, urging them to take effective action to promote this measure.

When Edward Grosse, the man who had introduced our first tenement house bill came up for re-election, we supported him. As a member of Typographical No. 7 and an active member of the old International Workingmen's Association, he was well known in labor circles even though he had become a member of the bar. He had taken the initiative in the educational campaign necessary to secure consideration of the bill by the Legislature. We called a public meeting to give Grosse an opportunity to state his position and policy before the workingmen. A number of Socialists, who came to the meeting to make trouble, repeatedly interrupted him. As they failed to break up the meeting, they finally withdrew.

The Socialists who were then thronging to New York were in marked contrast to the trade union Socialists who belonged to the old International and who were sincere in their desire to bring betterment into the lives of the workers. The great majority were Germans "exiled" under the Bismarckian rule. They were fanatics who believed in partisan political methods exclusively, for German Socialism was under the spell of Lassalle despite the counsel of Karl Marx. They preferred to see evils continue rather than see remedies from any other agencies than those prescribed by Socialism. The "party" was a fetish. In the fall of 1881 their obstructive tactics became a menace to our legislative hopes. Though the Socialist Party nominated no ticket that fall, it forbade its members to support the candidates of other parties. They were advised to stay away from the polls even though it was well known that the enactment of labor legislation was imperative in the cigar and other industries. They were willing to see the cigar industry absorbed by tenement-house production unless that fate could be averted by Socialism. This was the folly against which trade union cigarmakers had to contend for several years.

We made progress in the New York Assembly with our tenement bill. A young Assemblyman from New York City, Theodore Roosevelt, who was serving his first term, was conspicuous even at that time. I had met young Roosevelt while in Albany lobbying for the bill. He became interested in the measure and told me that if the conditions described really existed he would do everything in his power to help to secure the passage of the bill. Although he was what we called a "silk stocking," his aggressiveness and evident sincerity appealed to me. I offered to show him through the tenements, and he accepted my offer. Roosevelt was convinced and he made good his declaration. Our bill passed the Assembly, and got on the docket in the Senate. In the closing hours of the Legislature, a member called for consideration of the bill. It was significant that this member had been elected over an opponent of the bill in the previous Legislature. The clerk looked in the file where the official copy should have been, but the space was empty. The search continued, but meanwhile the legislative situation altered so that no action could be had.

The next year Senator Grady, a Tammany man, introduced bills to regulate convict labor and the manufacture of cigars in tenement houses. The Amalgamated appointed to co-operate with him a standing committee consisting of Lynch, McKenzie, Strasser, Eberhard, Salty, Gompers. The results of our political work were apparent in the presence of labor members in the Legislature. We had three trade unionists in that Assembly, David Healy (printer), Joseph Delehanty (textile worker), Godfrey Ernst (printer). This gave us direct representation, competent to advance our cause and keep us informed. Strasser was in Albany at least one day a week, and I was there once or twice a week. Our bill passed the Senate with one dissenting vote and the Assembly by a vote of 84 to 20.

The tenement cigar manufacturers were working hard also. They sent men with petitions among the tenement workers to get signatures to the statement that tenements were better than shops. Of course they got signatures among those whose employment they controlled, many of whom did not know enough English to understand what they were signing. The tenement manufacturers went *en masse* to Albany to urge Governor Cleveland not to sign the bill. Cleveland designated March 8 for a hearing on the measure. Both sides were well represented at the hearing. The tenement-house cigar manufacturers' associations were represented by Rufus H. Peckham and Morris S. Wise as counsel. In favor of the bill Senators Thomas F. Grady and James Fitzgerald and Assemblymen Theodore Roosevelt and George Roesch. Governor Cleveland sat stolidly as arguments pro and con were placed before him. He gave no indication of his opinion at the time, but on March 12 approved the bill. To celebrate this victory after ten long years of struggle, the Amalgamated arranged a jubilee demonstration for Cooper Union which was a tremendous, inspiring success. As a result of our method of political action, labor also secured from the 1883 session of the Legislature the abolition of hat making by convict labor and a law providing for the establishment of a Bureau of Labor Statistics.

Securing the enactment of a law does not mean the solution of the problem as I learned in my legislative experience. The power of the courts to pass upon constitutionality of law so complicates reform by legislation as to seriously restrict the effectiveness of that method.

The manufacturers shortly found a test case and employed William M. Evarts. The decision of the court declared our law unconstitutional. We found our work was nullified. The court had evaded the heart of the issue. There was no difficulty in getting a sponsor for our measure in the Legislature. All legislators were familiar with the case and cause. We met the check imposed by the court quickly and in a constructive way. Our machinery was still intact. A new bill passed the Legislature and was signed by the Governor in May 1884. The tenement-house manufacturers again carried the law into court.

In October the Supreme Court declared this second enactment null and void. The case was then appealed to the Circuit Court of Appeals. After the Appeal Court declared against the principle of the law, we talked over the possibilities of further legislative action and decided to concentrate on organization work. Through our trade unions we harassed the manufacturers by strikes and agitation until they were convinced that we did not intend to stop until we gained our point and that it would be less costly for them to abandon the tenement manufacturing system and carry on the industry in factories under decent conditions. Thus we accomplished through economic power what we had failed to achieve through legislation.

Following the Socialist demonstration against Edward Grosse, they held a meeting of their own in a neighboring saloon. Such meetings were repeated until they became an established practice and suggested secession. Because we were trade unionists and they Socialists and we had frustrated their attempts to convert the union into a Socialist body, they denounced us in the most abusive terms. The differences between the trade unionists and the Socialists made the semi-annual election of officers of No. 144 a very tense episode.

The election came early in the spring of 1882. We trade unionists felt rather apprehensive of the future as the unruly Socialist element increased in numbers. The candidates for the presidency were Pfrommer and Schimkowitz. The latter was a loud-talking German-American who was a politician by inclination and practice. He had been actively identified with the Socialist Labor Party and all manner of Socialist propaganda and had heartily endorsed the independent labor policy of the Central Labor Union, a new central body that had been organized. I had never regarded him as a bona fide labor man. In the election campaign it was freely charged that he operated a shop employing from one to five men and therefore was not a wage-earner and consequently ineligible to any office or even membership in the union. When the report of the election was made to our Board of Administration, there were conflicting claims—one group declared for Schimkowitz; the other for Pfrommer. Since there was also a doubt as to the eligibility of Schimkowitz, the question was referred to the International president.

Strasser made inquiries at the office of the Internal Revenue Department and also at Schimkowitz's place of business and held him ineligible to the office. This decision was transmitted to our Executive Board, and the vice-president called a special meeting. From the first it was evident there could not be an agreement. No one room could have been large enough for the two rival groups to function peacefully. Frequent altercations occurred—or rather were provoked to furnish excuse to call in police protection. Fifteen policemen were brought in by the Socialists to maintain peace. No action could have been better calculated to render adjustment of differences impossible. The leaders of the dissension all were found guilty and suspended for one year, as was Schimkowitz. The seceders notified cigarmakers to pay dues meanwhile to their treasurer and tried in every way possible to substantiate claims to the name and the authority of Union No. 144. They made a very clever imitation of our seal and carried on dual activities that were purposely confusing even to those who wanted to follow the regular organization. However, one strategic necessity the Socialists had failed to control. When they began their fight, we let them spar for control in the conspicuous field and concentrated our effort on retaining the sinews of strength—the treasury and legal authorization—the charter. We trade unionists won the first scrimmage. Then the Socialists preferred charges against President Strasser and demanded his immediate suspension.

The charges preferred against Strasser were sent to the first vice-president of the International, Fred Blend. He declared that the request to suspend Strasser was out of reason and unjustifiable and suggested that their remedy lay in an appeal from the president's decision to the Executive Board. He then wrote to Strasser and suggested that the Executive Board go to New York and investigate the situation. This suggestion Strasser vetoed as he had determined upon no compromise. Strasser had been brutally frank with the Lassalleans, but he knew their tricks and unscrupulous antics. He knew it was useless to spend time in trying to reach an agreement. The Executive Board yielded to bad judgment and consented to allow the Socialist faction in the controversy to pay the expenses of the Board's trip to New York to hear the charges. The Board was really anxious to restore unity in New York and gave advice which might have been good had the Schimkowitz faction been actuated by union motives.

The Executive Board made an *ex parte* investigation without securing a statement from the International president. Nor did they seek information of No. 144 and then render a decision accordingly.

It was generally supposed that Mr. Blend, who at one time was International president, had an ambition to return to that office, and inasmuch as the constitution of the International Union provided that the Executive Board's business should be transacted by mail or telegraph and made no provision for any Executive Board meeting, the only deduction was that an attempt to hold an Executive Board meeting under the direction of Mr. Blend was without any warrant of law and could not be and was not recognized. Every effort for conciliation was approved by us, but an attempt to over-ride our constitution and exercise of the duties of International president was effectively opposed. So there the matter stood, and the disrupters launched a rival union to No. 144 and undertook to establish a national organization in rivalry to our International union. A few local unions and several members of the International unions went over to the seceders. They maintained their organization for some time, but because of their small number and their low dues, they were unable to meet their obligations and carry on their work.

3

A NATIONAL
ORGANIZATION IN THE
MAKING

1880–1900

LOOKING BACKWARD I appreciate the significance of a little group called the Economic and Sociological Club. Our club was in reality a group of trade unionists who banded together for the purpose of extending and defending the principles of trade unionism. Each of us had his group of personal friends in which he wielded influence, so that the club served as a practical clearing agency in the development of trade union understanding. Without the slightest disparagement upon the active men in the earlier movements of labor—for I know that many of them were earnest and self-sacrificing—it was pointed out in our "talk" that there were altogether too many labor men who, having grown to some degree of prominence and having demonstrated their ability to serve their fellows, had been lured and weaned from the labor movement. Some had been elected or appointed to public office, others had entered business, and it must be borne in mind that at that time there were few salaried officers in the labor movement who were paid for services rendered.

65

The loss of these leaders had a most depressing effect upon workers and often resentful expressions were made by the unorganized.

Realizing this situation as an actual fact injuriously affecting the efforts to organize the workers, our group developed the thought and agreed: "Let us without any formality pledge to each other and to ourselves that under no circumstances will we accept public office or become interested in any business venture of any character or accept any preferment outside of the labor movement." In other words, that we would devote our entire activity and influence to the labor movement and in furtherance of the interests and welfare of the toiling masses. Perhaps the names of a few of the other members of that group may be of more than passing interest: Hugh McGregor (jewelry worker), David Kronburg, Conrad Carl (tailor), Fred Bloete (cigarmaker), J. P. McDonnell (printer), Fred Bolte (cigar packer), Ferdinand Laurrell (cigarmaker), Louis Berliner (cigarmaker), Henry Baer (cigarmaker), George Steiberling (cigarmaker), J. H. Monckton, Carl Speyer (cabinet-maker), Edward Speyer (printer), Edward Grosse (printer), James Lynch (carpenter). George E. McNeill and Ira Stewart of the eight-hour movement were very close to our group, though they placed more confidence in political activity than did we.

It was this little group that refused to subordinate the trade union to any "ism" or political "reform." We knew that the trade union was the fundamental agency through which we could achieve economic power, which would in turn give us social and political power. We refused to be entangled by Socialist partyism, not only because we realized that partisan political methods are essentially different from those of industry, but because legislation could affect the lives of men at work in a very few points—and those not vitally important for progressively improving conditions.

Some of our club, Kronburg and McDonnell, had tried to organize a national labor movement—the United Workers of America. The next effort toward national organization was the International Labor Union. Several members of our club initiated the effort. The movement failed of its national purpose and became an organization of textile workers. The suggestions for action to effect national amalgamation came from many groups and sources. The International Typographical Union undertook sustained work to promote such action. In 1879 the convention instructed its corresponding secretary, William White of New York, to open communication with the various international unions to ascertain views as to the feasibility of forming an international amalgamated union. The results of this correspondence were referred to a special committee by the next convention. L. A. Brandt reported to the next convention which met in June 1880 that he had not been able to secure the conference. Brandt stated that Strasser and I had given him hearty co-operation and W. H. Foster and Josiah Dyer had helped in publicity. During the spring and summer of 1881 Strasser received several communications from Terre Haute signed by Mark Moore, urging the need for an amalgamation of all trade unions and outlining a conference to effect such an organization. This proposal was the subject of considerable discussion in labor circles in New York and especially among the cigarmakers.

There were various real efforts to bring about conferences to discuss federation or amalgamation. All should be given due credit, though none was the exclusive agency. The Cigarmakers Union which felt keenly the need of an organization to replace the National Labor Union was an early promoter of federation. The advanced character of our organization and the constructive energizing spirit of the leadership that emanated from the New York office of our International had developed in our unions throughout the country really able and practical representatives. We cigarmakers had been hurried toward a realization of the necessity for union among internationals by legislative needs as well as by our appreciation of the dangers of secret organization, which was making headway and which had been interfering in New York strikes.

In addition we were contending against a menace to our trade federal legislation alone could remedy. In 1878, of forty thousand cigarmakers in the entire country at least ten thousand were Chinamen employed in the cigar industry on the Pacific Coast. Adaptability and power of imitation soon made skilled workers of the Mongolians. As their standards of living were far lower than those of white men, they were willing to work for wages that would not support white men. Unless protective measures were taken, it was evident the whole industry would soon be "China-ized." The Pacific Coast white cigarmakers at that time organized independently, were using a white label to distinguish white men's work done under white men's standards. But local organization was an inadequate protection against the strong tide of Chinese immigration that threatened to flood the West.

When the call came for conference for August 2, 1881, in Terre Haute, my international union voted to send a representative, and President Strasser appointed me. However, serious illness in my family and the death of one of my children prevented my presence. There were about fifty persons present at the first conference, and they spent the first day in discussing the situation and developing practical plans. They appointed a Committee on Arrangements for a labor congress to be held in Pittsburgh [in] November. After a brief meeting on August 3, the members of the committee went to their various homes and continued through correspondence to persuade organizations to send delegates to the Pittsburgh Congress.

The congress met November 15, 1881, in Pittsburgh. It was the first national meeting of labor men from all the trades that I attended. I was thirty-one at that time and was looked upon as one of the youngsters. One of the most important men there was John Jarrett, president of the Amalgamated Association of Iron and Steel Workers, then the strongest trade union. Others were Sam Leffingwell, a printer of Indianapolis, a veteran of the Mexican and Civil wars, who had long been active in the I.T.U. and the K. of L. and who later compiled a manual of parliamentary procedure which was extensively used; W. H. Foster, another printer, was widely known, who had served on the I.T.U. committee on amalgamation and was to give his few remaining days of activity to the new Federation; Robert Howard, secretary of the Cotton and Mule Spinners Association, an outstanding figure in any group, was able, resourceful, constructive, and held the respect of employers as well as fellow-workers; Richard Powers of the Chicago Lake Seamen's Union was conspicuous for his tremendous voice and volubility; R. D. Layton, the secretary-treasurer of the K. of L. (Bob Layton, as he was familiarly called) was more interested in a political future than in the labor movement.

One significant circumstance gave the trade unionists reason for serious thought—the number of delegates representing K. of L. organizations. Out of 107 delegates present, 69 represented organizations in Pittsburgh or Pennsylvania. R. D. Layton, representing District No. 3 of the K. of L., could not submit regular credentials. Circumstances indicated that the K. of L. organization had become concerned as to the purposes of the labor congress and had hurried representatives in to control decisions. It had been rumored that a new secret organization, a rival to the K. of L., was to be formed.

The report of the Committee on Organization and the minority report were then submitted and both laid on the table. The following nominations were then made from the floor for permanent president: John Jarrett, Richard Powers, and Samuel Gompers. I declined the nomination for president in favor of John Jarrett. Mr. Powers followed me in declining, and Mr. Jarrett was elected by acclamation. Powers and I were elected vice-presidents. Chairman Jarrett appointed the following Committee on Plan of Organization: Gompers, Brandt, Howard, Somers, and Lynch. We reported proposing that the name of the new association be Federation of Organized Trades and Labor Unions of the United States of America and Canada. Those who had been appointed by the Terre Haute conference to make preliminary plans had been greatly influenced by the British Trade Union Congress. It is significant that the thirteen declarations and the four supplementary resolutions constituting the platform adopted proposed industrial betterment by legislation. Little did that congress realize that the fundamental work of the labor movement was to be the development and inculcation of the principles of trade unionism—the understanding and the use of economic power.

However, three of the four objects of the Federation enumerated in Article 11, outlined action in the economic field—the encouragement and formation of trades and labor unions, of trade and labor assemblies or councils, and of national and International trade unions. This is the field that, when developed later, made the A. F. of L. the most powerful economic organization of the world.

Another important decision prescribed representation by national or International organizations when such existed. This provision was basic in developing regularity and responsibility. During discussion of this section, Mr. Rankin raised the question whether delegates should be chosen by local unions or Internationals. Delegate Cummings of Massachusetts wanted selections given to the rank and file, giving every state full and fair representation. I rose in protest against this unwarranted criticism of the delegate system. I objected to the proposed amendment of the committee's report because under that rule every national congress would be controlled by the delegates from the locality. Such local control would destroy the national representative character of the Federation. The issue was finally decided that the basic representation should be from national and international unions and that local trade assemblies or councils be allowed one delegate each.

Our report provided for a Legislative Committee of five members to act as the executive officers of the new Federation and for revenues to be derived from a per capita tax of three cents per member annually from trade and labor unions.

The Committee on Platform proposed legislation needed to protect wage-earners. That report shows so concretely what was in the minds of labor men of that day, that I wish to enumerate the subjects:

Compulsory education laws
Prohibition of labor of children under fourteen years
Licensing of stationary engineers
Sanitation and safety provisions for factories
Uniform apprentice laws
National eight-hour law
Prohibition of contract convict labor
Law prohibiting the order or truck system of wage payment
Law making wages a first lien upon the product of labor
Repeal of all conspiracy law
National Bureau of Labor Statistics
Protection of American industry against cheap foreign labor
Laws prohibiting importation of foreign workers under contract
Chinese exclusion.

A resolution urging Congress to enact legislation to establish governmental control over lines of communication and transportation in order to secure moderate, fair, and uniform passenger and freight rates, was held by Chairman Jarrett to be foreign to the purposes of the congress.

The dissension that can be created by the introduction of partisan politics in a labor organization was demonstrated in the heated discussion that occurred on a proposal to endorse a policy of protection for United States industries. The East and the West followed lines of divergent interests—one group felt the need of protection, the other did not and believed in free trade. The issue was then acute in the steel industry. Mr. Jarrett declared he wanted the issue settled then and there. He wanted the endorsement of the labor congress on Tariff. He asked if the delegates wanted the wages of workingmen dragged down; if they wanted foreign cheaply produced articles imported to compete with home manufacturers. Jarrett declared his willingness to debate the protective issue with anyone—and that was no idle declaration for I heard him debate the question with Henry George in a most able manner. The debate in our congress was heated and excitement ran high. Only by repeatedly banging the gavel did the chairman secure order to take a vote. The protective resolution was adopted. However, it is significant to note that when the Tariff declaration was repealed at Cleveland the following year, the Iron and Steel Workers withdrew from the Federation.

On the last day of the congress, Charles Burgman presented the situation on the Pacific Coast, showing the need of prohibiting importation of Chinese coolies. The Pacific Coast Trades and Labor Union of San Francisco sent him to the Pittsburgh Congress to present their most urgent difficulty. A declaration demanding Chinese exclusion was adopted by the congress. The Federation in 1881 was the first national organization which demanded the exclusion of coolies from the United States. The convention elected the following Legislative Committee: Samuel Gompers, Alexander Rankin, Richard Powers, and C. F. Burgman, with W. H. Foster, secretary, ex-officio member of the committee.

With no provision for a central office, there was grave danger that the organization would have no real existence, influence, or even records. I suggested that each member of the Legislative Committee purchase a blank book in which to record all official acts and also that each write to the secretary at least once a month.

Significant of past experience was the following resolution which I proposed and which was adopted by our committee:

Resolved, that it is the sense of this Committee that no member thereof should publicly advocate the claims of any of the political parties; but this should not preclude the advocacy to office of a man who is pledged purely and directly to labor measures.

This resolution reflected the conviction of our No. 10 Stanton Street group. We believed we ought to concentrate on the development of economic power and that political discussion would dissipate energy. Labor organizations had been the victims of so much political trickery that we felt the only way to keep this new organization free from taint was to exclude all political partisan action. My own mind was firmly convinced that progress for labor must come through economic agencies. I did not then have a clear idea of how it was to be done, but I sensed the fundamental principles and appreciated the dangers that lay in partisan methods.

During the year, correspondence between the members of the Legislative Committee of the Federation was extremely desultory and we had no meetings. Printing the proceedings of the first congress almost bankrupted the organization. Work of organization and all other activities were restricted by limited funds. But every organization that grows to real service is the product of insight and faith of the few who give devoted service. Secretary Foster sent out ten thousand copies of the circular drafted by our Legislative Committee which served to keep the idea of federation alive. The funds raised by the secretary during that year were less than $350. W. J. Cannon and I represented the International Cigarmakers' Union in the second congress held in Cleveland, beginning November 1, 1882.

It was a small group of men who convened in Schloss Hall. The Legislative Committee served as the Committee on Credentials. There were seventeen delegates present. Eight national trade organizations were represented. The contrast between this handful and the crowd of the year previous was striking. It was significant there were no representatives of Knights of Labor. That second meeting was an inspiration for those of us present. We were just trade unionists met to counsel one with another how to meet our trade and labor problems through trade union activity. Samuel J. Leffingwell was elected to preside over the congress; I, vice-president; Thomas H. Murch, secretary. We declined to commit our Federation to a free trades policy as against protection. In order that the Federation should not stand committed to either policy, we repealed the declaration of Pittsburgh and thence forward our Federation remained neutral upon this controversial question.

Toward the end of the Cleveland Congress a new note was introduced by a letter from P. J. McGuire. In 1881, just after he organized the United Brotherhood of Carpenters, he went to Europe to attend the International Workingmen's Congress. McGuire had in mind that the Federation had been modeled after the British Trade Union Congress, that its permanent officials constituted a Legislative Committee, and that practically all matters coming to the body for consideration were political in character. Fearful lest the original idea—a federation of trade unions—should be wholly lost, he sent an able letter of counsel pointing out the need and the possibilities of federated action in the industrial field, national and international. He declared: "We want an enactment by the workmen themselves that on a given day eight hours shall constitute a day's work and that they themselves will enforce."

The next congress of the Federation met in New York in August 1883. There were about twenty-five delegates present when I called the congress to order. I was elected by acclamation president of the gathering and I outlined the situation with which we had to deal thus: "The object of the assembly of the delegates is to discuss grievances and hardships workingmen are called on to endure from time to time in their respective trades. Employes are attacked by employers who would subjugate the workingmen and prevent them from organizing for mutual protection. In this city there is a recent instance in point wherein a vast corporation has tried to crush out their employes' hopes. The corporation's motto, with reference to their workingmen, is 'One man is no man.' The time fast approaches when workingmen will be required to determine what rights and liberties they really have. Employers not only try to crush the manhood of the employes, but they also use their vast wealth to take away their independence. The strong arm of the government is on their side and against us. The police and the military are used against labor and even the good will of order-loving citizens is employed to crush us. We do not receive a legal right to exercise our whole efforts to unite. Federal and state laws deny us the right to unite. They protect employers and their ill-gotten gains. When labor asks for protection, there is no response from the legislators in Washington or at the state capitals where their interests are presumably attended to. When the national eight-hour law was passed, it was at first obeyed in the spirit of its designer, but when trouble came to the government in consequence of obeying the law, then it was broken by the government both in spirit and in form. Now that labor is arousing and realizing its strength, the government is disposed to enforce this law. It is furthermore absolutely necessary that both national and state governments should adopt a law by which labor, when employed and meeting with accident, or injury, caused by employes, shall be recompensed by employers."

See the Capitalist inherently as the enemies.

The report of the Legislative Committee showed how inadequate our organization was to meet our needs. With no directing executive, the work was sporadic, depending upon the interest and opportunities of individuals. The report of the Committee on Standing Orders dealt with the problem of relations to the Knights of Labor and recommended that a committee of three be appointed to confer with the Knights of Labor and other kindred organizations with a view to the thorough unification of the working people of the country. I suggested as a substitute the Legislative Committee get in touch with the proper officers of national and international unions in order to ascertain their views upon unification and make a report. My suggestion was adopted.

Next year I was elected a delegate from the cigarmakers' union to the fourth congress of the Federation of Trades and Labor Unions which met in Chicago in November 1884, but owing to the very serious illness of my wife and two of our children, at the last minute I was prevented from going. That is the only annual meeting of our Federation during its forty-three years of existence that I did not attend, but I contributed in the form of communications and suggestions—one of which was the result of conferences with Gabriel Edmonston and which he presented to the convention—that is, the inauguration of a movement for the simultaneous establishment of the eight-hour workday May 1, 1886.

For the only time in the history of the Federation I was not elected to an executive office that year. The following year, however, I attended the fifth annual meeting of the Federation in Washington, D.C. I joined with Hugo Miller in proposing that the United States be urged to join in a conference of nations to consider an international agreement proposed by Switzerland for the limitation of the hours of labor of the working people, the regulation of female and child labor, and factory inspection and other measures tending to the amelioration of the conditions of the workers of the world. That resolution contained the germ of an idea that years afterward I helped to formulate and have incorporated in the Treaty of Versailles.

Another resolution which I introduced and in which I have always taken considerable pride was one urging and advising working women to protect themselves by organizing in unions of their trades. Women industrial workers were steadily increasing, and I felt it the part of wisdom for the labor movement to take constructive action early.

We all felt that the Federation had not become the organization that was urgently needed, and several plans were adopted for the purpose of strengthening it. Of course, money was indispensable to that end, and we asked all organizations to contribute what they could. We proposed that a representative of the Federation visit various labor conventions in order to secure new affiliations.

A *Fight to the Finish*

New Year's Day, 1886, dawned on the beginning of a momentous struggle in the history of American trade unionism—a struggle fateful for the cigarmakers' international as well as the national labor movement. The United Cigar Manufacturers' Association posted a new bill of prices for sixteen factories which reduced wages. Our strategy was to concentrate our efforts by calling a strike in one shop at a time. New York shops were the key to the cigar industry of the country, and two-thirds of the cigars made in New York were tenement products. The percentage of tenement work had been steadily growing with every check the courts gave to our efforts to abolish by law tenement cigar production. The secession situation described in a preceding chapter was a potential danger. A large group of these "progressives" under the leadership of Fred Haller had rejoined the International and arrangements were under way to adjust the whole problem. But the situation was so delicate that intrigue could readily find an opportunity and we had reason to distrust the Knights of Labor group then strong in New York. When strike approval was given us, we asked the Progressive Union to appoint a committee to co-operate with us. It was agreed that neither organization would enter into conference with employers without inviting the other to be represented. The tenement-house workers too held a delegate meeting and selected a representative committee.

The Progressive Union, then one of the foremost organizations in the Central Labor Union, a central body organized and controlled by the K. of L., asked that body to appoint a committee to assist the "progressive" cigarmakers.

A brief sketch of the labor situation in New York is necessary to interpret the conditions we had to meet. The K. of L. in New York City were organized in local assemblies which sent representatives to a delegate body called D.A. 49. This body had jurisdiction over all assemblies, and its executives had authority to supersede local assembly officials at any time. Many workers in addition to belonging to the union of their trade belonged also to a local assembly which, of course, had a membership of mixed trades.

The C.L.U. from the beginning had been hostile to Union No. 144 and the trade union movement. We first clashed because it was a central body dual to the Amalgamated Trade and Labor Union. Despite our protests, the C.L.U. was launched and as often happens declared itself progressive and the older body reactionary. It accepted delegates from trade unions, K. of L. assemblies, and open lodges or societies. It became the champion of "progressive" causes which all too often means willingness to depart from policies indicated by a fundamental philosophy based on facts. After a time the C.L.U. completely displaced the trade union assembly. It supported the "progressive" cigarmakers or the dual union in their fight upon our International union. The progressives allied themselves with the controlling group within the C.L.U., a Socialist group which in turn dominated D.A. 49.

When the charter of D.A. 49 was suspended in 1882 by the General Executive Board of the Order, Strasser and I organized an Assembly of cigarmakers [K. of L.] and got a charter as L.A. 2458 and adopted the public name of Defiance Assembly. The purpose of our assembly was obvious in the name. We had a special charter which made us independent of the jurisdiction of D.A. 49.

In 1886 a definite order went out from D.A. 49 to make war on the International Cigarmakers' Unions. It was the culmination of years of friction developing over K. of L. encroachments on trade union functions. The two movements were inherently different. Trade unions endeavored to organize for collective responsibility persons with common trade problems. They sought economic betterment in order to place in the hands of wage-earners the means to wider opportunities. The Knights of Labor was a social or fraternal organization. It was based upon a principle of co-operation, and its purpose was reform. The K. of L. prided itself upon being something higher and grander than a trade union or political party. The order admitted to membership any person, excluding only lawyers and saloon-keepers. This policy included employers among those eligible. Larger employers gradually withdrew from the order, but the small employers and small business men and politicians remained. The order was a hodge-podge with no basis for solidarity with the exception of a comparatively few trade assemblies.

When the order began to encroach upon the economic field, trouble was inevitable, for such invasion was equivalent to setting up a dual organization to perform a task for which they were entirely unfitted. It was particularly unfortunate when it endeavored to conduct strikes. The K. of L. was a highly centralized organization, and this often placed decision upon essential trade policies in the hands of officers outside the trade concerned. Strikes are essentially an expression of collective purpose of workers who perform related services and who have the spirit of union growing out of joint employment. The K. of L. never engaged in any dispute with employers, large or small, but that they received the support of trade unionists including myself.

Our union deliberated very carefully to determine the most effective plan to contest the wage decreases announced by the Cigar Manufacturers' Association. We were not in a position to conduct a general strike successfully. When we found that the progressives were trying to arouse the tenement workers to revolt without adequate funds to support the movement, we were apprehensive. The first strike was called at Levy Brothers—a large shop that did high-grade work where the majority of the workers belonged to the International. After the strike and lockout had been on for a few weeks, the Knights of Labor gathered enough cigarmakers and other workmen partially to man McCoy's shops and organized them in an assembly of the K. of L. and furnished the employers with their K. of L. label. Both these moves proved their undoing, for the organized labor movement of New York and vicinity resented this treasonable act against the workers. When the cigarmakers in other shops and in the tenements learned that it was the International unions making the fight against wage reductions, they flocked to our banner notwithstanding the fact that the C.L.U. and the K. of L. were antagonistic to us. The people who had been inveigled into entering the three factories revolted and quit. We held a great parade in which practically all the cigarmakers of New York participated. The demonstration proved to the manufacturers that the cigarmakers were again united under our leadership. They withdrew their wage reductions, and we came to an agreement, settling the strike within two weeks. The so-called "Progressive Union," the central body and D.A. 49 and the general officers of the K. of L. were unhorsed. The next struggle was to overturn their domination of the trade union movement, local and international.

We determined to find out whether the Order approved the efforts of D.A. 49 to destroy the International Cigarmakers. So we agreed that Strasser should go over to Philadelphia where with John S. Kirschner he laid before the Executive Board [of the K. of L.] the whole situation and asked for an investigation, with the result that a hostile committee was sent to New York. The committee called before it our assembly, the "progressive" assembly, and D.A. 49. The spirit of the investigation was relentlessly hostile, and its work interrupted by many trips and other duties. Finally, the charter of Defiance Assembly was revoked.

The work of the Investigating Committee was interrupted by the strike on the Southwestern Railroad, which made it necessary for the Executive Board to go to St. Louis. When the General Assembly met in Cleveland in May, the hearings were continued there. I took before the committee carefully collected comprehensive data showing how the K. of L. of New York had been trying to undermine the International and that the agreement which they had arranged would destroy trade standards which we had struggled, and starved, and fought to establish. The "investigation" closed, but we were given no intimation of the committee's findings. In July when the report was sent to the whole Order, I found that the committee exonerated D.A. 49 and maligned the representatives of the International.

We then undertook to rouse wage-earners to the gravity of the situation and the importance to trade union autonomy. We accepted the K. of L. challenge to battle and fought a straight fight. When the first round was over and we surveyed the field, the schism within our own ranks was healed; we had forced cigar manufacturers to deal with our union and had roused the trade unionists of the country to an understanding of the menace which the K. of L. interposed to trade unions.

During this period when the trade unions were being so severely attacked openly and covertly, the need for defensive measures grew in many minds. After many union representatives had been consulted, Strasser and P. J. McGuire took the initiative in calling a conference of trade unionists. On May 18 there gathered in Philadelphia in the Donaldson Hall on the corner of Broad and Filbert Streets the largest meeting of trade union executives I had attended up to that time. Forty-three invitations were sent out, which brought twenty delegates and letters of approval from twelve other organizations. About 370,000 organized workers were represented in this conference. One after another gave testimony of the necessity of finding some way to protect trade unions against K. of L. aggression. I participated and gave information not only from my trade but from the movement generally.

The conference prepared and adopted a treaty to be submitted to the General Assembly of the K. of L. to meet in special session the following week. The trade union committee and a special group of cigarmakers sent by the New York and Philadelphia unions were on hand when the General Assembly convened. It was an unusually cold spell, and we shivered around when the cold lake winds swept through. Strasser, P. Wolf, Kirschner, Haller, and I represented the Cigarmakers. The trade unions had warm friends in the Order; such men as Frank Foster, George E. McNeill, Joe Buchanan, Sam Leffingwell were heartily in sympathy with our cause. The attitude of trade unionists to the Order was pretty much this: We went into the Order understanding it to be an educational association for the uplift of labor. We saw need of such an order and joined. But the Order has been changed into a conglomeration of trades in mixed local assemblies, which are seeking to arrange the affairs of trade unions regardless of labor's interests. We protest against the change and insist upon the Order's confining its activity to its own jurisdiction.

As our trade union committee was not permitted to present our protest or treaty to the General Assembly, on the opening day of the session General Master Workman Powderly submitted the trade union treaty to the Assembly, and it was made public for the first time. The treaty was as follows:

> *First,* That in any branch of labor having a national or international organization, the Knights of Labor shall not initiate any person or form any assembly of persons following said organized craft or calling without the consent of the nearest national or International union affected.
>
> *Second,* That no person shall be admitted to the Knights of Labor who works for less than the regular scale of wages fixed by the union of his craft, and none shall be admitted to membership in the Knights of Labor who have ever been convicted of scabbing, ratting, embezzlement, or any other offense against the union of his trade or calling, until exonerated by the same.
>
> *Third,* That the charter of any Knights of Labor Assembly of any trade having a national or International union, shall be revoked, and the members of the same be requested to join a mixed assembly, or form a local union, under the jurisdiction of their respective national or International trades union.
>
> *Fourth,* That any organizer of the Knights of Labor who endeavors to induce trades unions to disband, or tampers with their growth or privileges, shall have his commission forthwith revoked.

Fifth, That whenever a strike or lockout of any trades union is in progress, no assembly or district assembly of the Knights of Labor shall interfere until settled to the satisfaction of the trades union affected.

Sixth, That the Knights of Labor shall not establish or issue any trade mark or label in competition with any trade mark or label now issued, or that may hereafter be issued by any national or International trades union.

The Assembly finally decided that since it was in special session it had no power to act upon our treaty, but was ready to receive and discuss grievances. The regular session of the General Assembly was held in Richmond in October, and it was generally understood that definite action would be taken on the trade union issue. The Richmond Assembly upon which we had been waiting convened early in the month. The Order had been growing rapidly. The number of delegates gathering in Richmond was several times the number at Cleveland. Because of its rapid growth, the membership was inexperienced and undisciplined. This condition made it easier for an organized minority to dominate. The Home Club, which won the first rounds in Cleveland, had a triumphant victory in Richmond. The Assembly formally ordered cigarmakers to choose between their unions and the Order and gave notice that Cigarmakers who were members of the International Union would be expelled form the K. of L. The treaty and grievances which trade unions had presented to the K. of L. were ignored. This action solidified trade union ranks.

Federation

Our [trade union] committee issued a call to national and International trade unions to send delegates to a conference to be held in Columbus, Ohio, December 8, 1886.

In a conference between McGuire, Kirschner, and me it was determined that the Federation of Trades and Labor Unions should meet at the same time and place in order that the delegates of affiliated organizations could meet with representative officials of the unaffiliated national unions to discuss the whole situation and formulate a policy and program. All were convinced that the old Federation could not do the effective work required. We needed a consolidated organization for the promotion of trade unionism under which work could go forward daily for the organization of all workers of America skilled as well as unskilled. We needed a central office and officers who could give all their time to the Federation work. The old Federation was committed to relief by legislation. As year by year we learned the inadequacy of our program, we tried to revise our constitution to authorize action in the economic field. Now the time had come to stop patchwork and rebuild. We had learned the need of an alliance for defense and mutual help.

As chairman of the Legislative Committee I opened the congress. We organized for business and heard the report of the Legislative Committee and extended the courtesies of our sessions to the trade union conference. When the trade union conference met on December 8, the Federation resolved itself into a Committee of the Whole to participate in the conference. John McBride of the National Federation of Miners was made chairman.

During the first day's session of the Federation, a telegram was received from Mr. Powderly giving the names of five Knights of Labor appointed to discuss trade union differences. Our Trade Union Committee met with them and found that they had not even the power of recommendation and that they declared the "treaty" had been rejected at Cleveland. The K. of L. committee suggested nothing but absorption by the K. of L. and loss of trade autonomy. The Order had reached a stage of intoxication with power that prevented clear thinking and wise action. Our committee reported inability to make any progress.

The Columbus meetings unanimously decided that a Federation should be formed and that all trade union organizations should be eligible, whether affiliated or unaffiliated to the Federation of Trades and Labor Unions and the conference appointed a committee of five to confer with a committee from the Federation of Trades and Labor Unions. Acting under instructions from the Federation, I met this committee and stated the Federation had resolved to turn over all moneys, papers, and effects to the new American Federation of Labor requesting only the publication of our Legislative Committee's report. Then the officers and delegates of the old Federation disbanded or merged in with the new Federation which was organized under the title of the American Federation of Labor. The revenue for the Federation work was to be derived from a per capita tax of one-half cent per member per month.

The convention provided for a president with a salary of $1,000 per year and added as part of its constitution, "that the president shall devote his entire time to the interests of the Federation." I was nominated for president, but I was greatly disinclined to accept any salaried labor office and therefore declined. John McBride of the Miners was nominated, and he frankly stated that he could not afford to accept a position to which he would have to devote his entire time upon such a meager salary. The office fairly went begging, and finally I was again nominated and persuaded in the interest of the movement to accept the nomination and election. That was the first salaried office I held in the labor movement. The convention elected as the officers of the Federation: George Harris and J. W. Smith, vice-presidents; P. J. McGuire, secretary; and Gabriel Edmonston, treasurer.

This was in November [sic] and the constitution was to go into effect on March 1 of the following year, and so there was no salary paid me for the intervening months. It was a difficult economic struggle for me to devote my entire time for those months without receiving salary or compensation for I had a wife and six children in addition to myself to support. Somehow I managed through it all. My family and I just put ourselves in the psychological position of a strike or lockout, and somehow the period was tided over. It was a bit hard to arrange for the family budget, but Mother never complained although there was a large family to care for. We simply did the best we could.

I was president of a Federation that had been created but yet had to be given vitality. I felt that the trade union movement stood or fell with the success of the Federation and gave everything within me to the work. The new movement had to establish itself as a working agency. This could be done only by rendering service and establishing a reputation for ability to do things.

The struggle between trade unions and the K. of L. was at high tide when I assumed the task of making the American Federation of Labor something more than a paper organization. I thought it best to continue my active participation in labor matters in New York City while developing opportunities for service as national executive as best I could. I was usually asked to speak at all important labor mass meetings, to participate in conferences in which policies were formulated. It was my custom to attend meetings of the Central Labor Union. After 1887 I did not serve No. 144 in any official capacity except as a representative delegate.

Early in January came the revolt of a powerful group of K. of L. labor papers. The *Philadelphia Tocsin* edited by David Pasco; *Haverhill Labor* by Frank Foster; *Brooklyn Labor Press* by Merrill; *Denver Labor Enquirer* by Joseph Buchanan; *Chicago Knights of Labor* by Bert Stewart; the *New York Union Printer* by a member of D.A. 64. These labor papers really created labor opinion. To the columns of each of these papers I contributed articles or letters on trade unionism, emphasizing the struggle which the trade unions had to make in order to defend themselves against attacks of employers all too often aided by the K. of L.

I presided over the first meeting of the Central Labor Union in 1887, that endorsed the blue label of the cigarmakers, a victory over the K. of L. This was a gratifying action which I hoped to use as a precedent for similar action by the State Workingmen's Assembly, the call for which I, as president of that body, had just issued. That meeting I knew would be a definite test of power. As the state organization had long been controlled by the New York group, the Home Club faction was pretty well entrenched in power. In my report to the convention, I presented a summary of the year's work. Upon the problem of the relation of the political branch to the S.W.A., I pointed out the way to make the political branch subordinate to the parent body, recommending that the political branch no longer initiate measures but merely follow the S. W. A. I recommended that child labor be prohibited under the age of fourteen; that the hours of railroad labor should be consecutive and limited to ten hours a day; authorization of a substitute for contract prison labor; fair representation for labor in the coming constitutional convention; tenement house legislation; a state printing office; that factory inspectors be increased; that workingmen as a class ought not to be discriminated against for jury duty; that no officials of the State Workingmen's Association ought to accept political office; and that labor ought to elect workingmen to office whenever and wherever an opportunity presented itself, and when that course was impossible "to stand by men who stood by our measures and to defeat those who opposed them." The range of these recommendations reflects matters with which labor was concerned thirty-six years ago.

On the last day the representatives of the K. of L., and some of the representatives of the trade unionists, I included, had a conference and agreed upon recommending to the convention the election of Thomas J. Dowling for president; John Phillips of the Hatters for treasurer; two representatives of the Knights of Labor and two trade unionists to constitute the officers of the Executive Board for the following year. This was unanimously adopted, and there was a great demonstration of joy. We felt assured that the best interests of the workers of the state would be furthered by this harmonious conclusion and once for all the organized labor movement of the State of New York had rid itself of the control of the corrupt element of the K. of L.

So I worked along, taking advantage of every opportunity to establish the name and service of the American Federation of Labor in national labor circles. Early opportunities came in requests for assistance in controversies between organizations in Brockton, Lynn, and other shoe towns. I went before newly organized unions such as the United Clothing Cutters' Union and explained to them the fundamentals of trade unionism. I gave considerable time to the organization of Jewish workers during 1887 and the next year following. These workers were coming in such numbers that the welfare of all was endangered if they remained unorganized. The clothing trade was largely in the hands of Jews who in every way within their power encouraged the Jewish Russian people, particularly those who were in the sections where oppression and cruelty obtained, to come to the United States and, coupling the possibility of profit with affection for their co-religionists, found employment for the new Russian-Jewish immigrants in the clothing industry. After the immigrants had landed in the United States and were employed by the clothing manufacturers, the latter lost interest in the welfare of their employes and paid them miserably low wages and had them make workshops of their bedrooms, where they worked from early morning until late at night.

Several conventions of the A. F. of L. directed that efforts be made to establish reciprocal relations with the K. of L. Conferences were held between K. of L. representatives and representatives of the Federation and others in which the railroad brotherhoods participated. Often it seemed something constructive had been accomplished, but always something developed to defeat the purpose.

The last really serious attempt to develop a working agreement between the K. of L. and trade unions was in 1894. Joe Buchanan, who had been a most ardent K. of L. but who recognized the right of trade unions to priority, had the confidence of both sides. In 1893 the K. of L. invited the A. F. of L. to participate in a conference. This invitation was accepted by the Chicago convention and three representatives chosen. Since the K. of L. failed to arrange for the convention, Buchanan suggested to me that inasmuch as he had the confidence of men in both organizations he might be helpful. Buchanan sent a call for a unity labor conference to be held in Philadelphia in April.

The conference lasted two days. There was much plain speaking, which clearly manifested desire to end internal fights. This conference had the effect of forcing the K. of L. to issue a call for a conference for St. Louis, June 1894. P. J. McGuire, Frank Foster, and I attended that unity conference for the Federation.

J. M. Bishop, on behalf of the Knights, submitted a proposal to maintain dual organizations perpetuating the Knights' invasion of the economic field, to endorse the People's Party, and to provide for general conferences to deal with conditions causing friction between the labor organizations. Immediately following this conference, Sovereign went to Chicago where he publicly endorsed the American Railway Union and officially supported the disruptive movement. Thus ended efforts to establish co-operation between the Knights and the Federation.

From the time that I became a member of the Knights of Labor and during all the years since and now, it was never my intention to do an injustice to that organization. The fact was that it was an organization with high ideals but purely sentimental and bereft of all practical thought and action.

My earliest official efforts were concentrated in promoting stability of labor organizations. This had to be done by making the idea an inseparable part of the thought and habits of trade unionists by establishing a business basis for unionism and then driving home the fallacy of low dues. Cheap unionism cannot maintain effective economic activity. Sustained office work and paid union officials for administrative work have become the general practice since the Federation was organized.

To build the Federation we had to secure members. Numbers give confidence not only to members but to outsiders. The membership problem fell into three divisions—affiliation of existing nationals and internationals; chartering of local unions, central bodies, and state federations of labor; when a trade was sufficiently organized we launched a national organization.

When a large number of workers were organized in local unions of the same trade or industry, then I called a conference or convention to create a national or international union of these locals. I endeavored to carry out the historic development of the United States. The territory in which no state government existed belonged to the United States, and out of this territory states were created and became part of the Federal government. Following this principle of development, I regarded the national or international unions as "territories" later to be formed into national and International unions and as such to form an integral part of the A. F. of L. The local unions not so organized in national or international unions hold the same relation to the American Federation of Labor as the territories had to the government of the United States.

At the meeting of the Executive Council in February 1887, I was authorized to examine applications for affiliation to the Federation and to issue charters. In March, Ed Finklestone attended the convention at Hartford to launch the Connecticut State Federation of Labor—the first child of the Federation. The next to follow was Massachusetts. Cigarmakers' Union 97 issued the call for the convention that authorized affiliation in that state. Sixteen unions responded through delegates who met in Dexter Hall, Boston. Henry Abrahams was elected president.

A speech I made in Brooklyn in 1887 is typical of the educational work of that time:

> The best way to defeat strikes and boycotts is to provide for them. There is no way of decreasing strikes so good as that of making men experienced. From a strong organization generous treatment follows and with fairness on the part of the employer there is no desire to strike or boycott on the part of the men. The best method to decrease strikes is to organize to defend men in the case of strikes. The stronger the union the fewer the strikes. We do not want strikes, but if men are not organized they will have to strike. First, one employer will cut wages, then another, until the rate has fallen so low that the men must strike. We are opposed to sympathetic and foolish strikes. Ignorance is not discipline. It requires more discipline to pay an assessment of $1 a week to help those on strike than to strike in sympathy with them. The first thing a new union does is to want to strike. They overestimate the power of organization without resources. The old unions do not strike, their strength is known. They do not have to strike to resist encroachment.

JAMES O'CONNELL,
Third Vice-President, A. F. of L.

AUG. McCRAITH,
Secretary, A. F. of L.

M. M. GARLAND,
Fourth Vice-President, A. F. of L.

G. W. PERKINS,
President, Cigar Makers' International Union.

SAMUEL GOMPERS,
President, A. F. of L.

MARTIN FOX,
President, Iron Molders' Union of North America.

JOHN B. LENNON,
Treasurer, A. F. of L.

P. J. McGUIRE,
First Vice-President, A. F. of L.

WM. B. PRESCOTT,
President, International Typographical Union.

OFFICERS OF THE AFL AND PROMINENT AFFILIATED ORGANIZATIONS
Composite portrait that appeared in the Chicago
Eight-Hour Herald. 1896.
U.S. Department of Labor.

GOMPERS SIGHTSEEING IN COLORADO
At Garden of the Gods. Probably 1894.
Courtesy of George Meany Memorial Archives, AFL-CIO.

Top
Adolph Strasser
1896.
Courtesy of George Meany Memorial
Archives, AFL-CIO.

Bottom, at left
P. J. McGuire
With an unidentified associate. 1890s.
Courtesy of United Brotherhood of
Carpenters and Joiners of America.

Above
ATTENDING THE
PRESIDENT'S INDUSTRIAL CONFERENCE
Left to right, Franklin K. Lane, secretary
of the interior; Judge E. H. Gary, execu-
tive head of the U.S. Steel Corporation;
Gompers; Frank Morrison, secretary,
AFL; and John D. Rockefeller, Jr. 1919.
Courtesy of George Meany Memorial
Archives, AFL-CIO.

At left
GOMPERS TESTIFYING BEFORE THE NEW YORK
CITY INDUSTRIAL COMMISSION
1915.
Library of Congress Portrait Collection

GOMPERS
1908.
Courtesy of the Chicago Historical Society.

I have helped in the organization and stabilization of unions and in the development of discipline among officers and the rank and file. With the mobilization of economic power, constructive program became possible.

Economic betterment—today, tomorrow, in home and shop, was the foundation upon which trade unions have been builded. Economic power is the basis upon which may be developed power in other fields. It is the foundation of organized society. Whoever or whatever controls economic power directs and shapes development for the group or the nation. Because I early grasped this fundamental truth, I was never deluded or led astray by rosy theory or fascinating plan that did not square with my fundamental. This firmly rooted conviction I owe in a large measure to Laurrell's oft-repeated injunction: "If it doesn't square with your due book, have none of it." This is the reason it was often hard to have patience with well-meaning, enthusiastic but misinformed persons who have wanted the trade union movement to forsake this simple truth.

Eight Hours

An eight-hour law [for federal employees] had been passed by Congress and signed by President Johnson in 1868. As officials ignored the law, President Grant issued an order directing that its provisions be executed. Various executives "interpreted" the law to mean that a reduction in wages must accompany a reduction in hours. A short time afterwards the President issued an executive order directing that no cut in wages should be made because of the reduction in hours due to the eight-hour law. The issue got into politics. A committee went to the Democratic Convention, which met in Philadelphia, and informed the platform committee of the situation as to the eight-hour law. The Democratic committee, apprehensive that whatever credit might come from establishing eight hours would be entirely absorbed by the Republican President and inured to the advantage of the Republican Party, adopted an eight-hour declaration as one of the planks of its platform. Later, the Republican Party Convention adopted a similar plank. When we asked for eight hours by law, the law was to apply only to government employes. Eight hours in private industry we undertook to establish by direct negotiations.

I became very well acquainted with George E. McNeill and Ira Stewart and familiar with their philosophy of the shorter workday. According to my own understanding, the eight-hour day was a revolutionizing force that altered all the workers' relations, both industrial and social, and raised standards of living and work.

All this served as preparation for my responsibility as president of the Federation in trying to establish eight hours in industry. I helped to draft the resolution to establish the eight-hour day, May 1, 1886, which was adopted by the 1884 Convention of our Federation. We proposed that the workers obtain contracts for the establishment of the eight-hour day in all industry. The plan was thoroughly discussed and finally adopted by unanimous vote.

In New York the first organized campaign for eight hours since 1872 got under way in the summer of 1885. Some of the veterans of the early movement were our most enthusiastic workers. Our program was strictly economic. Our first step was to send a circular to all unions. Even under most favorable conditions our campaign must have been chiefly valuable as an educational influence. There were then hardly twelve industries in the United States sufficiently organized to establish an eight-hour day. The movement of '86 did not have the advantage of favorable conditions. Also, it had to counter duplicity from the K. of L. Our eight-hour program was officially submitted to the Executive Board of the K. of L. with the request that they co-operate. No official reply was made. The leadership of the K. of L. was not in accord with the spirit of the working-class movement.

In February 1886, W. H. Foster, the secretary of the Federation, sent eight-hour circulars to all labor organizations, asking all to unite in achieving this first step in industrial betterment. Responses were generally cordial. Most of the unions began holding agitation meetings and inaugurated practical programs. There was scarcely a union in New York that did not hold a special eight-hour meeting and follow it by constant educational discussion. The Cigarmakers and the Building Tradesmen made demands for eight hours. Even the street-car drivers who had worked interminable hours demanded twelve as the limit. When T. V. Powderly, the head of the Order, was in New York early in 1886, he gave an interview in which he spoke of the eight-hour day in most glowing terms. That statement was generally interpreted to mean a sympathetic attitude toward our movement. Still, we did not feel sure that we knew what was being done in the inner circle of the K.

of L. Our apprehension was confirmed by the statement which Mr. Powderly made in April, "The Knights of Labor do not contemplate making an effort to enforce the eight-hour day at present."

The eight-hour movement of 1886 was general but most aggressive in New York, Chicago, Milwaukee, Cincinnati, and Baltimore. Of course, as president of the Federation of Trades and Labor Unions, I had general information of efforts in different localities. Paul Grottkau of Milwaukee, formerly of Chicago, who had been on a tour through the East in behalf of the movement, told me considerable of the Chicago and Milwaukee plan. Grottkau was an eloquent German speaker. Chicago was the headquarters of the active anarchist group headed by Parsons, Spies, and Schwab. Two anarchist papers were published there—one in English edited by Parsons, *The Alarm*, the other, *Die Flackel*, in German, edited by Spies.

We held a series of eight-hour meetings in New York for which we secured popular speakers like Henry George and S. E. Schevitsch. At these meetings the various unions reported progress of the movement in their trades. The Cigarmakers and Furniture Workers were the only organizations that had determined to establish eight hours for their respective industry. The Cigarmakers' Convention had recommended that course, and each local had made the necessary arrangements. We were then generally working nine hours, and the reduction was to be made without contest.

May 1 mass meetings were held all over the country. Our May Day meeting in New York was a complete success. All went away strengthened in determination to establish the eight-hour day. That mass meeting was to constitute not the termination of our eight-hour movement but only the end of the first period. The news that came next morning from Chicago indicated the extent of enthusiasm there. Forty thousand men were on strike, the railroads were crippled, and many factories closed. Just as there seemed to be a probability of trade unions being welded together for united resistance to long hours, there came the dynamite bombs at Haymarket Square, Chicago. In a strike at the Harvester Plant in Chicago, a number of men were ruthlessly clubbed and shot down by the police. On the following evening, a protest meeting was held in Haymarket Square and was addressed by Spies, Parsons, and Fielden. To that meeting, generally attended by strikers and sympathizers, a large force of police was assigned. After the meeting was in full progress, it was said and never denied, that the officer in charge of the police telephoned to headquarters that the meeting was being conducted peacefully. The Mayor of the city was present during the greater part of the meeting, leaving only when a gathering storm became very threatening. After the Mayor left, and hardly fifteen minutes after the above report was made, a squad of police formed to advance on the crowd. Spies, who was speaking, cried out in protest against disturbing a peaceful meeting. Then a bomb exploded and fifteen policemen were killed. Of course, the meeting broke up in a furor of excitement, and the anarchists were arrested on a charge of murder.

This catastrophe, coming so soon after the launching of the new Federation, halted our eight-hour program. It was not until 1888 that the convention again directed that we renew our aggressive campaign. This campaign was to culminate May 1, 1890. It was agreed to hold simultaneous eight-hour meetings throughout the country on July 4, Labor Day, and February 22. I wrote to practically every labor organization urging agitation for the eight-hour day. Most of these letters were written in long hand. After the Federation secured its Caligraph typewriter, letters were sent to the President of the United States, the Cabinet, forty Senators, seventy-five Representatives, and one hundred economists. My purpose was to create sympathetic understanding for the eight-hour movement and to forestall any association of the movement with anarchistic influences. It was decided to concentrate activity and to establish eight hours for one trade each year, the Executive Committee to select the one best prepared to secure the shorter workday each year. Of the several organizations that made application, the Carpenters were designated to be the standard-bearers for 1890.

In the meanwhile, I had had to watch the K. of L. lest they attempt to frustrate our movement as happened in 1886. Early in the year I saw a newspaper statement from Powderly that increased my apprehension. I squelched an incipient rumor that a general strike would be called May 1, 1890, by issuing a circular in which I said: "Nothing is further from our intention than a general strike. The date, May 1, 1890, was fixed in order to concentrate efforts on a certain point. In the present condition of labor, no movement for a general strike would have my support. The end of the labor movement will not come in 1890."

As plans of the eight-hour movement developed, we were constantly realizing how we could widen our purpose. As the time for the meeting of the International Workingmen's Congress in Paris (July 14, 1889) approached, it occurred to me that we could aid our movement by an expression of world-wide sympathy from that congress. My letter informed the Paris congress of our American efforts to celebrate the coming May Day by establishing eight hours for the Carpenters and urged them to co-operate. The proposal fell upon the ears of two bitterly warring factions; [but] eventually a resolution for an eight-hour demonstration in every country was adopted, and there was pretty general observance of the day. That was the origin of European May Day, which has become a regular institution in all European countries.

The Carpenters did their level best to win a complete victory. As their unions throughout the country did not have uniform strength or working standards, it was determined to try for a shorter workday instead of a uniform eight-hour demand. When carpenters were working ten or more hours and could reasonably expect a nine-hour day but not an eight, nine was made the objective. Practically every Carpenters' union in the country secured some definite betterment of working conditions as a result of the struggle. The results affected 137 cities and benefited 46,197 workers. The total membership of the Carpenters' unions was then about 73,000.

When the Detroit (1890) convention was considering the selection of an organization to make the next campaign, the Miners urged with eloquence and insistence that they were ready and anxious to make the demand for the eight-hour day and to fight for its establishment in the whole trade. The United Mine Workers were operating under an extremely difficult form of organization—part of the organization was secret and affiliated to the Knights of Labor. The convention, therefore, inquired what assurance the Miners could give that the secret bodies would co-operate in the eight-hour movement. The Miners' delegates stated they had just come from the General Assembly where approval had been given to the proposal. Upon that assurance the Convention approved the selection of the U. M. W. as the next trade to move toward eight hours.

In addition to sending letters and circulars to all affiliated organizations, the president of the A. F. of L. was instructed to make a wide tour of the country to carry a personal message to as many workers as possible. As the Federation was unable to finance such an undertaking, I asked our organizer in Denver, Adam Menche, to act as manager of the trip. He arranged with each central body to bear its proportional share of the expenses of the trip. On February 2, I left New York City on my first trip to the Pacific Coast. My main purpose was to unite all workers in behalf of eight hours for the miners [earlier legislation had been in behalf of federal employees], and thereby assure their moral and financial support. My second purpose was to strengthen the local movements. It was then only five years since the A. F. of L. had been organized out of the old Federation of Trades and Labor Unions. The purpose and the value of federated effort were a new idea; hence, the importance of educational work. Thirdly, at that time there was grave danger of a secession movement on the Pacific Coast.

The eight-hour educational work had been sufficiently thorough to enable each national union to carry forward the shorter hours movement in its own industry. Our work pressed home upon all the concept that the shorter workday is the initial step in better conditions for wage-earners. After the movement of 1891, it was no longer necessary for the national labor movement to sponsor specific eight-hour movements. The pioneer work had been done, and special groups from that time on assumed responsibility for establishing this standard in their own trades.

Henry George's Campaign

In the spring of 1886 New York labor began to discuss how to make its influence felt in politics. Among the chief promoters of the political movement was Father McGlynn, who was very popular among the workingmen and a great friend of Henry George, with whom he had been speaking at many public meetings for labor and for Irish freedom. So it was natural that when a Labor Party was considered, the name of Henry George at once presented itself as a suitable leader. The suggestion for an Independent Labor Party aroused enthusiasm. That was a time when municipal government in the United States was notoriously corrupt. Labor aspired to elect a reform administration—one that would more nearly approach the doing of justice. Even though New York labor determined to enter politics, I did not feel enthusiastic about the plan.

Not all were persuaded that an Independent Party was the way to deal with their problems. Many staunch trade unionists opposed the idea. On the other hand, various labor troubles added fire to enthusiasm for political party action. Political action had no appeal for me, but I appreciated the movement as a demonstration of protest.

The political movement was in inception a trade union movement. It was inaugurated by trade unions and conducted by trade unions. The Central Labor Union appointed a committee on plan. That committee recommended the fusion of all New York labor organizations in support of a common purpose. All delegates to the organizing conference were bona fide workingmen. The name of Henry George was repeatedly used in connection with the candidacy for the office of Mayor, and a resolution endorsing him was unanimously adopted by the Central Labor Union. The secretary of the organization committee, James P. Archibald, was authorized to write Mr. George to find out whether he would be willing to serve. George replied in a letter which outlined his principles, stating that he would accept the nomination provided the request was confirmed by a petition signed by 30,000 voters. Immediately began the work to secure signers to the petition. When these were secured, Henry George was formally proclaimed labor's standard-bearer at an immense mass meeting in Cooper Union. The political branch of the State Workingmen's Assembly met in Syracuse in September for its fifth annual session. The convention endorsed the Henry George candidacy and appointed an Executive Committee consisting of representatives from each assembly district to help in electing a Legislature friendly to labor. I served on this committee. Even in all this urge toward the political, trade union progress stood first in my mind. I found time to give a helping hand to the store clerks of New York in their efforts to secure an early closing. It was a struggle to establish the idea that retail stores need not remain open during all the hours purchasers are usually awake.

The political campaign was strenuous from the beginning. There were in New York City two factions in the Democratic Party—Tammany Hall and the County Democracy. The political implication was obvious when Tammany selected a candidate for Mayor from the ranks of the County Democracy, Abram S. Hewitt, a liberal and a humanitarian, who had already given distinguished service in Congress.

The Republicans also went outside the ranks of the regulars and nominated Theodore Roosevelt, then regarded as a "silk stocking" because of his aristocratic and wealthy relations. In his service as Assemblyman, Roosevelt had earned the reputation of supporting the people's rights against political corruption.

It was a tremendous campaign and, in addition to labor men, attracted a large number of men and women of all walks of life, particularly those who had been thinking in a broad way on municipal and social problems. Patrick Ford was one of those who worked unreservedly. No less earnest a worker was Father McGlynn, who was rector of St. Stephen's Church and had influence among wide circles of workingmen. It was unusual for a Catholic priest to take such a prominent part in a constructive labor movement, and McGlynn soon brought upon himself the surveillance of the Church. Father McGlynn preached many sermons that concerned themselves not with the orthodox creed but with practical religion. When the Anti-Poverty Society was organized after the campaign, McGlynn took an active part in its propaganda. Because of his utterances, he came into conflict with his superiors in the Church, and his case was taken to Rome. McGlynn was ordered to change his course, and when he refused was removed from his position and suspended. At length, however, a sort of peace was negotiated, and McGlynn was assigned to a rural diocese in the upper part of the state of New York.

The Catholic Church was fundamentally opposed to the Henry George movement. This opposition was increased by somewhat irresponsible radical statements of enthusiasts. Archbishop Corrigan prepared a letter condemning Henry George's theories, which was read in all the Catholic churches of the diocese.

Meetings continued until election day. Then there was no legal regulation of political parties. On election day, flying squadrons operated about the ballot box until results were finally determined. It is claimed with good grounds that in the afternoon of election day, word was sent out from Republican headquarters that inasmuch as there seemed no possibility of electing Roosevelt, instead of wasting additional votes on him, Republican voters ought to cast their ballots for Mr. Hewitt and thus assure the defeat of Henry George. In those halcyon days of the big Fourteenth Street organization, there were methods that effectively secured for preferred candidates necessary votes for the determination of contests. The election returns announced 68,242 votes for George; 91,215 votes for Hewitt; 60,597 votes for Roosevelt. There was, however, sufficient genuine encouragement for labor in the political field to continue the political organization.

Never was a more enthusiastic meeting of a defeated party held than the jubilee of the George workers in Cooper Union on November 6. The hall was overcrowded, and people swarmed outside. On the platform were temporary chairman, James Archibald, Mrs. Delescluze, Daniel DeLeon, David B. Scott, Charles F. Wingate, James Redpath, Cynthia Leonard, Dr. Cramer, and others, including me. The crowd was in a turbulent mood and would listen to nobody but George. At the close of his speech a declaration was adopted for a permanent political organization to be called the United Labor Party with a Central Committee consisting of John McMackin, Rev. Edward McGlynn, and Professor David B. Scott.

In New York the party organization was extended to cover the state. An internal struggle developed over membership of Socialists in the U. L. P. When the state convention was held in the summer of 1887, the issue was acute. Before the opening of the conference, Chairman McMackin's ruling was made known: No member of the S. L. P. shall be admitted to the convention of the U. L. P. John N. Bogert, trying to find some compromise, talked the situation over with me. I suggested that both parties give over the campaign to the trade unions, for I believed then as now that no separate organization was necessary for labor to advance any phase of its interests.

When I was asked for a statement after George had been nominated for Governor, I said: "The Federation of Labor as an organization is keeping its hands off this fight. The questions involved are purely political, not strictly affecting labor matters and call simply for individual expressions by men constituting the Federation. A great many of them are Socialists and are very bitter toward the U. L. P. Personally, I have nothing to say about the ticket."

The so-called Henry George Movement fell into the hands of some men who were not so scrupulous or so earnest as those who promoted the mayoralty campaign. A furniture dealer in New York named Coogan developed an ambition to become Mayor, and those in charge of the political organization catered to his ambition. It was a time before any Corrupt Practices Act was on the statute books, and the expenditures of Mr. Coogan were enormous. I was fairly reliably informed that Coogan spent over two hundred thousand dollars in that campaign. The whole affair became the laughing-stock with the people of New York, particularly among organized wage-earners who coined the phrase: "Was ist los mit Coogan?"

A Rope of Sand

My job as the president of the A. F. of L. was coveted by no one in the early days. There was much work, little pay, and very little honor. Though the Federation had been created by agreement, it had to be given reality by making it a force in industrial affairs. The necessary first step was to win for the Federation the good will of the wage-earners. The Federation was the unified activity of the trade union men. It was dependent upon good will and understanding of economic power. So I became a seeker of men. I wanted to win them for a labor movement which was sound philosophically, competent economically, and inspiring spiritually. At times I was well-nigh consumed with zeal, so that I gave little thought to anything else. My work was my life. So in recording the events of my life the labor movement is the controlling purpose.

I watched our local unions and gave them suggestions and advice. I fostered the organization of city centrals and state federations. I sent reminders to national officers urging them to pay per capita dues. In the case of national bodies which the Federation had fostered, local unions and members expected me to be a sort of fatherly supervisor of the organization. I wrote letters and talked to officials, diplomatically urging them to performance of duties and constructive policies. I got trade unions to put on their letterheads "affiliated to the American Federation of Labor" and thus helped advertise the name. All this work had to be done in such a way as to win men to the cause. The Federation had no compulsory authority—it was absolutely dependent upon voluntary co-operation.

Then there was the problem of establishing the custom of maintaining membership in the Federation. Unions wanted to come in and go out as best suited their temporary convenience. There was not then an understanding of the necessity for maintaining continuous membership in local trade unions, to say nothing of understanding the value and the service that a national labor movement could render. Without warning and for only fancied grievance, organizations withdrew from the

Federation. Sometimes I was fighting single-handed to hold the line of federated organization. The only other officer of the Federation who felt a real responsibility for the work was P. J. McGuire. Though McGuire's office was in Philadelphia and he was the mainstay of his own struggling organization, he found time for the problems and the work of the Federation. Somehow the organization struggled along, gaining a bit month by month. Finally, a period of development was reached when it was evident that I must be relieved of much of the office detail and routine.

Until 1891 I was the only full-time official of the Federation. This meant I had to be responsible for practically all the work of the Federation. Finally, I protested to the Executive Committee urging that I be relieved of the financial work and that a resident secretary be provided to assume full responsibility for that work. This was done in the 1890 convention, and Chris Evans of the Miners was elected secretary.

This reorganization of the Federation office made it possible to initiate a national plan for our work. I found it necessary to withdraw more and more from local affairs in New York City, both because I no longer had time for them and because I found that associating myself with local phases of problems made it more difficult for me to deal with problems as national issues affecting the welfare of all wage-earners.

The Federation had to win men by the authority of sound logic and results. It had less authority than national trade unions, for it was the voluntary banding together of those autonomous unions. Its continuous existence depended upon mutual service and welfare. It was at once a rope of sand and yet the strongest human force—a voluntary association united by common need and held together by mutual self-interests.

Legislative work demanded that I go to Washington occasionally. When I went and worked to the limit of my energy, I was increasingly conscious of the conviction that only a full-time Legislative Committee could protect labor's interests. Congressmen were not so much indifferent or hostile as they simply lacked knowledge of industrial problems and labor needs. It was not until there was an organized attempt to force Congress to oppose labor legislation that our legislative work became extremely difficult.

Though I realized that continuous work and watchfulness were necessary, I could give only a small portion of my time to legislative activity. Organization of workers in unions is always the first essential. Single-handed, I could not organize the workers of the United States into one compact, efficient movement. My problem was to secure the necessary co-operation. I conceived the idea of selecting labor men who were earnestly and unselfishly devoted to the cause of trade unionism and giving them an official commission to organize the unorganized and to help develop the American Federation of Labor into an effective agency for the betterment of wage-earners. During 1888, about eighty commissions were issued. Results came in membership increases.

The nineties brought no spectacular growth for the A. F. of L. There was steady progress, but it seemed painfully slow to my ardent hopes and boundless aspiration. Between 1890 and 1900, obviously the primary thing to do first was sustained effort to gather into the folds of the Federation national labor organizations that were eligible to membership. In those days the organization situation was pretty much that of England today—in the same trade there might be two or even three organizations with the same jurisdiction. The consequences were not so serious in those days as they would be today with our tendencies toward organization of industries on a national scale and standardization. However, our problems developed with changes in industrial organization. The nature and the scope of those problems were indicated in our first big struggle with a modern industrial corporation—Homestead.

The relations between the Carnegie Company and their employes at Homestead had been based on mutual confidence, but Henry Frick, who had been recently added to the firm, was known in his coke plants as an implacable foe of labor.

The strike at the Carnegie plant was precipitated by an announcement of reduced wages and rendered more acute by the fact that Frick was in charge and Andrew Carnegie was in Europe. The men resisted the wage reduction. Frick sent for Pinkertons to overawe them.

At the time of the strike, it was believed by many and was fully verified afterward that had Andrew Carnegie been in the United States during the annual negotiations, or immediately after the rupture, the strike would have been averted.

With the passing of Carnegie's personal management, Homestead became a non-union plant. This was the beginning of the policy of antagonism to trade unions followed by the Steel Corporation, which included maintenance of an excessive working force, the majority of whom were recent immigrants and hostile to organized labor.

The repercussions from Homestead, the A. R. U., and the financial depression of 1893–94 brought the labor movement squarely against the problem of holding its lines. This necessity bore fruit in new plans. We began to extend organization among groups that had been called unskilled workers. We inaugurated the period in which the field of organization was extended and developed the labor philosophy that there is no such thing as unskilled work *per se* and that the possibilities of organized labor are limited only by our development of the technique of organization.

For a number of years I had foreseen the necessity for paralleling in the labor movement the centralization that was taking place within industrial organization. I incorporated in my annual report to the 1888 convention a recommendation for organization based upon grouping of workers employed in related industries, or industries which squared upon some common basic need. I suggested such grouping as the iron, steel, and metal trades, the building trades, the railroad employes, etc. The first experiment in developing closer co-operation between trade organizations in the management of industrial matters was the Building Trades Department. The early Building Trades Council was organized independently of the Federation, and hence serious difficulties developed because it attempted to usurp the functions of the Federation. Our experience with that organization indicated that such councils or departmental organizations must be within the Federation and under its supervision. Later, departments were organized upon this basis. This new feature of our organization enabled us to parallel the industrial tendency for large-scale organization. Another development came through the unifying forces within industry. Industries in which there had been three or four craft organizations witnessed a merging of these. The action was voluntary and an inevitable response to the facts of the industrial situation. The labor movement does not act upon formulas or philosophies. It seeks a practical answer to an urgent need.

Denver Defeat and My Sabbatical Year

Eighteen ninety-five is the one year in which I have not been president of the American Federation of Labor since its organization in 1886. I was defeated for the presidency of the A. F. of L. at the Denver Convention in November 1894. Few have understood the circumstances which led to my defeat and the manner in which it was consummated.

From and including 1893 industrial depression all over the country was of such a character that large numbers of workers were unemployed. The poverty and misery of that period were most acute. That this caused dissatisfaction with men in any responsible position is without question. It may be a great pity, but it is a fact, that when conditions of life and of labor are keenly felt, those in responsible positions, whether in government or in organized labor, are blamed and criticized because they have not either averted such a condition or have not remedied it.

Just prior to the Denver Convention it was mooted that a candidate would be nominated for the presidency of the A. F. of L. to oppose my re-election. As the date of the Denver Convention neared, the name of John McBride, president of the United Mine Workers of America, was hinted at as being the candidate to contest the election. The Socialists came to Denver ready to make use of any instrumentality to secure my defeat. They figured that if the political program proposed by T. J. Morgan was adopted by the Denver Convention and I was defeated, the Socialists could control the American labor movement. As directed by the Chicago Convention, the political program was referred to affiliated unions for a referendum during the year. In addition I conducted an inquiry to determine the extent and effectiveness of independent political action as practiced by trade unionists. The results of my inquiry revealing the devastating consequences of ill-advised political action, were published in the *American Federationist* and incorporated in my report to the convention. This made the Socialists all the more eager to displace me. They came to Denver with high hopes. As the election of officers approached in the convention, the Socialists arranged for a rousing mass meeting in the largest hall in Denver. Eugene Debs sent a telegram of greetings to that meeting. The vote in the election for president resulted in: McBride, 1170; Gompers, 976.

John McBride, president of the U. M. W., was not a delegate to the convention. The four delegates from the United Mine Workers of America were Phil H. Penna, N. R. Hysell, Patraick McBryde, and John Nugent. Phil Penna was at the time first vice-president of the United Mine Workers of America, and in the case of a vacancy in the presidency would automatically become president. When McBride resigned in order to begin the duties of the president of the A. F. of L., Penna became president of the United Mine Workers. August McCraith of the International Typographical Union, R. H. Metcalf of the International Molders' Union, James Lanahan of the Brotherhood of Carpenters, and J. M. Barnes of the Cigarmakers' International Union voted for McBride. They kept their bargain, and thereby hangs the tale. Each of these men had been approached and offered an agreement that if he voted for McBride as president, the Miners' delegation would vote for him for secretary of the American Federation of Labor. This is the way the bargain was carried out. After McBride and the other officers had been elected, the nominations for secretary of the Federation were then in order. McCraith, Metcalf, Lanahan, and Barnes were all nominated for secretary, and during the balloting each of the four delegates for the miners voted for one of the four nominated for secretary.

When the election of John McBride was announced, I arose and offered a motion to make the election unanimous, and it was adopted. I deemed it to the best interests of labor and the organized labor movement that the president should hold office by unanimous consent.

Soon after my return from Denver occurred an incident that touched me deeply. A group of about thirty men active in the labor movement about Boston tendered me a breakfast at the old Quincy House. Their purpose was to manifest their affection for me and an expression of their regard after my defeat as president of the Federation at Denver. At that breakfast these friends presented to me a set of Herbert Spencer's works, signing their names on the blank pages of the first volume. When Spencer was in this country, I met him and heard him speak several times. I read with great care and deep interest the works of Herbert Spencer.

Then I turned my attention to earning a living. A great weight seemed to roll from my shoulders. My inclination was to return to the cigar bench, for I had never enjoyed life so much as in the days when I worked at my trade. I had a number of urgent requests for lectures and articles for magazines and newspapers. The proceeds for this work averaged more than my regular salary had been. But I was not to escape the responsibility of organizing work.

Charlie Reichers came to me and urged that I make a trip through the South for the United Garment Workers. I knew just how badly the organization needed a traveling organizer, and I could not refuse the workers to whom I had always given of my best thought and energy. The trade with its deplorable conditions would appeal to anybody's sympathy, and I had been associated with the formation of the

Garment Workers' Union. I accepted the commission for the Garment Workers and started on a long trip through the Atlantic Coast states, the Gulf states, and up through Missouri and back to New York. That trip constituted my first real acquaintance with the South. It brought me face to face with facts which no intelligent person could ignore. Of course, I never entertained the thought of anything approaching social equality, but I did believe, and still to a very large extent believe, that equality of opportunity in the economic field should be accorded to colored workmen. At least, they ought to have the right to organize for their common protection and mutual interests, and every assistance should be given them by our labor movement in the furtherance of that purpose.

At the 1891 convention of the Federation held in Birmingham, we changed the hotel headquarters of the Federation in order that all delegates should be treated equally. There were several Negro delegates. It had been our pleasant custom to arrange an annual dinner as part of the convention program. This was turned into a reception in deference to local feeling. That southern trip made me realize the difference between racial problems as theories and practical situations.

P. J. McGuire and I were elected by the Denver Convention to be the first fraternal delegates to the British Trades Union Congress, which met that year in Cardiff. For a number of months in advance I planned to get the most out of that experience. The Federation allowed me $225 to pay for the passage on the trip, including compensation and living expenses. I traveled second class both ways. I left New York about the last week in August. That was my first return to England which I left in 1863. In London I visited my old home in Fort Street and my relatives, of whom there were still many, though the majority had moved to New York.

The week before the opening of the congress we went to Manchester, Liverpool, and Dublin. In each city we addressed meetings of wage-earners and found many opportunities to acquire information. Both McGuire and I were intensely interested in the Irish effort for freedom. At the time all Irish workingmen were divided between the Parnell and anti-Parnell wings of the Irish National Movement. Despite the fact that every delegate to the Dublin Trades Council was ardently devoted to one of the causes for Ireland, the council in its sessions remained neutral. I addressed this body.

The Trades Union Congress convened September 2. I was interested in studying the proposals that came before the congress as well as their method of procedure. They covered a wide range. I was particularly interested in a proposal for the nationalization of land and the means of production, which had been referred by the previous congress to the Parliamentary Committee. When the proposal came before the Cardiff Congress, it was defeated by a vote of 607,000 to 186,000. The proposal was almost identical with Plank 10, which had been defeated at the Denver Convention of the Federation.

When we had finished our work in Great Britain, we went to the Continent where we visited Paris, Hamburg, and Amsterdam.

The Federation convention at the end of 1895 was held in New York City. During that year, as I have elsewhere recorded, President McBride had publicly and consistently advocated compulsory arbitration "as a settlement of all labor troubles." To this policy the trade union movement was emphatically and decidedly opposed. McBride's position on this question alienated a large number of trade unionists from him. I had not the slightest idea of again being a candidate for the presidency of the Federation. But I was none the less, as much as anyone, opposed to allowing compulsory arbitration to constitute one of the tenets of the American labor movement. During the early days of the New York convention, a number of representative men came to me and urged my acceptance of the candidacy for the presidency of the American Federation of Labor. Finally, I yielded, and at the convention was elected to the presidency over McBride, who had occupied that position one year.

Acceptance of the call to further official duty meant something of the nature of sacrifice to both my family and me. When I went west to take charge of the Indianapolis office, January 1, 1896, I did not feel enough permanency in the relationship to warrant the expense of moving my family to that city. Besides, it would have meant the rending of many ties that made New York a very dear home. The factional divisions within the Federation that worked for my defeat at Denver and for the removal of the headquarters from New York City made me doubtful whether the Federation development would continue along the trade union lines upon which it was founded, and if constructive practical policies were not maintained, I could not, in good conscience, remain spokesman for the organization.

When I reached Indianapolis, I found [that] the office of the Fed-

eration was directly opposite the offices of the International Typographical Union on the same floor. William V. Prescott was then president. It
was the time of the introduction of the Mergenthaler typesetting machine in the printing trades. The union had not determined its official
policy. Again and again I talked through the problem with Prescott, urging him strongly to advocate a policy of not opposing labor-saving machinery, but to plan so that the workman could control the use of the
machine through the union instead of permitting the machine to control
the printers. The wisdom of the printers in dealing with this issue gave
the union a strategic advantage in the development of the printing industry.

The work of the Federation progressed in a most satisfactory
way. A few months after I got back into the harness we added a second
stenographer, a typist, a shipping clerk, and an office boy. In 1896 the
Federation was established as a permanent organization and had no
competitors. We had developed discipline as an essential of trade unionism. With discipline the movement emerged from confusion of thinking
and practice to a definite trade union philosophy. A practical business
administrative system within unions had provided offices, salaried officials, and the beginnings of systematic labor records. All these things
were necessary to sustained contractual relations with employers. The
trade agreement we had found to be an important instrumentality in advancing toward the goal of trade unionism.

Not only was the Federation serving as a clearing house for existing trade unions, but we were helping to gather unorganized workers
into unions and out of local unions to develop national trade organizations. The growth and problems of autonomy of our Federation were
much akin to the problem of sovereignty growing out of our Federal
government. The stability of the Federation was due to our insistance
upon voluntary principles and practices of non-partisan political policy.

It was this convention at Cincinnati [1896] that [resulted in] the
complete justification for my course by unanimously re-electing me to
office.

It was about the first of January 1897, that I came to Washington
to find suitable office rooms. The task was difficult, for wherever I made
inquiries rents had been raised to disproportionate sums. The Federation changed quarters as it outgrew its housing. The 1908 (Denver) Convention authorized the building of a national labor headquarters. I was

one of the committee of three entrusted with carrying out that mandate. To my mind the building was to be of the nature of a Labor Temple, so I opposed the customary plan of letting the ground floor for stores lest the money-changers should filter into the temple.

Our building is a seven-story structure, the product of union labor, standing on a commanding site on Massachusetts Avenue at Ninth Street.

I omitted no ceremony that would serve to emphasize the sentimental and spiritual significance of the building; at both the breaking of ground and the corner-stone laying we had fitting services. My son, Henry, a union granite cutter by trade, who had been the first office boy of the Federation, asked the privilege of contributing the cornerstone. On it is an inscription which I formulated and which he carved: "This edifice erected for service in the cause of Labor, Justice, Freedom, Humanity."

Substantial proof of stability and the influence labor has achieved is presented in the contrast between the one room back on East Eighth Street, New York, donated rent free, and our seven-story building at whose dedication President Wilson was present and spoke appreciatively of the national service of labor. That was a proud day for me. There were gathered in Washington representatives from labor organizations all over the United States and Canada, representing orderly self-development in the ranks of America's workers. As I watched labor men gather that day I thought of the old days when the morning of a labor gathering found travel-stained labor men sleeping on the benches in the station. Then we got no pay for the work we did and thought ourselves lucky if traveling expenses were refunded. It took many of us years to get away from our somewhat impractical feeling that to take money for serving the cause of labor was a desecration.

When we moved into our office building, I gave orders that each morning the American flag should be raised on our flag pole and under it the pennant of the A. F. of L. and that at sunset they should be lowered. The order typified my conception of the relationship of the A. F. of L. to the Stars and Stripes.

4

OPINIONS AND POLITICS

1890–1910

Socialists as I Know Them

MY PERSONAL KNOWLEDGE of Socialists extends over a period of six decades. My judgments have not been based upon second-hand information. As I have stated in earlier chapters, I early became acquainted
with two opposing factions of Socialism in the old International Workingmen's Association, the Marxian Socialists who understood that labor
activity must rest upon the trade union as its foundation, and the Lassallean group which placed the emphasis on political activity. I have known
Socialists who were personal students under Karl Marx—those who
knew the movement from its source. Among these were F. A. Sorge,
J. P. McDonnell, Conrad Carl, and Ferdinand Laurrell.

There were many others in the labor movement who in the early
days called themselves Socialists, because the term was used then very
loosely, but who came inevitably to the practices and policies necessitated by the growth of American trade unionism. Many of those who

113

helped to lay the foundations of the trade union movement were men who had been through the experience of Socialism and found their way to sounder policies. They were always men of vision, to whom the spiritual implications of fellowship made a strong appeal, but their instincts for the practical carried them safely beyond the emotional to principles based upon a better understanding of human nature. They were far removed from the professional Socialists of later years.

I have known the later leaders in American Socialism from S. E. Schevitsch, Daniel DeLeon, Hermann Schleuter, down to Eugene Debs, Victor Berger, and Morris Hillquit. In the early days I used to argue with Socialists. I told them that the *Klassen Bewustzsein* (class consciousness) of which they made so much was not either a fundamental or an inherent element, for class consciousness was a mental process shared by all who had imagination, but that primitive force that had its origin in experience only was *Klassengefühl* (class feeling). This group feeling is one of the strongest cohesive forces in the labor movement.

The Socialists within the Federation tried in many ways to control our declarations and policies. The first big battle came over a barefaced attempt to get a trade union standing for the Socialist Party made in connection with the charter of the central body of New York City. The old Central Labor Union had become corrupt, and a new organization was formed—the Central Labor Federation which applied for charter from the A. F. of L. After the charter was granted, differences with the older organization were adjusted, and the charter returned. Trouble developed again, and Ernest Bohm, the secretary, asked to have the charter returned. I ruled that the old charter was surrendered and application must be filed for a new one. After many protests, this course was pursued. To the charter application was appended a list of the unions of which the C. L. F. was composed. In it was "New York section of the Socialist Labor Party." It would have been easy for me to have granted the charter automatically. However, I knew that course was wrong—no political organization had a right to representation in the trade union movement. A trade union card was the only claim to membership in the A. F. of L. which I would recognize. I refused to grant the charter. An appeal was made to the Executive Committee which sustained my ruling. A veritable tumult of Socialist rage clamored against my position. I was charged with trying to drive the Socialists out of the labor movement. The Socialists declared they would appeal from my decision to the coming convention [1890] which was to be held in Detroit.

In my report to that convention I stated my action upon the case and clearly set forth the issue—maintenance of trade unions. I used a phrase that became a current term in labor circles during the next few years. I said: "I am willing to subordinate my opinions to the well being, harmony, and success of the labor movement; I am willing to sacrifice myself upon the altar of any phase or action it may take for its advancement; I am willing to step aside if that will promote our cause; but I cannot and will not prove false to my convictions that the trade unions pure and simple are the natural organizations of the wage workers to secure their present and practical improvement and to achieve their final emancipation." The phrase "pure and simple" has been often used in a derogatory sense against trade unions and trade unionists.

The issue came squarely before the convention when Lucien Sanial, one who had never belonged to a trade or labor union, presented credentials from the C. L. F. and asked to be seated as its delegate. The Socialist faction, led by Thomas J. Morgan, fought hard for their contention. Many concurred in the opinion voiced by Mr. Morgan, who said: "In my judgment it is one of the greatest mistakes the New York men have made." The vote in the convention was 1574 for the committee's report, 496 against, and 5 not voting. Thus, the Detroit convention gave a decisive rebuff to the Socialist Labor Party's effort to worm its way into the labor movement.

The longer I live the more grateful I am to Ferdinand Laurrell, who saved me from the quagmire of Socialism. Yet many of my utterances in those days could not be classified as conservative statements, for the fire and vigor of youth grow very hot against injustice. I never tried to delude myself into believing that men in authority were not often prejudiced against the labor movement, and I made few concessions to official prestige.

The second effort to commit the Federation to Socialism came in our 1893 Convention held in Chicago. T. J. Morgan was spokesman for the Socialists who launched a vigorous campaign to gain control of the Federation immediately after their defeat at Detroit. Morgan introduced a number of "radical" resolutions in the convention, one of which was a political program consisting of eleven planks. With one exception, the program was a summary of legislative measures in support of which the Federation was on record. The exception was Plank 10: "The collective ownership by the people of all means of production and distribution." Morgan proposed that this political program be referred to affiliated organizations for favorable consideration in order that they should instruct their delegates to the next convention on the proposal.

When the resolution came before the convention, the convention voted to strike out the word "favorable" and automatically referred the program for consideration. After that action the Socialists became very bitter and vindictive and made their attacks personal, charging me with responsibility. I knew that for a year the labor movement would be in ferment, considering the Plank 10, not the question of twenty cents an hour more or a shorter workday, but Plank 10. And it was so. The Socialists laid their plans to prevent my election as president that year. Should they fail in that, they proposed to remove national headquarters from New York intending that action as a vote of discredit. John McBride was nominated against me. When I was declared elected, I took the chair and immediately wrote on a piece of scratch paper, which I laid on the desk of Secretary Evans:

> I hereby tender my resignation as President of the American Federation of Labor to which I have just been elected.
>
> SAMUEL GOMPERS

The resignation was to be submitted if the offices were moved. However, the Socialists could not secure enough votes to put through their program.

During the following year I published the proposed political program in each issue of the *American Federationist*, the publication of which was authorized by that same convention. Copies of the program were sent all affiliated organizations, and the proposition was discussed during the year both in the *Federationist* and other labor publications and by labor organizations. The Socialists were active in seeing that the largest possible quota of Socialists were sent to Denver. They came in numbers with high hopes.

The political program was made a special order. It was taken up section by section. Very methodically and conclusively the consideration proceeded. Many of the planks were changed to make them consistently trade union, and in that form each was adopted. No time of the convention was wasted in making speeches against Socialism, but the Socialist trick program was demolished by ridicule. Each separate plank was adopted (after amendments), and then the convention refused to adopt the program as a whole. The Socialists raged helplessly. Only one part of their program was a success, and elsewhere I have explained how that was accomplished. They elected John McBride president of the Federation for the following year.

Year after year the Socialists continued their efforts to get endorsement for their propaganda. To the trade unionists their talk program became a wearisome repetition, which gradually lost even its educational value. In the Boston convention came a sort of a climax. After the Socialist oratory had cleared away, I asked for the floor and made one of the most incisive speeches I have ever made, closing with this statement:

> I want to tell you, Socialists, that I have studied your philosophy; read your works upon economics, and not the meanest of them; studied your standard works, both in English and German—have not only read, but studied them. I have heard your orators and watched the work of your movement the world over. I have kept close watch upon your doctrines for thirty years; have been closely associated with many of you and know how you think and what you propose. I know, too, what you have up your sleeve. And I want to say that I am entirely at variance with your philosophy. I declare it to you, I am not only at variance with your doctrines, but with your philosophy. Economically, you are unsound; socially you are wrong; industrially you are an impossibility.

The roll-call vote on the recommendation of the committee to non-concur in the resolution was adopted by a vote of 11,282 to 2,147.

Outside of other considerations, if there were anything required to demonstrate the absolute accuracy of my Boston convention statement, the Soviet régime in Russia has fully established it, for there are no bolder exemplars of Socialism in its fullest ramifications than are Lenin, Trotzky, and their associates. Under their régime they put the philosophy of Socialism into practice with the resultant failure, brutality, and the reintroduction of compulsory labor. There, after five years, the Soviets have demonstrated beyond question that Socialism is economically unsound, socially wrong, and industrially impossible.

After Boston, the Socialists gave up hope of committing the Federation to the socialistic program and began a sniping campaign against labor officials they considered especially obnoxious to their purposes.

They succeeded in defeating James O'Connell of the Machinists and John B. Lennon of the Tailors. They were most energetic in their efforts to defeat me. Failing in that, they sought to discredit my policies. They attacked and denounced my relations with the National Civic Federation.

The N. C. F., with its practical efforts to bring about conferences between employers and wage-earners in order that there might be face-to-face discussions of industrial relations, was striking at suspicion bred of isolation in which class conflict has its roots. The Socialists were so ardent to take the world by storm at the ballot box that they preached without cessation the doctrine of irreconcilable interests and class war. They rigorously opposed any organization or any movement to secure betterment under the existing industrial order. When labor representatives attended meetings of the N. C. F. and became actively identified with its Bureau of Conciliation and Mediation, the class-conscious comrades in horror declaimed that we were being blinded and chloroformed. They set industriously to work to spread propaganda discrediting the organization and sought to get action by labor unions instructing officers and members to withdraw from the N. C. F. Such a resolution of instructions was adopted by the United Mine Workers. The attempt was made in the Atlanta (1911) convention to get similar declarations by the Federation. The convention emphatically rejected the resolution.

The next big issue between the Socialists and the trade unionists grew out of the World War. Again it was my part to lead the fight against Socialist tactics and position. The story of that I shall tell in later chapters.

Efforts to Disrupt the Federation

No one can organize a successful movement without stimulating desire in others to do likewise. For years my life was a relentless fight to maintain cohesive forces within the Federation against disintegrating tendencies. In addition, I had to combat organized movements to destroy. At first, this phase of the work was concerned chiefly with overcoming the dual activities of the K. of L. The first threat of serious geographic schism in the Federation ranks developed over a secession movement within the brewers' organization. The first attempt to displace the principles of the trade union came with the American Railway Union.

With the A. R. U. [Pullman] strike Eugene V. Debs loomed on the horizon as a leader of irregular movements and lost causes. I had known Debs for a number of years while he was editor of the official journal of the Brotherhood of Locomotive Firemen. Our relations were cordial and friendly. The Grand Chief of the organization, Frank Sargent, I also knew very well, and whenever opportunity presented itself I had suggested to these men union with the federated movement of trade unions. Both of these men as well as W. S. Carter, who succeeded Debs as editor, heartily favored affiliation with the A. F. of L. Several times I addressed the convention of the Firemen, urging them to do their part to unify the American labor movement and to remove the weakness resulting from "independent" labor organizations. In 1892 I invited Debs to address the Philadelphia Convention of the A. F. of L., but he was prevented from speaking by illness.

The first I heard of the American Railway Union was in 1891 when I was in Kansas City on my way to the Pacific Coast. George W. Howard came to see me at the hotel and told me he had a comprehensive plan for the organization of railway workers which he wished to present to me. Howard offered the plan to me and asked me to assume the initiative in launching it and become its president. The plan provided for amalgamation of all railroad workers in one organization. Although the railroad men were not well organized, they had remained outside the Federation. Neither had they developed a plan for concerted action among the brotherhoods. The Engineers were the best organized of railroad workers, but Grand Chief Arthur was opposed to an alliance with any other organized body of laborers. His policy, of course, did not facilitate the organization of the great mass of the railroad men. I told Howard that his plan was impractical and could not possibly succeed and that it would be wrong to try to undermine the railroad brotherhoods, for that was what his plan amounted to. I felt it was better to let the brotherhoods correct their own mistakes rather than to foster a dual organization with the hope of bringing railroad unions into the Federation. "Well," Howard remarked, "then I shall have to go to Gene Debs." I told Howard that if I knew anything about Debs he would repudiate the offer just as I had and resent the proposal.

Debs, as I have said, was one of the earliest members of the

Brotherhood of Locomotive Firemen. His ability was soon recognized, and he was made secretary of the Brotherhood; and then upon his own initiative he was relieved of the office of secretary to become editor of the Brotherhood's magazine. In that journal there was disclosed a bitter controversy between him and Chief Arthur upon the narrower policy of Arthur and the broader vision of Debs, who desired a greater co-operation among the labor movements of all trades and callings. However, I had felt that his loyalty to his Brotherhood would influence him not to engage in any such impractical venture, for I knew it could not succeed, or even if it could, that it would be treacherous to the organization which had placed its confidence in him. So when it was announced that Debs had accepted the position of leader and become president of the American Railway Union, I was truly shocked; though I bore Debs no ill will, I never could quite forgive him for his action and particularly for retaining the position of editor of the official magazine of the Brotherhood of Locomotive Firemen while undertaking to establish a rival organization which aimed for the disintegration and destruction of the brotherhoods, his own included.

Then genial Gene Debs, with much avowed idealism, tried to fit the labor movement into a different shape from that into which it had naturally developed. It is hard for the reformer to realize that the labor movement is a living thing and that it must develop by passing through the normal stages of growth. It is not transformed by any dictum or overnight resolution, but it must grow into something different. When Debs began to discount his judgment in favor of his emotions, he ceased to play a constructive part in the labor movement.

The organization was launched in a period of deep discouragment when the formula "One Big Union" was artfully used to imply that mere difference was a proof of effectiveness. The problem of type of organization is one that the Federation has repeatedly discussed and carefully considered. Under our system groups of workers are free to determine the form that best suits their needs with due regard, of course, for the interests of other groups.

I was chairman of the special committee authorized by the Scranton Convention to draft the Federation's policy upon this point. We pointed out the impossibility of establishing hard-and-fast lines between trades, and recommended that closely allied or subdivided crafts give consideration to amalgamation. The Federation, having no power of compulsion, could not enforce practices contrary to the wishes or rules of affiliated unions. The Federation does not instruct unions as to the structure of their organization. Unions may select the industrial form if they so desire, but we do not make the mistake of restricting unions to one model.*

In June 1893, a convention of railroad men in Chicago launched the American Railway Union with Debs as president, Howard, vice-president, and Keliher, secretary. Keliher in 1888 had founded the Brotherhood of Railway Carmen and served as its secretary-treasurer.

The A. R. U. made some progress during its first year. On the Great Northern there was a strike; and for a moment circumstances were to their favor and they won an agreement. It was not due to the A. R. U. that they won; it was due to influences brought to bear other than the organization. However, the success brought over-confidence.

The second convention of the A. R. U. occurred simultaneously with a strike in the Pullman car shops. These workers revolted against the arbitrary control which prevailed in the shops and social life of Pullman. The company refused to confer with their representatives or to arbitrate grievances. These unorganized workers turned to the nearest agency that promised aid, which happened to be the A. R. U., and that organization assumed control of the contest.

The strikers planned to bring every sleeping car in the country to the side tracks and to hold them there until George M. Pullman capitulated. Active co-operation of all in the operation service was needed. The grievances of the Pullman employes had the sympathy of every employe, as wage reductions had been declared in all trades. A sympathetic boycott spread through the Northwest. Trains carrying Pullman cars were stopped all along the way. In July freight and travel to Chicago were practically at a standstill.

Even papers that had never been friendly to labor conceded that no effort was spared to precipitate violence and then to give the impression it was due to strikers. Thus an opportunity was created for sending in troops. The Federal government intervened in this situation to main-

*The student's attention is called to the fact that the report of the Special Committee on Trade Union Autonomy as published in the Scranton printed proceedings was corrected by the subsequent convention of the American Federation of Labor held in New Orleans, and in its corrected form this report has been used in the official proceedings of the American Federation of Labor for several conventions.

tain interstate commerce and mail service. President Cleveland issued a proclamation to that effect. Attorney-General Olney plastered mail cars with injunctions enjoining the officers of the A. R. U. and railroad employes from "interfering with the mails or obstructing interstate commerce." Federal troops and United States marshals were mustered to crush the strike.

Information of conditions in Chicago came to me from many sources, but the Federation was not officially concerned until on July 9 I received a telegram from representatives of Chicago trade unions informing me that at a meeting held on Sunday a resolution had been adopted insisting that it was my duty to go to Chicago immediately and there to call a general strike. I have never had any delusion as to the real nature of a general strike. I consulted those members of the Executive Council whom I could reach and by telegraph called a meeting of the Executive Committee for Chicago, July 12, and telegraphed to the executives of national and international organizations to meet the Council in Chicago for conference.

Our conferences were held in the Briggs House. Some Chicago locals had already responded to the call of the A. R. U. with strike and boycott. Many others throughout the country were waiting upon the decision of the conference. We were asked to order a general strike. Of course, we had no power or right to order a strike, but any recommendation we might make would have tremendous influence. It was a serious responsibility. To decide unwisely might mean the disruption of not only the railroad organizations but the shop unions and all other organizations that might co-operate.

After hearing Debs and other representatives, the conference considered the situation carefully. We thought it not inappropriate to ask President Cleveland to use his influence to adjust the difficulties. No answer was ever received.

We asked Debs to confer with us as to how we could be most helpful to the strike. He came and gave us an account of the strike situation. He asked that I be authorized to present to the Railroad Managers' Association the proposition that the strikers return to work at once in a body upon the condition that they be restored to their former positions, or in the event of failure to call a general strike. After asking that his request be considered at the earliest possible time, he retired. It was understood that I should advise him of our action that same night.

After a prolonged discussion in which it was pointed out that the proposal was a confession of failure and asked only for reinstatement, the conference agreed that Mr. Debs might select me and such other members of our conference as he might desire and a committee of citizens to act with him in presenting his proposition to the Railway Managers' Association.

It was after 1 A.M. when the conference adjourned. When I called at the Revere House, the clerk informed me that Mr. Debs had retired and could not be disturbed.

The conference met again at nine-thirty to consider the request to call a general strike. There was no authority vested anywhere to call a general strike. To recommend to various labor organizations to strike in sympathy with the A. R. U. movement was unfair to those wage-earners, as the A. R. U. statement confessed failure and that the strike was a lost cause. Such a course would destroy the constructive labor movement of the country. The conference appointed a committee consisting of four others and me to draft a statement expressing the position of the conference in the crisis. The conference recommended to the Executive Committee that $1,000 be appropriated for the legal defense fund for Eugene V. Debs.

The course pursued by the Federation was the biggest service that could have been performed to maintain the integrity of the Railroad Brotherhoods. Large numbers of their members had left their organizations and joined the A. R. U. It meant, if not disruption, weakening to a very serious extent. The chiefs of these organizations have had so little regard for the general welfare and protection of all workers, for the moral obligation of giving assistance as well as helping to maintain the agency through which assistance could be assured—that they have persisted in remaining apart from the Federation.

The Pullman strike had grown bigger than anyone had supposed possible. Its cause appealed to the consciences and hearts of even those who could not approve its methods and agencies. The boycott exceeded all expectations.

Debs was sent to the Woodstock jail for a year, and the A. R. U. shriveled and died. He came out of jail a changed man. He had lost all faith in the power of constructive work and became the advocate of revolt. As he had lost faith, he had lost his usefulness and became the apostle of failure and later of secession. Debs was emotionally intellectual. He had high ideals, but was without the practical or constructive mind to put even the least of them into effect. In the economic field he championed and lost the A. R. U., the Western Labor Union, the American Labor Union, the Socialist Trade and Labor Alliance, the I. W. W.

No more sinister force ever appeared among the Socialists than Daniel Loeb or DeLeon, as he later called himself. He was first a single-taxer and then embraced Socialism, which became a fetish with him. When I first heard of him he was a professor in Columbia University; but Socialism became an obsession with him, and he gave up everything else for the Socialist Labor Party and its paper *The People*. He infused vitriol into Socialist propaganda. It was DeLeon who invented the epithet "labor fakirs" for application to trade union officials. He used his intellectual ability and training to embitter the differences between Socialists and trade unionists. DeLeon gathered round him a group devoted to warfare on trade unions. They could not content themselves with efforts to capture the labor movement or with the S. L. P. but determined to create a labor union of their own.

DeLeon again raised the slogan "the trade union is obsolete" and under this common slogan sought to salvage the bankrupt K. of L. When this failed, he drew up blue-prints and specifications for the "new unionism"—the Socialist Trade and Labor Alliance.

This Socialist union was to be a general hodge-podge or a perversion of the industrial union. It proposed to ignore the industrial and human forces which had generated the trade union. It was a movement that imperiled the American trade union to the development of which I had devoted so much of my life. I did everything within my power to resist these efforts at disruption.

The Western Federation of Miners composed of workers in the metalliferous mines for obvious reasons was one of the few labor organizations that originated in the West and had western headquarters. After the W. F. M. affiliated with the Federation [in 1896], there were continual rumors of its plans to withdraw. Many of these rumors were founded upon statements of Ed Boyce, president of the organization. There were natural forces which tended to separate the labor movement of the western states from that of the eastern in those days when means of communication were not so good as now. For a time I was able to counteract Boyce's influence, but he was so determined to subordinate the labor movement to Socialism that reason could not prevail upon him. So without authority he directed that no per capita tax should be forwarded to our Federation nor reports made to it—this despite the order of his organization.

When I heard that Ed Boyce was making the statement in public speeches that trade unions were obsolete, his line of talk was so familiar to me that I knew what policies to expect. Through the many avenues of information open to me came rumors that the metal miners intended to withdraw from the Federation. Such a step meant, of course, the beginning of a schism along regional lines. Realizing all the weakness and difficulties that come from division, I reasoned with Boyce and wrote the convention of the W. F. M., urging harmony and uninterrupted progress. I sent representatives of the Federation to their conventions. Nevertheless, the W. F. M., in 1897, withdrew from the A. F. of L. and began sowing seeds of disruption. It was not very long before they launched the Western Labor Union and fostered dual unionism.

The Western Labor Union was chartering unions in rivalry with the unions of the regular trade unions. The western movement was sadly honeycombed with dual unions. It was common information that the W. L. U. had under consideration plans to invade the East with its propaganda of division and misunderstanding of economic power. In 1902 the Executive Committee sent a committee to the convention of the Western Federation of Miners. That committee spent three hours with the convention. However, Eugene Debs followed them with an eloquent, glowing appeal, pointing to the East as the promised land which they might enter and possess if they would endorse Socialism and launch a dual organization along national lines. Debs won the day for secession. The American Labor Union was launched but was short-lived. Debs, the invincible leader of lost causes, had twice failed to develop his conception of organization for American labor and then offered his services to lead a movement to organize a world labor movement. He was aided by prominent "radicals"—those who were unable to work with the regular labor movement. William Haywood, a lieutenant of Ed Boyce, joined the group forming the Industrial Workers of the World.

This organization was to be "truly" international, gathering within its protecting circle and into its sectors the workers of all countries organized by industries. This organization was launched as a rival to the A. F. of L. Some of these men were the victims of bad judgment, others were guided by the rule or ruin idea. They launched an organization which denounced trade agreements and which glorified violence and waste. They failed to attract the dependable American workers. They made an appeal to the reckless, the unprincipled, the uneducated, the unstable. The "wobbly" movement has never been more than a radical fungus on the labor movement, those who could not fit into a normal, rational movement. The I. W. W. was frankly revolutionary and had an appeal to a limited number of wage-earners. Now and then I encountered the I. W. W.'s in my work.

Women's Work

I have known a number of remarkable women both within and without the labor movement. Nothing has been more essential to the sustained progress of the labor movement than the conscious and unconscious co-operation of the womenfolk of union men. My daily observation taught me the meaning of the sacrifices made by the wives of men who have devoted themselves to the labor movement. Not only did the wife share privations and actual want, but she lived the spiritual sacrifice of being helpmate to a man who gives an absorbing cause first demand on his life. I have often said that labor leaders ought not to marry—but I did not follow that advice. Neither my wife nor my daughters ever made a murmur against the hardships of our life, which included even hunger.

There have been within the labor movement, in addition to those who sustained this sort of auxiliary relationship to the labor movement, wonderful women trade unionists, for the labor movement, like all primary human movements, is neither male nor female—it is the instrumentality of unity. So I have never felt that there was properly a sex phase to the fundamentals of trade unionism. Trade unionism is to protect all who work for wages, whether male or female.

Devotion to trade unionism leads to interest in movements for freedom in all relations of life; consequently, I was early interested in the movement for equal suffrage. Equal rights for all brought me logically to endorse the women's struggle for equal political and legal rights. At that early day, the cause was at the height of its greatest unpopularity. I was one of the early advocates of woman's suffrage even at the time when Victoria Woodhull was confusing the cause with all manner of wild ideas. In 1891 I secured the signature of over 229,000 organized workmen to a petition which I presented to Congress asking for the Susan B. Anthony constitutional amendment providing suffrage for women equally with men. In later years I found myself in harmony with the suffrage movement as led by Mrs. Carrie Chapman Catt, and it was a source of considerable gratification to me to co-operate with her from time to time until the equal suffrage amendment was finally passed.

Women were not employed in all industries when I first entered the industrial field, but I was accustomed to thinking of women as industrial employes from daily seeing them employed in the cigar industry. Girls worked as strippers and on the less expert work, and women were employed where molds (the early machine process) were in use. The natural and safe thing seemed to me to organize these women workers into unions of the trade. This idea has been the basis of all my thinking concerning women and the industrial problem. I did not see how the welfare of wage-earners could be most effectively promoted in an industry where the men were organized and the women unorganized. I firmly believed that the problem was economic and that the development and organization of the economic power of women wage-earners were essential to the permanent economic betterment of all.

While the large number of women were advocating equal suffrage, but few of them devoted any attention or activity to a movement in which I was deeply interested—that is, the movement to secure to women and girls equal pay with men and boys who were engaged in the same work. It was one of the principles for which I strongly contended within the labor movement. I believed, and as time goes on, I have become more fully convinced, that political equality without some degree of industrial independence would be more of a fantasy than a practical reality. In so far as was within my power, I endeavored to help women workers to understand principles and methods of economic power and self-help. In 1885 I helped to prepare a call issued by the Legislative Committee of the Federation urging all women workers to unite in trade unions.

Early the names of women appear in the list of organizers of the Federation. The first of these was Mary Kenny. In 1891 I had, upon one of my visits to Chicago, met Mary Kenny, a member of the Bookbinders' Union, whom I found to be an intelligent union woman with much to learn of the labor movement but anxious to learn and anxious to be of service. As we accumulated a little money in the treasury of the Federation, I determined to inaugurate a special effort to organize women workers. I wrote to Mary Kenny and asked her whether she would not spend several months in and around New York. She readily assented. She was anxious to help. I sent her a commission and with it a check to pay her immediate expenses. She came on to New York and worked there for a few months. I had also commissioned Dora Sullivan of Troy to organize the women workers of Troy. She organized a strong union of starchers.

In the early nineties there were in New York and in other cities working women's clubs and associations. These clubs which were not formally identified with the labor movement were not essentially economic and were generally organized by persons of the type we now call social workers. Women of intelligence and broad sympathies became interested in the problems of working girls and tried to help them. Grace Dodge and Ida Van Etten were active in this work in New York, both of whom were participants in the Henry George campaign. That campaign inaugurated a sort of humanitarian renaissance. It was from persons of this sort that there came proposals for legislation to improve the environment of women wage-earners. Practical measures resulted from their activities such as the enactment of legislation regulating the hours of work in factories for women and minors.

It was the beginning of the twentieth century when the Women's Trade Union League was launched—a somewhat different type of working-women's organization—for the purpose of organizing women into trade unions. As before, the leaders in this movement were largely social workers. I was in sympathy with the movement and gave it my cordial co-operation because I hoped it would lead to genuine trade union work.

William English Walling—a longtime friend—came to the Boston convention full of enthusiasm for the league of women workers. Mary Kenny O'Sullivan's quick mind caught the possibilities of the suggestion. When they submitted to me a proposal, I gave it most hearty approval and participated in the necessary conferences. It was a step toward the realization of the economic organization of women. I defended the movement against the dubious and tried to contribute counsel for its guidance. Under the leadership of Jane Addams and Mary McDowell, the movement became of national importance. The tendency has been steadily toward the domination of trade union influence. I have attended many of its regular conventions which were really national conferences on women in industry. In more recent years, Mrs. Raymond Robins, as president of the league, exercised good influence in promoting the organization of women workers into trade unions.

Some of the staunchest workers in the labor movement have been women. Some few of them, such as Sara Conboy, Mary Anderson, and Fannia Cohn have been rewarded by official position in unions whose membership is composed of both men and women. Of the service given, none was more remarkable than that of Lucy Robbins who gave up everything to establish a better understanding between the "radicals" and the labor movement. The concrete issue was pardon for political prisoners imprisoned for acts growing out of the War and not guilty of acts involving moral turpitude. With simple faith in men and women and in her cause, she refused to accept any negation and mobilized a demand for the release of conscientious objectors that compelled attention.

My Economic Philosophy

The first economic theory that came under my eyes was not calculated to make me think highly of economists. My mind intuitively rejected the iron law of wages, the immutable law of supply and demand, and similar so-called "natural laws." As a matter of fact, the laws had no connection with nature or economic forces, nor were they laws but merely theories which sought to justify existing practices. Everywhere those directing industries were seeking to bring about a control that served their purposes. Those who did not participate in determination of policies were treated as industrial spoils. As the control built up by holders of capital rested upon strategic economic advantage, I saw no reason why it was not just as practical for employes to mobilize and control their economic power as a counter-move. The force of such economic organization would interpose a protecting barrier against arbitrary employers who failed to understand that those who supplied human labor for industries were human beings, and thus make possible the development of constructive methods. My unfailing support of voluntary principles reflects my aversion to any theory of economic fatalism.

My span of life includes a series of industrial periods marked by panics, business depression, and wide-spread unemployment followed by a period of recuperation leading gradually to a return of "prosperity," better wages, and general employment. The period of depression was often called a period of so-called overproduction, which was really a period of underconsumption for the people I knew, a period of hard times. In a country as big and as fertile as ours, with so many willing workers seeking the chance to give service, the periods of unemployment accompanying depression in the business cycle have seemed to me an unnecessary blot upon American institutions.

During the fall and winter of 1893, there was widespread unemployment such as I had never seen before. When the session of the New York Legislature began the winter of 1893, I watched its deliberations carefully. Thomas C. Platt, president of the United States Express Company, was then a member of the Senate and controlled the Republican state party machine. When adjournment was approaching, there was no evidence of any constructive thought upon the unemployment problem. Even the appropriation bills carrying funds for public works were unpassed. Now I had no love for Platt and knew he had none for labor—but regardless of this, if Platt could do anything for the unemployed I was willing to use him as an instrumentality. I wrote him, asking that he consider the advisability of enacting legislation to appropriate money for public work, for I reminded him it would be bad policy to add to unemployment by failure to act upon the measure.

As I considered these facts, they seemed to me to indicate the necessity for a sustained policy of wage-increases in order that consumption levels should be maintained commensurate with the increases in production levels, and that credit control should be based upon production needs rather than upon speculative gain.

Wage-earners had to bear the consequences of the mismanagement and wrong-doings of others. In 1903 I noted indications of a recurring period of depression and in my report to the Boston Convention declared it the height of economic unwisdom to curtail the consuming power of the masses, because no industry or country could become great if founded upon poverty. Based upon my conception that wage rates can be used as a stabilizing force, I recommended that the working people should resist any attempt to reduce their wages or increase their hours of work.

When the business crisis came in 1907, I was prepared to make good use of my experiences. One of the functions of the annual meetings of the National Civic Federation is a dinner which is attended by important employers, big financiers, trade unionists, and many people well known nationally. The dinner furnished an extraordinarily advantageous stage from which to make a declaration for which I wanted national consideration. There were fully four hundred there talking conventionalities, men and women in evening clothes, the women gorgeous in gleaming jewels. Never have I felt more peculiarly alone. I was conscious that I was the spokesman of the "working class," and I didn't care how I startled or shocked the millionaires if I protected my fellows. I was ruthless in what I intended to do. The fire of the revolutionary was burning through me as I rose to make labor's reply to the careful, smug suggestions of retrenchment and wage reductions as the way out of the industrial stagnation. I fairly flung defiance at the buccaneers of industry as I declared, "Labor will not submit to any wage reductions."

The result of the 1907 experience convinced me that panics and business depression can be controlled, perhaps avoided, if we know contributing causes. I felt there must be certain fundamental principles of industrial order to which we could cling at such times. But I had to wait many years before I saw a comprehensive effort launched to study periods of depression and to determine principles of intelligent control. That came with the World War aftermath. Again labor opposed wage reductions and was fairly successful in holding normal increases. By this time management had begun to appreciate that maintaining wage levels means maintaining a stable purchasing demand and hence is a stabilizing force. Wage reductions by decreasing demand adds impetus to the trend toward business depression. On the other hand, gradual wage increases tend to absorb increases in production. It is my opinion based upon six decades of experience that the future will bring progressively high wage levels with gradual price decreases. When I contrast industrial conditions of the ten years following the War between the States and the conditions now, I am convinced that tendencies can be controlled in accord with principles developed through experience and study. As our knowledge widens, we shall be able to establish a stable industrial order in which organizations of wage-earners will be an integral part.

My experience has extended over periods in economic development in which the whole nature and organization of industry have been transformed. Within my span of life have come inventions that have been revolutionizing in effect. Electricity both for lighting and power, the telephone, the wireless, the submarine cable, the radio, the transcontinental railroad, aeroplane, electric street cars, internal combustion engine, cold storage, are a few of the changes that I have seen come. Methods of work, methods and agencies of communication, and facilities for travel have brought society so close together that merging of economic interests and activities has been an inevitable result. The consolidation came so gradually that many did not see the trend of development until some of the new trusts were exercising their newly found and rapacious powers. American spirit rebelled against it as a new form of tyranny, and the trust problem became a foremost issue in public discussion. The reformers in state Legislatures and Congress began to discuss legislation to protect the people. Most of the politicians seemed to think that by making a law they could prohibit trusts.

From the first I mistrusted the proposal to take the trust problem into the political field. It seemed to me we could not safely trust policies of repression, and furthermore, the economic field was competent to deal with policies of regulation. Regardless of anti-trust agitation, consolidation remained the trend. Quite contrary to the prevailing economic dogma that free competition was the necessary basis to industrial progress, the economies and efficiency of consolidation presaged tremendous strides.

When both in transportation and industrial organization there came pooling or merging of interests, the problem of financing the combines made the older financial game seem like child's play. Only central banks were competent to finance the large-scale undertakings, so the control of industry gravitated into the hands of Wall Street. The development seemed to me natural. The trust was a phase of the new industrial organization where groups replaced individual effort. Our problem was not to try to prevent a normal development but to find the principles and technique for utilizing group action and group production in furtherance of general welfare. It is a problem to whose solution the groups concerned should jointly contribute. The organization of management, finance, and producing workmen is the way to develop discipline and information within those groups. The next step, to my mind, is cooperation of all the groups with the pooling of information to determine control of the industry. The industry would thus become self-regulated and disciplined while checks interposed by organized consumers would deter non-social tendencies. As my contribution to this development, I have promoted the organization of workers and opposed attempts of politicians to bungle the economic development.

Organization was response to economic forces, and therefore I did not believe that arbitrary limitations especially by law could prevail against it. When the Sherman Anti-Trust Law was proposed, I did not believe it would be effective in curbing trusts, but fearing that attempts would be made to use the law against collective action by wage-earners, I went to several members of Congress and told them my fears. The bill originally introduced by Senator Sherman considered in the debates of 1890 was an anti-monopoly bill intended to restore full and free competition. Senator Sherman did not share [the] apprehension, but in order to avoid confusion accepted a proposal made by Senator [James Z.] George which specifically excluded arrangements, agreements, and combinations between laborers made with a view of lessening the number of hours or increasing their wages. Similar exemptions were provided for persons engaged in horticultural or agricultural pursuits who were seeking to increase the prices of agricultural or horticultural products. The Sherman Anti-Monopoly proposal with the exemption proviso was referred back to the Committee on the Judiciary with instructions to report within twenty days. When the bill was reported at the end of that time, it had been changed from an anti-monopoly to an anti-combination bill. In view of this change, the Senators did not believe it necessary to include the labor exemption proviso. Events soon demonstrated that the law was to be applied to labor unions and that it was not effective in curbing trusts.

In addition to proscription of trusts, our government began to develop a system of state regulation of privately owned and operated enterprises—such as railways. To this effort I gave my hearty support and co-operation, but I have resisted unswervingly all proposals to inaugurate government ownership and operation for two reasons: first, because I believe our main dependence lay in individual initiative; and secondly, because I believe the economic field is essentially different from the political and the legal.

I reached this conclusion gradually after discarding proposals to which I temporarily subscribed. Some which I have discarded have not infrequently been suggested again by "progressives" who dub me "conservative" or even reactionary. My method of evolving my philosophy has been intuitive.

The principles of political freedom worked out in our Republic have been based upon political equality. If the rights of any individual are infringed, he has the right of counsel. But where political conditions touch a man's daily life once, economic conditions will affect it fifty times. To insure economic justice, therefore, I hold that the principle of the right of counsel maintains. By economic counsel, I mean an agent expert upon the matters in question selected with the approval of the individual. Thus the economic organization of the workers is basic. This economic organization, in addition to its defensive service, is free to develop constructive functions as soon as it is accepted by the management and its spokesmen admitted to conferences considering various problems in which their work is concerned. This procedure provides a way to utilize the experience and the information of workmen, which in turn can be collected and systematized only through organization. Ultimately perhaps, those things which concern all industry may be determined by a national economic body, truly representative, competent to make decisions and to secure compliance, or political regulation must develop a new technique and more competent personnel.

The methods and the agencies for progress in the economic world must be evolved out of economic experience and life. It is a serious mistake to confuse the two fields or to carry the problems of one into the other. Trade unions or voluntary associations of wage-earners constitute one of the essential agencies for establishing procedure of control. The development of large-scale production, the increasing authority of science in determining processes, and the more recent investigations of management for the purpose of making it truly scientific, together with the marked tendency toward trade associations, are to me a most gratifying exemplification of my thought that discernment of the essential difference between the economic and the political clarifies the problem of progress.

Several times the plain question has been put to me by members of the Senate Committee on Judiciary: "Mr. Gompers, what can we do to allay the causes of strikes that bring discomfort and financial suffering to all alike?" I have had to answer, "Nothing." My answer has been interpreted as advocating a policy of drift. Quite the contrary to my real thought. Foremost in my mind is to tell the politicians to keep their hands off and thus to preserve voluntary institutions and opportunity for individual and group initiative and leave the way open to deal with problems as the experience and facts of industry shall indicate. I have, with equal emphasis, opposed submitting determination of industrial policies to courts. But it is difficult for lawyers to understand that the most important human justice comes through other agencies than the political.

Though frequently impatient with existing wrongs, I am not impatient with what sometimes seems the slow progress of the labor movement. My patience has rested upon realization of facts, not upon lack of idealism or sentiment. I realized that since the labor movement is a living, sentient thing, growth comes from life within. It can be aided, directed, but not forced. Just as a plant may be cultivated and pruned, cared for in every way, still it cannot be compelled to grow or flower, so the labor movement cannot be handled or computed as material quantities. I have worked a lifetime for the labor movement, and I feel that I know it as few others do. Out of that knowledge is born faith in its destiny and its high service.

Foreign Friends

During the six decades in which I have been identified with the organized labor movement, I have met the labor leaders of practically every country of the world. Though I was very young when we left London to join the immigrants in the New World, I was strongly imbued with the spirit of internationalism which the English factory workers of that day, at the cost of personal privations, were making the basis of the policies of their labor movement. Without understanding why, I accepted the principle that human freedom is a world-wide struggle.

Later years gave me the reasons for the interdependence of all nations. Yet on the other hand, as the years have passed, I have become increasingly American although I never fully plumbed the depth of my feeling for America until the World War came; but it never occurred to me in all the years that I have lived in this country to question that I am an American. The spirit of America took possession of me so completely that I have never felt alien and I used the term "foreign" as a native American would use it. So, many among those whom I regard as my foreign friends are those who were born in the land of my birth.

My earliest foreign friends were men in the labor movement in New York City but whose vital interests were still in the land of their birth. For the most part, each of these was still in correspondence with fellow-workers "back home." From these sources I got information of labor movements in various countries and some knowledge of individual leaders. The labor movements in many European countries were identified with efforts to overthrow the government; thus, many in New York were refugees, not a few of whom continued from that sanctuary to help the revolutionary group back home. These efforts always appealed to me, for I could never think of human freedom dispassionately.

The movement of this type with which I was longest associated was that for Irish freedom. New York was headquarters for the Irish Land League and a succession of efforts of a similar nature. The early organization was identified with the paper, *The Irish World and Labor Agitator*, the office of which was the Irish headquarters. Patrick Ford, the editor of the paper, was a very warm friend of mine, as was O'Donovan Rossa who wrote for the paper and served as the direct connection with the agitation work in Great Britain and Ireland. When J. P. McDonnell sought refuge in this country, I, of course, met him both at that office and in labor circles. Through this group I became actively identified with the movement for Irish Home Rule, and I came to know all of the Irish patriots and through them the Irish labor leaders.

I met De Valera through P. H. McCarthy and Andrew Gallegher while in San Francisco in 1920. An arrangement was made by which we spent an entire evening together, talking over the Irish situation. At the next convention of the A. F. of L. held in Denver, the Irish question was one of the pivotal issues. The Federation went the limit in support of "Free Ireland"; but as the Irish cause approached its goal it fell into the hands of those who were not so unselfishly dedicated to the cause as the old leaders, and achievement was handicapped by professional Irishmen in America.

As the German labor movement was numerically the strongest of all countries, it had much to do with shaping the international labor thought. The Socialist movement developed in Germany before the trade union movement. The conception of relationship between these two movements that existed in Germany was reflected in the international movement. In the early days, I had no special fight with Socialism. I maintained an open mind and was willing to learn from Socialists and to adopt any thought of theirs in which I could see constructive possibilities.

Through my German friends and many German publications I had a fairly good knowledge of the German situation. I was eager to meet German leaders, Socialists or trade unionists. My first contact with Carl Legien came through my friend A. von Elm, who left New York and returned to Hamburg, Germany, in the early eighties after working at his trade in New York twelve years. I met Legien first when I was in Hamburg in 1895 and again when I was in Europe in 1909. In 1911 he wrote me of his plans to come to the United States. He was anxious to know something of our country and our labor movement. He indicated his financial difficulties in making the trip. I at once offered to arrange a lecture tour under trade union auspices.

Like most German workingmen, Legien was a Socialist and a member of the party. The Socialist Party made an offer similar to mine. It so came about that I arranged with the trade unions a lecture tour for Legien across the country, and a return trip was arranged under Socialist Party auspices. As Legien was a member of the Reichstag, I arranged with W. B. Wilson to secure for him the courtesy of addressing the House of Representatives, a courtesy usually extended to a member of a foreign parliament. Mr. Wilson introduced the necessary resolution, which Victor Berger, the only Socialist member of the House, nearly ruined. He made his usual *faux pas*. He made a number of wild, radical statements. It required unanimous consent for the privilege. On account of Berger's "eloquence and logic," objections were raised by two members of the House who, upon Representative Wilson's appeal, withdrew them. Legien submitted his address to me before it was delivered and made several revisions upon my suggestion. It was interpreted in English to the House by Baumeister. After the delivery of the address, Legien, Berger, Baumeister, and I met in Berger's office and had quite a "pow-wow," at which I took opportunity to demonstrate the misrepresentations that Berger had uttered in regard to the American Federation of Labor during his then recent visit to Germany. From that time I could never see Mr. Berger, and he never wanted to see me.

We then discussed another proposition urged by the Socialist Party of the United States, the election of the officers of the American Federation of Labor by the system of the initiative and referendum. Mr. Legien said that such a system did not obtain in Germany nor in any other general federation of trade unions in the whole civilized world, that such a proposition was impractical, impossible, and ridiculous. Berger's discomfiture was so manifest that he left our little company abruptly.

We arranged a luncheon for Mr. Legien so that the representative labor men might have an opportunity to meet him. Legien was a very able man and seemed to be making a serious endeavor to understand American labor. However, upon his return to Germany he published a report of his trip through the United States which I thought in many respects very unfair. Legien selected a few pictures of workingmen's homes to illustrate his report. Some were shacks in outlying districts as homes for workingmen in the packing house district of Chicago. The workingmen who lived in those houses were immigrants who had not yet become Americanized and did not conform to American standards of living. The impression created through these pictures and certain portions of Legien's report were not calculated to do credit to the American labor movement. However, I think they were the natural mistake of a traveler who could stay only a few weeks in our immense country and who did not speak English.

My interest in conditions in Russia was first aroused by Russian immigrants who came to New York in the early eighties. Those wretched, hunted people seemed for a while just as likely to be exploited in the New World as in the Old. Their exploiters were largely their own fellow-countrymen. The danger to the Russians was also a menace to working standards in some of the trades in which they worked and thereby to American standards of life for all the workers in those trades. It was the labor movement of New York that first undertook the practical problem of Americanizing the immigrant workers. We set about Americanizing the Russians. The most effective agency to that end was the trade union. I worked both with the Baron Hirsch Fund and with the Hebrew labor organizations. I did not approve of organization along racial lines, but we all realized that to organize Hebrew trade unions was the first step in getting those immigrants into the American labor movement. Three men who were prominently identified with this work over a long period of years and with whom I became intimately acquainted through our work were Gregory Weinstein, Joseph Barondess, and Abram Cahan. Weinstein and Cahan were employed in a form of unskilled labor in the Stachelberg factory where I was working at my trade. They had but recently come from Russia to the United States. Cahan has rendered as great service to the Russians of this country as any other one individual. That relationship has been more or less similar to that of the old Jewish patriarch. He has been father, counselor, and spiritual advisor. Through his work as editor of the *Jewish Forward,* he has exerted a tremendous influence in New York City and in the Jewish labor movement of our country. We have not always been in harmony on policies, but of late years there has been no stauncher defender of the American trade union than Abe Cahan.

There were many Englishmen who took a prominent part in the American labor movement, and through them and through my reading I was early familiar with the leaders of the British labor movement. The Dockers' strike in London attracted world-wide attention. It developed a number of new men, among them John Burns, Ben Tillett, James Sexton, and Tom Mann, and as a result I immediately began correspondence with them and received replies of a most fraternal character. That movement had done much to raise the standards of the Dock Laborers. One of the results of this correspondence was that in 1894 there was established between the Federation and the British Trade Union Congress, the custom of exchanging fraternal delegates annually, which constituted a powerful influence making for better understanding and friendliness between the labor movements of the two most important English-speaking countries.

My personal acquaintance with George Barnes began on his first trip. Mr. Barnes was then secretary of the Amalgamated Society of Engineers (now the Amalgamated Engineering Union). The members of that organization in the United States constituted a rival or dual body to the International Association of Machinists. More and more as time went on, it became evident that the trade union movement of America would develop its own entity and character and under conditions and circumstances particularly affecting America and the diverse character of her population.

The members of the American branch of the Amalgamated Society of Engineers were unable to maintain anything like a permanent existence. In the year 1888 the International Association of Machinists was formed at Atlanta, Georgia. It was regarded as a southern organization, and only after some years of its existence did it establish organizations in the eastern and northern parts of the country. With the election of

James O'Connell as its president, new energy was injected, and after a
few years I convinced O'Connell of the advantages of affiliation to our
Federation. He had no difficulty in having the convention of the organization adopt the proposal and make application. The situation as it existed in the English and the American organizations of machinists was
duplicated in the Amalgamated Society of Carpenters and the formation
later of the United Brotherhood of Carpenters and Joiners of America,
with this exception — that the Brotherhood of Carpenters was one of the
organizations which formed the American Federation of Labor. In the
full swing of rivalry between the American and English organizations,
feeling became very bitter, and it fell to my lot to conduct much correspondence with the officers of the Amalgamated Society of Engineers
and the Amalgamated Society of Carpenters and Joiners to bring about a
recognition of the principle that the American trade union movement
must have the exclusive right and jurisdiction over wage-earners of the
trades in America. Similarly, without the slightest prejudice to England
or Englishmen, I know that I carried that thought from the experience
of my young manhood into the labor movement to which I have referred
when with Alonzo B. Caldwell, I started the Independent Order of Foresters with authority vested in officers elected by citizens of America
and with the American administrators for the functions of the fraternity.

Japan was over-populated, and everywhere her people were
coming in increasing numbers to the western coast of this country and
were taking possession of whole localities in California. In addition to
the differences in standards of life, there was a racial issue which made
the situation critical. Organized labor of California determined to protect American workers. They united with other indignant Californians in
demanding that the Legislature of California pass a law denying Japanese the right to own land in California. This agitation reached its height
shortly after the World War had begun. In accord with the Anglo-Japa-
nese Alliance, Japan became an active belligerent against Germany. The
proposal of California to enact legislation that would precipitate difficulties between the United States and the government of Japan made the
situation very acute. The Wilson administration was extremely anxious.
The Secretary of State, William J. Bryan, went to California in person to
effect a compromise. During this critical time it was necessary for me to
see the President. When I called up Mr. Tumulty to make an appointment, he told me that there was an urgent matter which he would like

to discuss with me, and it was arranged that I should go to the White House in advance of my appointment with the President in order to have a talk with his secretary. Mr. Tumulty told me of the international implications of the California situation and asked me whether I would not request the California State Federation of Labor to withhold for the time being its demand for the enactment of anti-Japanese land laws. I told him I would do the best I could and drafted a telegram to Paul Scharrenberg which I showed to him. Mr. Tumulty took the telegram in to show to the President and returned with the statement that in his opinion it would be materially helpful.

Shortly afterwards, Dr. Gulick, who had been in Japan for thirty years, came to urge my co-operation in promoting a more friendly attitude toward the Japanese. He thought that considerable of the feeling against the Japanese was due to a hostile press. Dr. Gulick, as he was preparing to return, asked me if I had any advice to send to the working people of Japan. I dictated for him the philosophy underlying the labor movement organized upon principles of voluntary co-operation. [That] the wisdom to use freedom and power must develop through experience was the keynote of the message I sent to Japanese workers.

There had long been Cuban cigarmakers in New York City, and some of these were identified with the Cuban junta. At the solicitation of some of these workers who were shopmen of mine, I at first attended their meetings. As I became more interested, I went more frequently. It was there in that work that I met Charles A. Dana, whom I came to know very well. Through Mr. Dana I met José Marti, a writer and a member of the Cuban junta. Then I met Estrada de Palma, the first President of free Cuba, and many others prominent in the long struggle.

The Cubans with whom I worked in the factory were usually skilled workmen and belonged to our union. Cuba, which was the chief foreign market from which the United States imported tobacco and finished cigars, was of special interest to cigarmakers. In order to evade high tariff on cigars, Cuban cigar factories not infrequently opened shops in New York. Cuban workmen followed these shops. It was important for us that not only Cuban cigarmakers in New York should be organized but that we should spread the gospel of unionism in Cuba. But a labor movement was practically impossible under Spanish rule, which was at variance with the idea that the poor have rights. The Cuban revolutionary movement found the free masonic lodges effective

agencies through which to work. I had not at that time joined the masonic movement, but this experience was one of the chief reasons which
influenced that action.

When the Spanish-American War began in 1898, I was glad of
aid for the Cuban revolutionaries, but I was very apprehensive lest the
United States inaugurate a régime of imperialism.

In 1900, during the convention of the A. F. of L. meeting in
Louisville, I received a communication from Santiago Iglesias, who was
at that time in New York. Iglesias, Spanish by birth, had been living a
number of years in Porto Rico and had been active in the revolutionary
movement. He was a carpenter by trade, and his understanding of the
labor movement was based upon the Spanish school. He was then working in Brooklyn at his trade. In his usual resourceful way he got in touch
with what were known as the radical centers in New York. He met
Theodore F. Cuno, who was at the time working on the *New Yorker
Volkszeitung* and told him about labor conditions in Porto Rico. Cuno,
although a "radical" by profession, thoroughly understood that the only
agency that could help develop the labor movement in Porto Rico was
the American trade union movement. He advised Iglesias to get in
touch with me, and as the convention was then in session, some official
action might be secured in regard to Porto Rico.

The convention directed that the labor movement declare for the
right of fair trial, freedom of assembly, speech, and press for the workers of Porto Rico. Under this pledge of assistance, Iglesias returned to
Porto Rico where he was met at the docks by a government representative with a warrant for his arrest. He and other workmen were sentenced to terms of imprisonment on the ground that they had attempted
to increase wages and better working conditions. Under authorization of
the A. F. of L., I went to Porto Rico in 1904 where I made a thorough
investigation of conditions on the Island. Under the Spanish régime, labor unions had been illegal and were disbanded. With the coming of the
American flag, Porto Ricans had expected the rights and opportunities
for which our flag stands.

During our war with Spain, the Porto Rican people, believing in
the justice and democracy of our Republic, hailed with delight and enthusiasm the opportunity of aiding our army of occupation in Porto Rico,
Iglesias acting as a guide and interpreter for General Brooks. When
Porto Rico became a possession of the United States, her people had

neither the right of citizenship nor of representation in either house of Congress of the United States. Its international trade relations and regulations in so far as tariff was concerned were determined by the United States. They were bound by the same conditions as prevailed in any part of the United States. This reacted to the disadvantage of the people of Porto Rico both industrially and commercially.

Politics

Only once have I ever been a member of a political party. When I became of age I joined the Republican organization in the district in which I lived. To me it was an organization which still had a great purpose to fulfill. Lincoln typified that purpose in my mind. I received citizenship papers October 4, 1872, and have always tried to live up to the serious obligations of citizenship. My first vote was for Grant for President.

When I left the Republican Party I joined no other. In view of the fact that I have been charged with belonging first to one party and then to another, it may be of some interest to have the names of those for whom I have cast my ballot for president. As I have stated, my first vote after naturalization was cast for Grant; in 1876 I voted for Peter Cooper; in 1880 for James B. Weaver whom I knew personally and with whom I was on terms of good friendship. In 1884 I voted for Ben Butler; in 1888, for some cause which I do not now remember, I did not vote; in 1892 for General Weaver; in 1896 for William J. Bryan; 1900 for Bryan; 1904, Judge Alton B. Parker; 1908, Bryan; 1912, Woodrow Wilson; 1916, Woodrow Wilson; 1920, James B. Cox.

It will be observed that in recent years, I have voted for the presidential candidate on the Democratic ticket, and this has been interpreted by many to mean that I am a member of the Democratic Party. Anyone who will doubt the sincerity of the non-partisan policy which I have endeavored to pursue may compare the platform declarations of the Democratic and Republican Parties and judge for himself whether I was not justified as a labor man and, I hope I may say, as a forward-looking citizen, in casting my vote for a candidate nominated upon the Democratic platform. In the elections for Senators and Representatives, there is better opportunity to exercise the non-partisan policy, for I have supported or opposed the election of men aspiring to those offices with absolute impartiality, basing my course upon the pledges, attitude, and records of those candidates. That in recent years more Democratic candidates have been favorably disposed toward the cause of labor and freedom than have Republicans, is not the fault of my associates or myself.

In addition to our interests which we as citizens have in the outcome of elections and legislation, we have a primary interest in the protection and promotion of the rights interests, and welfare of the toiling masses of our country.

I have always sought to use political situations for labor's advantage. In the days when I was working at my trade, before the Australian Ballot system was adopted, it was hard for a workingman to maintain his right to independent use of his ballot. No one will for a moment deny that even to the present day employers, particularly in big business, exercise altogether too much power and influence over the votes of their employes, but that does not indicate to any degree the former power and coercion of employers to control the votes of their workmen. It was not an uncommon practice in establishments employing a large number of men that the workers, under the leadership of some overseer or foreman, were marched to their various voting precincts to cast their votes under immediate surveillance. It was due to these conditions that organized labor initiated a movement to bring about secret voting, then known as the "Australian Ballot."

Following the industrial depression and financial panic of 1893, the money problem became the paramount issue in the presidential campaign of 1896. The monetary system of our country had, from its formation, been the free coinage of silver at a ratio of sixteen to one. The Republican Convention which nominated Mr. McKinley for President declared for the gold standard. The Democratic Convention nominated Mr. Bryan upon the silver platform. It is not necessary for me to discuss the wisdom of either declaration. However, a large mass of our people were "greenbackers," and a much larger portion of them had been swept upon an enthusiastic wave for the free coinage of silver.

The 1893 convention of the A. F. of L. had declared in favor of free coinage of silver. This position was reaffirmed in 1894 when the issue still had no partisan bearings. There was a greater tenseness of feeling accompanying the presidential campaign of 1896 than any other within my experience except that of 1916. Free silver meant to the masses who were not capitalists, liberation from the goldbugs of Wall

Street, who seemed to have a stranglehold on the nation. Feeling was so intense as to play havoc with party regularity and to make dispassioned judgments impossible.

I was active in that campaign as was necessary in order to carry out the mandate of the Federation in favor of free silver. The Federation found itself in danger of being drawn into partisan politics. I had been directed to issue a bulletin relating labor's position on silver coinage. This produced a storm from the Bryanites because it failed to endorse the Democratic Party and a protest from the Republicans who interpreted it as favorable to Bryan.

During that summer I made a number of speeches. I was for free silver, not the Democratic Party. If the Democratic Party favored free silver, well and good, for legislation is altogether too frequently enacted by partisan sponsorship. Throughout the campaign I refused to let the labor movement be annexed by a political party, and I refused to lead them into a policy from which it would take decades to recover. I was attacked by the silver people, but I refused to yield my responsibility to the American labor movement.

I have accepted political appointments to which no salary was attached. One which afforded most genuine satisfaction was membership on the New York State Factory Investigating Commission.

The needless loss of 145 lives in the Triangle fire in 1911 shocked the public into a realization that something ought to be done to eliminate the preventable hazards of industry. The New York Legislature authorized the appointment of a commission to inquire into factory conditions and make recommendations to the Legislature. The following were appointed by the Governor: Senator Robert F. Wagner, Chairman; Assemblyman Alfred E. Smith; Charles M. Hamilton; Edward D. Jackson; Cyrus W. Phillips; Simon Brentano; Robert E. Dowling; Mary E. Dreier, and I. Abram I. Elkus was our chief counsel with Bernard L. Shientag as his assistant; Frank A. Tierney, Secretary.

Beginning with its organization in August 1911, until our report was filed in 1913, I gave intensive service. We, of course, had an adequate staff of technical experts and tried to mobilize all of the information which science and experience had developed as the basis for our recommendations and report. The deliberations and findings of our commission were an important event in the development of industrial safety, sanitation, and hygiene. We recommended to the Legislature bills to establish the necessary administrative governmental machinery. This involved re-organization of the state Department of Labor. Other measures dealt with safety standards, hours of work for women and children, and other measures to conserve human life and health.

After our report and recommendations had been submitted, February 19, 1913, was designated by the joint committees of the Legislature as the day upon which hearings would be held on bills prepared by our commission and also upon Workmen's Compensation Bills. A hearing was later to be held before Governor Sulzer in the executive chamber. The executive chamber was crowded, and Governor Sulzer delivered an address, declaring his purpose to aid in having the best laws enacted so as to benefit and protect not only the working people but all of the people of the sovereign state. There was little opposition to the commission bills except the one prohibiting thereafter the construction of bakeshops below the street level. In 1914 the Legislature passed a Workmen's Compensation Law to be administered by a commission of three.

5

THE NATIONAL
ORGANIZATION ESTABLISHED

1900–1915

THE COMING of the twentieth century found the Federation with well-developed polices and methods. The vicissitudes which had beset our Federation in the early years, the antagonism, the rivalry of the Knights of Labor, the lagging confidence and support of the rank and file of the organized, and the lethargy of the unorganized made it a most difficult task to lay a firm foundation for growth in numbers, effectiveness, and power.

The first step in securing permanent betterment for wage-earners of America was to organize them into bona fide unions of trades or callings, skilled or unskilled, to unite and federate them so that they might exercise influence and power upon the economic field to maintain what they had and to drive on and on for a better day. Wage increases, reductions in the hours of labor, at least one rest day in the week were more potential in the meaning of the life and progress of the workers of our country than the voting for any candidate of any political party. In making these purposes the compass of the labor movement, we had entered

147

a period of stabilization and expansion made possible by the firm foundations we had laid.

By the beginning of the twentieth century, our Federation had developed concrete and comprehensive methods of work. With the period of industrial prosperity which accompanied the new century, our work of organization was extended along lines paralleling industrial developments. Our agitation work had to do with problems arising out of sustained and organized opposition which employers began to interpose through their organizations. It was the period of rapid development of large-scale organization and trusts. Industrial corporations introduced a system under which the actual owners had practically nothing to do with management. The corporation substituted a fictitious person for the old-time employer who knew each of his workmen, and thereby dehumanized industrial relations. There were the beginnings of the technology of management, the rudiments of so-called efficiency. Like many another field of activity, the first attempts failed to find all the fundamentals. It proposed to treat wage-earners in just the same fashion that it treated the materials of industry. Against this mechanistic trend the labor movement interposed a demand that the human factor in production be considered and workers treated as men and women.

We had developed the machinery and the discipline of the labor movement. Discipline and regularization supplemented other cohesive forces that sustained it. We had developed self-imposed discipline that enabled us to go through a period of financial depression with our lines pretty well intact. We had established the leadership of the Federation in the labor world and as a national force.

With the twentieth century there came a period of extraordinarily rapid growth in the American Federation of Labor. It was the harvest of the years of organizing work which were beginning to bear fruits. Increase in numbers took the form of affiliation of national trade organizations and the extension of the principle of organization to workers in what were then called the "unskilled" occupations.

There were many more national trade organizations in those days than now. The structural bases of unions have varied with the development of machinery, new processes, and changing materials. Many national trade unions have consolidated, merged unions in allied trades, or passed out of existence. It was obvious that the keystone to sustained constructive service by the labor movement was the trade agreement reached through collective bargaining. In a large measure the work of establishing collective bargaining as a part of industrial procedure was educational. To have the support of public opinion was of strategic advantage in arguing for recognition as a normal industrial agency. The growth and expansion of the twentieth century multiplied the contacts between the labor movement and outside agencies and directed the activity of the labor movement as a constructive force in society as well as in industry.

Among the pioneer organizations which recognized responsibility for developing national industrial policies was the National Civic Federation. This organization brought together individuals committed to the policy of recognizing the necessity and service of organized labor. It arranged personal contacts between three groups: labor, employers, and the so-called public. It helped to establish the practice of accepting labor unions as an integral social element and logically of including their representatives in groups to discuss policies. I entered the organization with many reservations and with a distinct attitude of alertness, if not suspicion. I was not in the habit of meeting employers except for the purposes of avoiding labor troubles or effecting labor agreements and adjustment of labor difficulties.

In N. C. F. conferences, wage-earners were on an equal footing with employers. Such contacts contributed to the making of a new concept of human relations in industry and to laying the foundation for the rule of reason. Such an organization was possible only because of the progress that the labor movement had made. Of course, the N. C. F. was useless without the support of the A. F. of L. The first president was Mark Hanna, an outstanding employer of that day who stood for the principle of collective bargaining before others were ready to accept it. By common consent I was made first vice-president, an office which I have held continuously.

I was very closely in touch with the work of the organization through whose general conferences I found innumerable opportunities to present labor's story to employers while we were talking as man to man. The contacts helped me to reach the men who controlled the making of industrial policies. There were representatives of the biggest business interests in America in the N. C. F. and in attendance at its general meetings.

Although I have gone freely and frequently among meetings of employers and to any sort of a conference that they might invite me, I have gone as the spokesman for labor and have always felt that I had to be on guard, for I have feared the Greeks even when bearing gifts. The way that I have been able to best maintain most complete alertness has been to defer gratification of any physical appetite or pleasure. At [the] dinner of Charles R. Flint as at many similar dinners and banquets I did not eat the food served. After the dinner [Sam] Donnelly and [Henry] White went with me to a restaurant where I got a bite to eat. My practice about eating, however, was never extended to prohibition of smoking, if good cigars were available.

In all my relationships with the National Civic Federation, I have been on the alert, but in all justice to that organization, it should be understood that no position it has taken upon labor has been adopted in which I did not have an influencing vote. If any mistake in policy was made, it was not through a desire to injure labor but because there was not a complete understanding, and such mistakes have been remedied when I have submitted the good reasons why the policies ought to be revised. My association has been conditioned upon the helpfulness of the relationship. Undoubtedly, the forum instituted under the auspices of this organization made possible a wider understanding of labor issues and afforded a rather dramatic background for important statements. Before the Federal Department of Labor was authorized by Congress, the N. C. F. undoubtedly rendered a constructive service in its corps of conciliators whose services were available in industrial disputes. However, my relationship with the N. C. F. has not been viewed without suspicion by some of those within and without the labor movement.

Objections have come chiefly from those who relied upon declarations on "class consciousness" as a claim to leadership in the labor movement. These self-advertised radicals have time and again tried to force me to withdraw from the N. C. F. Because I knew I was advancing the interests of the labor movement through that relationship, I steadfastly refused to withdraw; several times the issue was injected into the conventions of the American Federation of Labor, notably at Atlanta, but after full discussion on the issue, my course has uniformly been heartily endorsed.

The changing industrial tendencies of the twentieth century were first manifest in the basic industries. Impersonal management supported by concentrated economic power presented difficult problems to our scattered and comparatively weak unions. The coal industry had been partly organized. Out of the coal strike inaugurated in 1897 came the agreement for collective bargaining in the central competitive field in 1898. On the other hand, union development did not keep pace with rapid consolidation in the steel, textile, and packing industries. Our progress was conditioned by many human factors which determined action by the rank and file as well as leadership.

The second big achievement in coal came through the anthracite strike of 1902, which was an epoch-making event in labor history. Since the nineties, there had been no trade unions in the anthracite district, and the Coal Trust was in control. It was a combination of mines and coal-carrying roads. When I was in the district in 1897 with George Chance and P. J. McGuire, we discovered very definitely that one of the chief conditions by which the operators prevented organization was the power they exercised through company police and detectives.

After the United Mine Workers established collective bargaining in the bituminous field, they undertook to secure a similar agreement in the anthracite region. There followed a battle royal with the anthracite trust. John Mitchell, who had become president of the United Mine Workers in 1898, was then a young man and comparatively inexperienced.

Control of the anthracite mines and the coal-carrying roads of Pennsylvania was in the hands of two Wall Street groups unfriendly to each other. J. Pierpont Morgan was at the head of one group. The partner of his firm who was closest to him was George W. Perkins, who was very active in the work of the National Civic Federation. Perkins had a broad human understanding of the problems of industrial relations. The group with which he was associated had submitted a three-year agreement which was receiving attention until the Miners' convention, contrary to the advice of President Mitchell and his Executive Board, declared solidly in favor of a sympathetic strike of the bituminous miners in support of the anthracite union. As the bituminous miners were working under an unexpired contract, the very discussion of a sympathetic strike aroused unfavorable criticism even though it was never approved. The anthracite operators at once seized this action as an opportunity to declare that labor agreements were worthless. Because there has been need for so much militancy in the labor movement it has not always been possible to maintain an even balance of judgment which makes against violation of contracts.

I knew that a strike was inevitable in 1902 unless the operators conceded the Miners' demands. It was improbable that they would concede, so we prepared to gain the utmost of advantage in the way of the support of public opinion. The National Civic Federation had just organized its Division of Conciliation and Mediation. I was asked to draft a statement of the purposes of the Division that would be acceptable to labor, and I remember performing that particular duty, going downtown to a meeting of the Civic Federation in one of the New York street cars. It was as follows: "To do whatever may seem best to promote industrial peace and prosperity; to be helpful in establishing rightful relations between employers and workers; by its good offices to endeavor to obviate and prevent strikes and lockouts; to aid in renewing industrial relations where a rupture has occurred." All agreements were to be mutual, and no power of compulsion was permitted.

When the anthracite coal situation became acute, it was arranged that this Division should call conferences of the operators and the Miners. Two such conferences were held before the existing agreement expired. On May 12 work was suspended in the mines. All mine workers remained out until October 23. During the summer months, no one worried about the strike. The American Federation of Labor helped to finance the strikers, for the United Mine Workers did not have big resources. We issued an appeal to all wage-earners. The anthracite miners showed no signs of weakening, but week after week maintained a solid front.

About the middle of September, when public interest in the strike was keenest, occurred the first formal meeting of the Coal Trust under its official name "Temple Iron Company." The group comprising this trust were the anthracite operators and representatives of the coal-carrying roads. The meeting was attended with the kind of publicity that made it an affront to public intelligence. It was deliberate defiance of the Sherman Anti-Trust Act as well as public opinion and welfare. There had been arranged for the evening of that same day a gigantic protest meeting to be held in Madison Square.

When it became time for coal consumers to lay in the winter supply, anxiety developed, but it was significant that no one questioned the position of the miners. The politicians became anxious, particularly the two Senators from Pennsylvania, Quay and Penrose. On October 1, President Roosevelt sent telegrams to the miners and mine operators asking them to come to Washington for a conference. Although President Roosevelt put the case bluntly and insisted that public interest was primarily concerned, the operators refused absolutely to make any concessions. President Roosevelt asked the representatives of both sides to submit the issues in dispute to a commission to be named by him. Again the operators refused. Following this suggestion, John Mitchell made the proposal that the entire controversy be submitted to J. Pierpont Morgan. Morgan was heavily interested in the anthracite situation, but the miners had confidence in his fairness and confidence in the justice of their demands. In a few days, conferences were called in New York. Morgan was working indirectly to bring about an adjustment. Again the operators rejected all suggestions. Then Mr. Morgan came to Washington.

Before naming the personnel of the anthracite coal commission, Roosevelt had a series of conferences with John Mitchell, Frank Sargent, and me. Mitchell made a strong plea to have a representative of the mine workers on the commission or in any event to have a representative of organized labor. Roosevelt did not feel that he could force the operators to go along in case he made such an appointment. The commission was not only to make recommendations upon the industrial controversy but was to point out methods by which the industry itself could be better organized in order to avert future industrial ruptures. The work of that commission was one of the pioneer studies of an industry from the approach of scientific organization.

Several times I have been asked what in my opinion was the most important single incident in the labor movement of the United States, and I have invariably replied: the strike of the anthracite miners in Pennsylvania. The conditions of the miners in the bituminous and anthracite fields were terrible. The 1897 strike formed the beginning of the movement for the regeneration of the miners, and then the anthracite fields were affected, but there were so many varieties of nationalities, of politics, of religious antagonisms that concerted action was practically impossible; neither trusted the other, and all lost confidence in themselves. The shacks and huts in which the anthracite miners lived and the "pluck me" stores were in full blast. The miners' families had not only to pay rent to the corporations which owned the shacks, but they had to make their purchases of all the necessaries of life, meager as they were, from the company stores at double the prices for which they could be had elsewhere. If the full amount earned had not been purchased, they were hauled before some overseer and threatened with eviction and discharge. The tools, gunpowder, and clothes, such as they were, all had to be purchased from the company. There was the company doctor for which the men had to pay, the company graveyard, the company parson or preacher, so that it was a common saying that children were brought into the world by the company doctor, lived in a company house or hut, were nurtured by the company store, baptized by the company parson, buried in a company coffin, and laid away in the company graveyard. Boys of ten, eight, and six years of age were employed as breaker-boys in the mines. The strike of the miners abolished that whole system. They secured the shorter work-day with higher pay, and from then on the miners became not merely human machines to produce coal but men and citizens, taking their place among the fairly well-paid, intelligent men, husbands, fathers, abreast of all the people not only of their communities but of the republic. The strike was evidence of the effectiveness of trade unions even when contending against trusts.

In steel, the second basic industry, the elements in the problem were slightly different from those of coal, and the union policies practically the opposite. In that industry came the culmination of the trust idea, with the formation of what was then regarded as a super-trust, the United States Steel Corporation. Up until that time labor organizations maintained their standing in the steel industry.

In the eighties and the early nineties the Amalgamated Association of Iron and Steel Workers was the strongest trade union in America. It had been officered by able men. Its membership had been chiefly English, Irish and Welsh. The Amalgamated Association had been accepted by employers as one of the necessary agencies in the industry. The Association united with employers in furtherance of protective tariff. When the flood of new immigration began sweeping into the steel industry, the Amalgamated refused to organize the unskilled workers who were increasing rapidly in numbers. At the time of the Carnegie strike, the Amalgamated controlled eighty per cent of the workers in the industry. When the steel corporation was organized by J. Pierpont Morgan and Company, Shaffer, then president of the Amalgamated, contrary to my advice, made a demand upon Morgan for the establishment of the closed union shop. Morgan resented Shaffer's demand and flatly declared he would oppose him and break him if it took five years. The

Steel Corporation adopted a policy of opposing extension of trade union organization. The steel workers called strike after strike, but made no progress. In the much-discussed strike of 1904 I made use of every agency available to me to assist Shaffer by getting conferences for him with the powers of Wall Street and by trying to further mutual understanding.

Things went on from bad to worse, until in 1909 I made the proposal that we launch a new campaign for organizing the steel workers. My plan was to have a committee of representatives of those organizations immediately concerned and to accompany the work of organization with a demand upon the government to investigate the United States Steel Corporation. I did not believe in the Sherman Anti-Trust Law because I did not believe that legislation would prevent normal, necessary development of industry; but since the law was on the statute books and the practices of the steel corporation were in open and flagrant violation of that law and since the corporation denied to wage-earners the right of collective action which they arrogated to themselves, it seemed to me that the labor movement was in a strategic position to call attention to the situation.

However, the organization campaign did not succeed. Under its cheap labor policy, the steel industry filled its mills with workers from eastern and southeastern Europe, creating difficulties of Americanization and unionization. It was not until the European War and stoppage of immigration that another real opportunity arose that made an organization campaign seem feasible.

Compulsion

Compulsory arbitration has been suggested at one time or another since the middle eighties when strikes were in progress or impending and before committees of Congress. After I have opposed bills for compulsory arbitration and compulsory enforcement of the terms of arbitration, I have frequently been asked what I proposed as a substitute. My invariable answer was: "Strikes are due to resentment against deterioration in the workers' conditions or an aspiration for a better life. There is nothing you can do by law to prevent these normal movements and actions of the working people." The proponents of compulsion are invariably those whose relation to industry is indirect or inimical to labor.

In truth, I have never looked hopefully upon arbitration as a method for achieving satisfactory industrial results. Satisfactory industrial agreements must, it seems to me, be evolved out of a mutual experience and understanding between the parties most concerned. Arbitration injects influences not immediately concerned in production. But disinterestedness should not be confused with equity. Absence of industrial dislocations does not necessarily mean industrial peace. Nor does industrial peace necessarily indicate industrial progress. The suggestion is deceptive because it seems an easy way to accomplish a difficult task. Some trade unionists were deceived by the suggestion. These were chiefly men whose thinking was not directed by a well-grounded economic philosophy, and usually they worked in trades that were not well organized.

The first proposals within my experience for compulsory arbitration were suggested with reference to transportation. But there was no unity in the thought of the labor movement upon that point at that time. The chiefs of the Railroad Brotherhoods favored the proposals, and they were representing the workers chiefly concerned. The Brotherhoods were then weak organizations with little promise of their present splendid strength. The situation involved difficulties.

During 1895, the year McBride was president of the Federation, the first Erdman Bill with its compulsory features was introduced in the House. He was in favor of the principle, having written several newspaper articles advocating the adoption of legislation to establish compulsory arbitration. The New York Convention [1895] adopted a resolution drawn up by Furuseth and me, making earnest and emphatic protest against compulsory arbitration of labor disputes—compulsory compliance with award and decision which would make it an offense to quit employment.

However, the Railroad Brotherhoods made up their minds they wanted the Erdman Act. When the bill was introduced in the next Congress by General Grovenour of Ohio, P. J. McGuire, Furuseth, and I went before the House Committee on Labor in opposition. As the members of the railroad unions would be most affected by the measure, I could not well maintain my opposition to the bill. My effort was turned toward excluding other groups of transportation workers from the scope of the legislation and toward preventing further acceptance of the principle of compulsion.

The Erdman Act, approved June 1, 1898, provided for mediation, conciliation, and arbitration in case of industrial disputes affecting railroad employes engaging in the operation of trains in interstate commerce. Contrary to expectations, it was the mediation and conciliation service that proved to be important and effective. Voluntary adjustment prevented for a number of years any railroad strike of considerable importance.

I saw in the proposal to establish arbitration carrying any degree of compulsion a blow at the fundamentals of voluntary institutions which to my thinking are the heart of freedom. I felt we had to keep open opportunities for freedom and initiative. All worthwhile achievement is based upon progress of individuals. My idea of voluntary institutions has been my most dependable measuring stick in many perplexing problems which the years have brought. Many have thought me over-insistent upon this point because they failed to grasp the directing vision. My insistence has made me not a little obnoxious to some within the labor movement and others without who have advocated short cuts to desirable objectives.

My resistance to the entering wedge of compulsion in industrial relations in America probably was a deterrent to efforts to bring the railroad organizations into the Federation. A proposal to affiliate had been discussed with Frank Sargent, the Grand Chief of the Order of Railroad Firemen, and W. S. Carter, who succeeded Eugene Debs as editor of the official journal of the Firemen. Upon their urgent request I went to Galveston in 1896 to address their convention. James O'Connell of the machinists was there at the same time. I felt sure that if the Firemen decided to affiliate, the other Brotherhoods would follow as a natural result. The chief difficulty was to get somebody to make the break. Though my address was received cordially, the desired action did not follow.

Discussion of compulsory arbitration paralleled the development of the idea that the public has an interest in industrial disputes. Compulsory arbitration enforced by the government sounded well to the intellectual groups. Compulsory arbitration was launched as the panacea for industrial ills. It fell to my lot to tell the other side of the story.

When next the issue of compulsory arbitration arose, it was in the shadow of the World War. The railroad men in the operating service, the four Brotherhoods acting together for the first time, demanded the eight-hour day in 1916. The railroad executives tried to force them to submit the eight-hour day and all other issues to arbitration. The refusal of the Brotherhoods brought the country face to face with a nation-wide railroad strike as a declaration of war was impending. Fortunately, there was a real man in the White House. He asked the 640 railroad representatives to come to the White House to confer with him. The President met first the railroad managers and the presidents; then he talked with the Brotherhood Chiefs. Then Mr. Wilson declared that the eight-hour day had been accepted by society and was not properly an issue to be arbitrated. He announced as part of the governmental program: To add to present agencies of mediation, conciliation, and arbitration full public investigation of disputes before a strike or lockout may lawfully be attempted.

The eight-hour law for private employment and compulsory arbitration were at variance with the policies of the labor movement. It was an embarrassing situation. Labor did not wish to jeopardize the nation at a time when foreign difficulties were imminent nor did it wish to seem unappreciative of the magnificent endorsement of the eight-hour day which the President had expressed. The Brotherhood Chiefs asked for a conference with me and my colleagues. This was the first conference held in the new A. F. of L. Building. They asked me to appear with them before the Senate Committee on Interstate Commerce. This I readily agreed to do. In that hearing I dealt only with the principles of compulsory arbitration as I could not give my approval to regulating by law hours of work in private industry. The Adamson Eight-Hour Law was approved just prior to the date designated for a strike to attain that purpose, but the compulsory arbitration measure was not enacted.

The Brotherhoods at this time were not advocating compulsion. They had had experience with that principle in Canada under the Lemieux Act, and the labor movement was united in opposition to compulsion.

The Adamson Law was for a basic eight-hour day to become effective January 1, 1917. The railroad executives secured an injunction, preventing the law from becoming operative and challenged its constitutionality. In March the four Brotherhoods declared that if the law did not go into operation on the evening of March 17 they would declare a strike. The strike threat came just at a time when we were daily expecting a declaration of war on Germany. I felt that the Railroad Brotherhoods had made a mistake in not striking on January 1, the date when the law was to become operative, but I did what I could to help present that case. At the time, I was a member of the Advisory Commission of the Council of National Defense. On March 16, Mr. [Newton] Baker, then Secretary of War and Chairman of the Council of National Defense, wrote that the Council had appointed Secretary Lane, Secretary Wilson, Mr. Daniel Willard, and me as a commission to bring about an adjustment of differences in the railway situation. The four Brotherhood Chiefs were present, and Elisha Lee, representing all the railroads, authorized by them to make a settlement in order not to interfere with necessary war-time activity. It was a hard, long session lasting all through the night until early dawn. As we watched the light breaking in the east, W. S. Carter remarked it was the breaking point for which he had long waited, the dawn of the eight-hour day for railroad men.

When the railroads were about to be returned by the Federal Rail Administration to private control, the thought was uppermost in many minds how to retain improvements in management that had been worked out in war-time. The railroad workers understood that their welfare was dependent on better management that made possible concentration on production and service problems. As a result of this desire a plan was suggested under which those in railroad work could control all decisions. With this purpose were associated government ownership and kindred suggestions that were at variance with industrial experience. While I was in attendance at the Peace Conference in Paris, this new railroad proposal was launched. The proposal which unfortunately was labeled the "Plumb Plan" was heralded in such a way as to create a sensation. The "intellectuals" filled the highbrow organs with praise, "Labor to operate the railroads!" The hard-headed and practical saw the old frame of government ownership in a new dress. Again it was my unpleasant task to point out the pitfalls lurking under appealing phrases. The Montreal Convention followed quickly, and the Federation at the request of the railroad unions endorsed government ownership of railroads. So when the Esch-Cummins Law was in the making, these unions were not in the most strategic position to oppose compulsory measures or the substitution of governmental agencies for voluntary methods. However, there was nothing to curb my expression of opinion, and I forcefully opposed compulsory arbitration and government boards. As the legal mind dominates Congress, it is hard to make a congressional committee understand that there is no way that Congress can create industrial good will by law. We succeeded in preventing the incorporation of compulsory measures. The Labor Board authorized was a colorless agency which would either accomplish nothing or repeatedly demand "more power." After giving the plan a trial, the railroad men are asking for the abolition of the Railway Labor Board.

Under our Federal system, the power of legal precedent is tremendous. An idea that gains a hearing in any legislative circle may travel the whole circuit. Every effort was made to develop an industrial cult out of compulsory arbitration. I regard no public service of mine of greater importance than my efforts extending over forty years to prevent the enactment of legislation of this character. I have tried to help others to understand that this type of legislation would only complicate industrial problems by introducing outside control. There is now practical unanimity among all labor men against all forms of compulsory arbitration, and employers and the general public have come to the same conclusion.

On the other hand, voluntary industrial institutions must come through the development of organization, the utilization of the intelligence of all concerned within the industry and the accumulation of industrial records.

The causes of strikes can largely be eliminated by the organization of working people into bona fide trade unions and by the organization of the employers, followed by provisions for chosen representatives to sit around the table and there discuss and determine the problems of industry, transportation, of standards of life and work and service. It is something not yet understood, that industrial agreements reached by negotiations between the organized workers and organized employers are a real product of industry, developed through experience and experimentation, unrestricted and competent to adjust themselves to the growth of the industry out of which they have developed.

Immigration

In my boyhood home in London, emigration to the New World was regarded as a very special opportunity for those who were able to make the journey. We heard that there was land in plenty for everyone, work in manifold abundance for everybody. The song of the day, "To the West, To the West," represents the sort of vision that we had of the vastness of the United States. When I reached the New World, never for a moment did I think of myself as an alien. I spoke the same language as the citizens of the United States though around about our little home in Attorney Street were to be heard many more different languages than could have been found in East Side London. Instinctively, I thought of those speaking other languages as the foreigners. As for myself, I felt identified with the people of my new home, and it was without a question that I accepted American customs and American institutions and the American life. To my mind the foreigner was the one who did not identify himself with American life and purposes.

So when I went to work in David Hirsch's shop, I found myself surrounded by fellow-workers who spoke little but German. However, I never thought of them as foreigners because they had identified themselves with the effort to work out the problems of our industry and participated in the common life of the city. But when the Bohemians began to come to New York in large numbers and allowed themselves to be used by the employers to build up the tenement-house factory system which threatened to submerge standards of life and work that we had established, I felt that those tenement workers were foreigners. The first step in Americanizing them was to bring them to conform to American standards of work, which was a stepping stone to American standards of life.

The next big industrial problem in immigration with which I came in contact resulted from the enormous influx of Jewish workers into New York in the eighties. Very few of the Jews who came had industrial training. Those who did were handicapped by not speaking English. Consequently, those immigrants crowded into any available employment where training and language offered the fewest obstacles. They were strangers in a new land. They had to provide subsistence for tomorrow in whatever opportunity it could be found. They crowded into unskilled callings and worked at starvation wages. They undermined standards and labor organizations, but they were under the urge of dire necessity. They were the products of decades of persecution. Even trades that had previously not been organized, under the need of protection against foreign workers, began to struggle to establish an agency to maintain definite standards.

We found it practically impossible to organize these Jewish workers in unions with other nationalities and, in fact, very hard to get a language by which we could give them an understanding of unionism. It was through an extraordinary little group which included Abram Cahan that Yiddish became the medium of propaganda. Joseph Barondess, Gregory Weinstein, Henry Miller were among those most active in this organization work. Despite many difficulties, we organized several Hebrew trade unions. There was a racial emotionalism and aspiration that both helped and hindered unionism. The Jews were fairly ravenous for education and eager for personal advancement, so that all industrial work was merely a stepping-stone to professional or managerial positions. We formed unions of cap makers, chorus singers, cutters, cloak makers and others. Individual unions fluctuated sharply, but the union movement grew steadily. I gave a great deal of time to this work and finally assisted in organizing the United Hebrew Trades—a policy that was theoretically bad but practically necessary and has eminently justified itself.

By the beginning of the nineties, the racial problem in the labor movement was beginning to assume serious proportions. Our problem was part of the larger national problem, for the majority of immigrants no longer came from Western Europe where language, customs, and industrial organization were similar to those of the United States but from the countries of Eastern Europe where lower standards of life and work prevailed. As these immigrants flooded basic industries, they threatened to destroy our standards.

I approached the immigration problem with the somewhat mixed feelings of one who had been an immigrant himself. Grateful that no barriers prevented my coming to this new country, I have always felt that restricting opportunities for others is a grave responsibility; yet as the number of immigrants rapidly increased and the admixture of various races was too rapid for assimilation, I could not escape the conclusion that some way must be found to safeguard America. America is the product of the daring, the genius, the idealism of those who left homes and kindred to settle in the new land. It is an ideal typifying a haven and an opportunity. In the early days, boundless and undeveloped resources made possible and expedient a policy of stimulating immigration. It was not until industrialism developed and there were evidences that the newer immigration was not being assimilated that as a nation we began to consider policies of regulation. The labor movement was among the first organizations to urge such policies. Our first proposal was the contract labor measure under which we hoped to prevent employers from importing strike breakers or workers to lower the standards by overcrowding what was termed the labor market.

In addition to the difficulties which confronted all immigrants, the Italians had to combat a system under which they were exploited by their own fellow-countrymen. Italians with some knowledge of American conditions and with some influence and financial backing would offer to secure for Italian immigrants employment under paternalistic supervision. These men were called padrones. They made contracts with employers in this country to supply labor. The padrone was to collect and pay wages to his group of workers and, of course, took his fee before distributing compensation to the immigrants. Vicious exploitation and the worst sort of graft resulted. As the majority of the Italian immigrants were illiterate, the padrones' grip was very strong.

The steady development of industrial interests in this country made demands for increased number of wage-earners more rapidly than could be supplied by the normal increase in population. Stimulated immigration resulted. Immigrants to this country are the raw materials out of which the labor movement has to develop an organized disciplined industrial machine. We immediately realized that immigration is in its fundamental aspects a labor problem. However, the earliest immigration proposals of the Federation were concerned only with honest administration of immigration bureaus and contract labor legislation which was intended to prevent the use of immigrants to disrupt the trade union movement.

The number of immigrants coming into this country had been growing steadily. Not only were the numbers increasing, but the character of immigration was changing. They were largely undisciplined in trade union policies and practices in their own country. This flood of immigrant workers drifted to so-called "unskilled" work. Practically, all of the basic industries were revising their production methods to substitute machine work in the place of previously indispensable craft skill.

The Nashville Convention [1897] adopted the report of its committee recommending that inasmuch as the majority of organizations favored restriction, the convention declare itself in favor of reasonable restriction, such as the educational test contained in the Lodge-Corliss measure. The discussion on this report was spirited. The convention declared in favor of a policy of restriction with educational tests. Upon no other proposal did we encounter more persistent or better organized opposition. The big employing interests of the country were determined to maintain a huge reserve of common labor which in their language meant low-waged labor. These propagandists for "big business" were abetted by idealists and sentimentalists who believed in the "open door" policy. That was a day before there was general understanding of the principle that maintenance of the nation depended upon the maintenance of racial purity and strength.

I realized that continual progress in organizing the wage-earners of the country involved the education and Americanization of the hordes of immigrants coming through our ports of entry. I did not believe that our national interests would be furthered by granting to the trusts unrestricted right to import cheap labor that could not be Americanized and could not be taught to render the same intelligent efficient service as was supplied by American workers.

Among the great economic and social problems which gripped me was Chinese coolie immigration to the United States. When Charles Bergman, with such clarity and force, laid the whole Pacific Coast situation before the Federation Convention at Pittsburgh in 1881, the convention declared without a dissenting vote the necessity for restricting Chinese coolie immigration and for their exclusion from the United States. Later, when Dennis Kearney came to New York, I had several conferences with him and with Hermann Gudstadt. I fully aligned myself with the California movement for exclusion and at every opportunity aided in safeguarding the people of America from the dangers which confronted us.

In advance it is my desire to state emphatically that I have no prejudice against the Chinese people. On the contrary, having some understanding of their history and the philosophy of their early sages, I have profound respect for the Chinese nation.

I have always opposed Chinese immigration not only because of the effect of Chinese standards of life and work but because of the racial problem created when Chinese and white workers were brought into the close contact of living and working side by side. I had a conference with President Roosevelt at Sagamore Hill. James Duncan and John Mitchell accompanied me. After we had discussed some other matters with the President, I called his attention to the increased immigration of Chinese laborers. The President declared emphatically that under no circumstances must Chinese workmen be permitted to enter the United States whether they were skilled or unskilled. I called the President's attention to the discontent of the people of the United States, particularly on the Western coast, with immigration of Japanese and Koreans. Roosevelt remarked that we must approach the question of Japanese immigration in an entirely different manner from the method used in regard to the Chinese. The Japanese had shown themselves to be great fighters and sailors, and if they were angry the United States would find itself in a serious situation as we were not prepared for aggressive warfare and also would find it necessary to protect the Philippines and Hawaiian Islands.

The state of California undertook to deal with the Japanese immigration problem within its own borders. The great majority of Japanese immigrants settled in localities close to the point of entrance until the proportion of Japanese began to grow in an alarming fashion. The white citizens objected to indiscriminate mingling of the two races in schools. When E. E. Schmitz became Mayor of San Francisco, the labor people naturally expected him to take action as Schmitz was a labor candidate and elected on a labor platform. Schmitz did not evade the issue, but with his School Board began the work of segregating Japanese children from the white children in the public schools. This was done under the Enabling Act of California.

Since many of the Japanese were not American citizens, it was necessary to take up with the Federal government such phases of the problem as were complicated by rights insured under foreign treaties. Mayor Schmitz kept me confidentially advised of all developments of the problem, and I was able to be helpful in conducting the necessary negotiations with President Roosevelt.

Roosevelt, as I have said, was of the opinion that the Japanese could not be summarily dealt with by legislative enactment as the Chinese were. I had several other conferences with him. In one of these conferences the President stated that he would emphatically censure California's treatment of the Japanese and hoped thereby to placate the Japanese government and to create the groundwork for the negotiations of the treaty between the two governments for the mutual exclusion from both countries of the laborers of each country.

I wrote to Olaf Tveitmoe, laying before him the whole situation in order that he might take it up with his fellow-unionists and friends who constituted the Chinese, Japanese, and Korean exclusion movement. Mr. Tveitmoe wrote me the problem was temporarily solved when Mayor Schmitz and the School Board of San Francisco worked out a plan of segregation so far as the schools were concerned.

In the 59th Congress immigration legislation was given unusual prominence. Senator Lodge and Representative Gardner were co-operating to have incorporated in the law a literacy test. Uncle Joe Cannon was opposing this feature of the bill with most diligent persistence. We were able to get through Congress that year a measure which placed control of Japanese and Korean immigration in the hands of the President. The law also provided for an immigration commission consisting of three members from the Senate, three from the House, and three to be appointed from the citizens of the country by the President. This commission was to report findings to Congress.

Public opinion moved just as slowly to accept the proposals for restricting immigration as did the organized labor movement. Throughout the intervening years I continued my effort to secure an Immigration Restriction Law for the United States. The literacy test remained the accepted method for setting up the restrictive standards. The two members of Congress who became distinctively identified with the literacy test were Senator Henry Cabot Lodge and his son-in-law, Augustus P. Gardner.

So far as I remember, this is the only issue upon which I have ever found myself in accord with Senator Lodge. I made a number of trips to the Capitol and the White House. On the "Hill" we encountered the same organized opposition which blocked the way of our injunction regulation proposals. It came, of course, from organized employers, such as the National Association of Manufacturers which inaugurated a campaign of hostility.

When President Wilson had under consideration the Burnett Immigration Bill to establish a literacy test, the last week in December 1914, he called a public conference in the White House for those most actively interested in the formulation of the legislation. About three hundred attended including both those who were opposed to the bill and those who favored it. Shortly after President Wilson vetoed the bill and returned it to Congress with his objections. [But] the dangers etched on a background of war had been sufficiently conclusive to convince a two-thirds majority of both houses in Congress that it was necessary to conserve American institutions. The bill passed the Senate by a two-thirds majority, but failed to pass in the House. It was introduced again at the next session of Congress and passed both Houses by over two-thirds majority. Again vetoed by President Wilson, it passed both houses over the President's veto.

Injunctions I Have Encountered

One of the first injunctions which came under my observation was that issued by a judge in the Cigarmakers' strike at Binghamton, New York, in the early eighties. The second was the injunction issued by a Federal court in New Orleans in connection with the Cotton Screw Workers' strike and the strike of many workers in several trades. That writ, so far as I can recall, was the first issued by a Federal court based upon alleged interference with interstate commerce in violation of the Sherman Anti-Trust Law.

The use of the injunction in industrial disputes by Federal courts made the issue acute. The lower courts had long followed the practice. Under this system the discretionary power of the judge supplanted government by law and substituted personal government by discretion. Overwhelming realization of the power of this governmental agency came with the American Railway Union strike of 1894. We were appalled. A placard bearing the seal of the U. S. Government made crimes of lawful and normal activities necessary to make the strike effective. The injunction converted the strike of the American Railway Union against the Pullman Company into a strike against the government. That is the effect sought by practically every injunction used in industrial disputes, and labor resents being tricked into such a false position. When the employer tries to sidestep and induce the government to make his fight for him, the working man feels he is the victim of conspiracy.

From that time, injunctions came in rapid succession, from both state and Federal courts. The great difficulty in testing the injunction cases is, that as a rule those writs are issued during a period when the workers seem to have the most favorable outlook for a successful termination of the dispute with the employers. For a time the injunction itself, instead of overawing the men, gives them a renewed spirit of determination, and they hire attorneys; but these attorneys usually take the position of entering a plea of not guilty not only for unlawful but lawful acts of the men and do not raise the fundamental issue involved—the right of the courts to issue injunctions forbidding the doing of lawful and normal acts. When the strike or lockout is ended, either by victory, defeat or compromise, the injunction appeal to higher courts ends; the writs, however, stand as the edict of the courts.

Such injunctions regulating industrial relations I hold to be illegal. Many injunctions have sought to prohibit workers from exercising their constitutional rights. Such injunctions can and ought to have no real authority. I believe that those to whom such injunctions are intended to apply ought to pay no attention to them whatsoever, but should stand upon their constitutional rights and take the consequences whatever they may be. "Resistance to tyranny is obedience to God," and resistance to the tyranny and injustice of injunctions which have been issued by our courts is necessary for a clear understanding by all our people of the principles involved.

My most grilling experience with injunctions came in the Buck's Stove & Range Company case. The foundry employes, as well as the metal polishers, declined to submit to an increase in the hours of their labor, and they were peremptorily dismissed by the company. Of course, the unions resented this action against their men and brought the subject to the attention of our succeeding convention and asked that the company's products be placed upon the "We Don't Patronize" list. Before so doing, as is the usual practice, the matter in dispute was referred to the Executive Council and in turn to me for investigation and an effort was made for an adjustment. James Van Cleave, president of the company, was also president of the National Association of Manufacturers. Finding all chances of an adjustment impossible, the Executive Council decided to publish the Buck's Stove & Range Company on the "We Don't Patronize" list in the *American Federationist*. It did not call upon anyone to refrain from purchasing any product—it merely stated a fact—that the company in question had acted unfairly toward the workers involved in the dispute. However, the company secured an injunction from the court forbidding the publication of the statement in the *American Federationist* or elsewhere. It enjoined all reference to the dispute in circulars, letters, or the spoken or printed word. It enjoined even our attorneys from discussing the principles involved.

Of course, as president of the A. F. of L., I could not ignore the terms of the injunction. It was absolutely essential to report the history of the case, including the injunction, to the following convention of the Federation, and this report, as well as the other evidence, was used in the contempt proceedings showing the violation of the terms of the injunction. This I held was manifestly in violation of the constitutional guarantees involving the right of free speech and free press. The injunction process denied that right in advance, preventing expression of opinion by individual or group.

Abuse of the injunctive writ had grown in frequency, until it had become the paramount issue in labor problems. It was at my suggestion that the Federation determined to select a particularly flagrant injunctive abuse to make a test case. Soon after that course was determined, the Buck's Stove & Range Company instituted injunction proceedings against the A. F. of L. This case was selected as it contained practically every phase of the abuse we wished to remedy.

After the injunction became operative, I gave orders to discontinue the publication of the "We Don't Patronize" list, but I refused even to consider suggestions that I should restrict my discussion of economic issues or place limits to my freedom of speech—written or spoken. In 1908 remedial legislation to prevent abuse of the injunctive writs was the crucial issue for which labor launched an intensive national campaign. We urged organized intelligent use of wage-earners' ballots. We presented labor's cause to the platform committees of both parties and then to the voters of the United States.

Following that campaign, contempt proceedings were instituted against John Mitchell, Frank Morrison, and me in the court of Judge Wright. Mitchell's offense was that he presided over the convention of the United Mine Workers which adopted a resolution to boycott the Buck's Stove & Range Company; Frank Morrison was charged with the act of distributing copies of the *American Federationist* and the official proceedings of the convention in which the history of the case was reported and discussed. My arguments in the presidential and congressional campaign, urging my fellow-citizens to take into consideration in casting their votes for the candidates for the presidency and the members of Congress the principles involved in our injunction suits, were held to be in violation of the terms of the injunction.

The court sentenced us to the following terms of imprisonment: Gompers, one year, Mitchell, nine months, Morrison, six months.

The new year 1909 found us with two appeals pending in the District Court of Appeals—upon the validity of the original injunction and Justice Wright's decision with the punishment affixed. The higher court modified the Gould-Claybaugh injunction. The modification eliminated the most flagrant violations of free press and free speech, which forbade printing or discussing anything in relation to the Buck's Stove & Range Company boycott or even the injunction itself. With that change, Justices Robb and Van Orsdel reaffirmed the injunction. The court of Appeals opinion was made November 2, 1909; Justices Robb and Van Orsdel reaffirmed the sentences, holding that regardless of whether the injunction was valid it must be obeyed. Chief Justice Shepherd dissented.

We wanted the United States Supreme Court to pass upon the fundamental principles involved, and counsel for the A. F. of L. asked for a writ of certiorari to have the record of this case brought before the Supreme Court. The request was granted.

When the Supreme Court rendered the decision in the Buck's Stove & Range Company case, May 15, 1911, it held that the petition was civil in nature and that criminal penalties could not properly be affixed. The court reversed the judgment of the lower court and remanded the case to the Supreme Court of the District without prejudice to the power and right of that court to punish by proper proceedings, contempt if any, committed against it.

Justice Wright reaffirmed his original sentences of prison terms of twelve, nine, and six months for Gompers, Mitchell, and Morrison respectively. An appeal was immediately taken to the District Court of Appeals. Our counsel took the position that since the contempt proceedings were criminal in nature, the rule of criminal procedure and the Statute of Limitations should apply. On May 15, 1913, the opinion of the court was read. It was written by Justice Van Orsdel and concurred in by Justice Robb. The court sustained the judgment of Wright in holding us guilty of contempt, but declared the sentences a violation of judicial discretion and changed them to thirty days for me and a fine of $500 each for Mitchell and Morrison. Chief Justice Shepherd believed the case should be dismissed.

Justice Wright filed a unique petition with the Supreme Court, charging that the Court of Appeals had exceeded its authority in mitigating the sentences. As labor had been pressing this case in order to se-

cure a judicial ruling upon the fundamentals involved, counsel for the
A. F. of L. was instructed to ask the Supreme Court for a writ of certiorari in order that the highest tribunal of the land should review the case.

On May 11, 1914, the decision of the Supreme Court was handed
down. It considered the nature of contempt trials and held that criminal
contempts should be tried according to usual criminal procedure. Under
this procedure the acts specified could not be presented after a lapse of
three years. The court, therefore, reversed the judgments.

The case had been doggedly contested through every stage up to
the highest judicial authority. For seven long years we were either presenting briefs or awaiting court decisions. The litigation was expensive
and absorbed money, time, and energy that were needed for constructive work. When finally the U. S. Supreme Court came to pass upon our
case, it evaded the fundamental issues and declared the case outlawed
by the Statute of Limitations.

However, because of the discussion growing out of the case and
because judicial perversion had solidified labor's forces in the political
field, we were able to press for remedial legislation. The case disclosed
the lines along which relief must be drawn and the basis for the labor
sections of the Clayton Anti-Trust Law.

Even after the enactment of the provision of the Clayton Act intended to protect labor against an invasion of its rights by injunctions or
anti-trust procedure, such cases continued. The two most conspicuous
with which I have been concerned were the Anderson injunction against
the Miners and the Wilkerson injunction against the striking Railroad
Shopmen.

National Politics

Before the headquarters of the Federation were moved to Washington,
it was my custom to arrange with the chairman of the House and the
Senate Committee on Labor to hold hearing upon labor measures at
some time when I could be in Washington. Usually, other members of
the Executive Council or official representatives of trades interested in
special matters arranged to be present. The arrangement was far from
satisfactory. The formulation of legislation is a development, and during
the whole discussion of measures affecting labor, there was need for labor advisers to keep in touch with changing proposals.

So in 1895, Andrew Furuseth and Adolph Strasser were selected to serve as the legislative representatives of the Federation to remain in Washington during sessions of Congress. Furuseth served for several years until his organization was able to keep him in Washington to give full time to promoting seamen's measures. The law held seamen liable to imprisonment for violation of contract. Seamen quitting their ships in safe harbor were liable to arrest and return to their ships for desertion. The seamen demanded the right of all free men—the right to quit ships in safe harbor. They were bondmen—who could be hunted down like serfs of old. They were the only workmen compelled to perform the specific terms of a contract. The issuance of a writ of injunction to regulate personal relations is postulated in the same principle—that the worker is property and hence unfree. The parallelism between the injunction and seamen's problems continued in the interesting fact that desired legislative remedy for each became law within a few months of each other. The Seamen's Act was signed March 3, 1915, and the labor charter (contained in the Clayton Anti-Trust Act), October 15, 1914.

During 1897 the Committee on Labor of the House of Representatives under the chairmanship of Mr. Phillips introduced in the House what we believed would be an effective eight-hour bill. Eight-hour legislation had been the paramount labor demand for many years, for the first law proved ineffective. When that law was restricted by interpretations to a very limited field, labor at once undertook to secure adequate legislative remedy. The purpose of the Phillips bill was to extend the eight-hour law to contractors and sub-contractors to whom government works were let.

The bill was introduced regularly in each session of Congress and just as regularly was defeated at some state of legislative procedure. From 1902 when the National Association of Manufacturers joined the opposition forces, resistance to all labor measures became definite and regular. I knew the source of the influences brought to bear upon congressmen, but did not have proofs. They were afterwards produced before the Lobby Investigations Committee (Mulhall exposé). In the meantime, labor inaugurated its non-partisan political campaign, and our eight-hour bill became law in 1912, after twenty years of work.

Our measures before the Committee on Judiciary fared no better. When Mr. [Charles] Littlefield was elected to Congress, he was regarded as a public-spirited tribune of the people. We presented to him labor's amendment to the anti-trust bill which he was then, with his committee, perfecting. In 1902 the House Judiciary Committee had under consideration a bill to amend and make more drastic the provisions of the Sherman Anti-Trust Law. The bill was referred to a subcommittee of which he was chairman. We had prepared a section of the bill so that the normal activities of workers in industry, agriculturists as well as horticulturists, should be excluded from the provisions of the bill and of the law to which the bill was intended to be supplementary. Without much ado, Mr. Littlefield declined to consider the subject further.

In 1906 the situation was so serious for labor that I knew some new factor had to be brought to bear. Since the Homestead strike in 1892, organization in large-scale industries had been increasingly difficult. The use of professional strike breakers supplied by detective agencies injected a lawless element in strikes that caused me much concern. There had been a number of important strikes that had been waged with unusual ferocity. In the courts, suit had been brought against the officers and members of the Hatters' Union under the Sherman Anti-Trust Act which threatened the very existence of organized labor.

It was of paramount importance that labor unions be specifically removed from the application of anti-trust law and that injunction use be defined and regulated. Such legislation would free us from harassing court litigation and enable us to fight out our economic problems in the economic field. To secure this result it was necessary to break the stranglehold which enabled organized employers to control legislation.

In order to get action by Congress, I knew we had to make an appeal to congressmen and that no appeal would be stronger than a threat of action at the ballot box. In order to give that appeal the proper authority and to focus attention upon our action, I sent a letter to the responsible executives of the various labor organizations, asking them to attend a conference in Washington late in March 1906. The conference called was something altogether new in the annals of the Federation. From the beginning, the Federation had been committed to a policy of independent political action, but there had been no effort to develop organization discipline for the most effective use of the political power of labor. As a result, labor men were identified with political parties and guided by the same sense of loyalty to them that influenced so large a part of the American citizens. At that time, party regularity was the rule. It was an appreciation of party regularity which made the Federation's action seem audacious in the eyes of the ordinary politician. Nevertheless, our conference convened, and the declaration known as "Labor's Bill of Grievances" was ratified and ordered submitted to responsible heads of the Administration.

In the spring of 1906, I was in the state of Maine attending the convention of the Maine State Federation of Labor. During my address to the convention, I related the history of Mr. Littlefield's opposition to labor measures. A number of the men discussed the situation with me and suggested that a campaign be inaugurated to elect someone from Maine more fairly inclined toward labor. In a mass meeting held in the evening, a committee was appointed to confer with me and to inaugurate the campaign.

Preparatory to the Littlefield campaign I sent into Maine a group of the organizers of the Federation who were to make the arrangements. In August the campaign began actively. As conducted by labor, the campaign was entirely educational. We gave the voters of Maine the facts about Mr. Littlefield and his record in Washington. We addressed meetings and distributed information. Nothing else was necessary.

The Maine election has always been regarded as a political barometer. The Republican Party became exceedingly concerned as to the outcome in Maine. They sent into the state and district some of the most important party orators. Speaker Cannon, particularly, was very abusive, and some of his statements on the platform and in private conversation were practically vituperation. President Roosevelt himself sent a letter to Maine, stating that the defeat of Littlefield would be a national calamity. We did not defeat Mr. Littlefield in that campaign, but we reduced his majority from 5,000 to 1,000. Mr. Littlefield gave out the statement that Mr. Gompers had helped him in his campaign, but there were no other congressmen of Littlefield's type requesting my "help."

Our labor campaign was followed very closely both here and abroad. The report was that the Federation was going into partisan politics. Both the politicians and the intellectuals hoped we would. The former knew that it would be an easy way to dispose of the labor vote, and the latter wanted us to become "progressive" like European labor. But I felt I understood American labor and knew something of American politics, and I insisted upon a policy that would secure results and at the same time maintain the independence and dominant economic character of the wage-workers' movement of America. I have not regretted my course.

Early in 1908 the Supreme Court of the United States rendered its decision on the demurrer in the hatters' case [*Loewe* v. *Lawlor*], ruling that labor organizations came under the operation of the Sherman Anti-Trust Law, thus making them liable to dissolution or the affixing of three-fold damages. Knowing how incompatible the judicial point of view was with procedure involved in industry, no other conclusion was possible but that disaster awaited the hatters' union. Nor could we expect to avoid similar catastrophes in other organizations. That decision was conclusive proof that labor must become active and insistent in order to secure legislative relief. In this case and in the test injunction case of the Federation then pending were involved issues fundamental not only to labor but to the citizenship in other walks of life, for the injunctions issued in labor disputes established a precedent in conflict with American concepts of equality of opportunity and justice. Nor were we willing to subscribe to the notion that unlawful acts should be restrained by the process of injunction. If acts are in themselves unlawful, then it follows that there is an existing law making the acts unlawful; and if such laws do exist, as they do, then men charged with the unlawful acts should be tried upon charge and indictment by a jury of their peers and not by the process of injunction forbidding the performance of unlawful acts and enjoining the commission of acts which are in themselves normal and lawful.

The right to organize I found challenged by injunctions and by perversion of law against illegal conspiracies to apply to trade union activity. This war on labor assumed the appearance of a concerted program shortly after David Parry was elected president of the National Association of Manufacturers. Under Mr. Parry and his successor, James Van Cleave, the opposition to the work of the organized labor movement in the legislative and economic fields became more aggressive. The situation in Congress prevented our getting relief there. In seeking a way out of these difficulties, I found myself concerned more and more with national problems, national determining forces, and national policies.

During the years we had patiently sought legislative relief, I found a number of congressmen who had some understanding of industrial conditions and who were willing to sponsor bills which labor approved. I got hearings, sympathy, and promises, but not labor laws. Then [1906] I called a national labor conference and put before organized labor plain facts of the congressional situation. The conference submitted to Congress a protest against its treatment of labor legislation and asked specifically for amendments to the Sherman Anti-Trust Law excluding wage earners and farmers from its purview, the enactment of the Pearre bill to regulate and limit the use of the injunction, the employers' liability and eight-hour bills. We communicated to labor organizations throughout the country urging them to defeat their enemies, whether candidates for president, Congress or whatever office, and those organizations in turn wrote their respective Representatives and Senators warning them that they would be held responsible for failure to legislate upon labor matters. At once a feeling of apprehension began to pervade the minds of the Republicans, and the Democrats began to sense the political opportunity in the situation.

The [1908] Republican Convention was to meet in Chicago in June, and the Democratic Convention in Denver in July. The Executive Council of the A. F. of L. met in Chicago just prior to the Republican Convention, to prepare the planks and platform which we would urge be inserted in the convention's declarations. In that meeting we considered the report of our legislative committee. Additional workers had been detailed to the legislative committee in order that we might have the labor record of every member of Congress and that there should be no misunderstanding on the part of any members of Congress as to the gravity which labor attached to its grievances and its demands for remedial legislation. The report of this committee was a recounting of the records compiled from votes on labor measures, but in effect it was an indictment of those in control of Federal legislation.

There were two members of our Executive Council who were known as adherents to the Republican Party, James Duncan and Daniel J. Keefe. Mr. Mitchell was generally regarded as more closely allied with the Democratic Party, but with a strong personal feeling for President Roosevelt.

James Duncan, Daniel J. Keefe, and I were selected to appear before the Committee on Platform. Mr. Keefe arranged for two interviews with Mr. Wade Ellis, and we discussed labor planks. Mr. Ellis was fairly confident that he would be able to secure the adoption of Mr. Roosevelt's proposals on labor issues.

It was pretty general knowledge that the personal influence of President Roosevelt was very strong in that Chicago convention. Although Roosevelt was for progressive policies, he desired to maintain party leadership, and that led to compromise with the reactionaries in the Republican Party. The platform contained an evasion on labor's paramount issue, and the convention nominated as its standard-bearer William Howard Taft, known as the "injunction judge." James Van Cleave and the Republican reactionaries jeeringly told Labor to "Go to Denver."

That was in accord with our program; and our Executive Council proceeded to Denver, and we presented the identical propositions which we had presented to the Republican Platform Committee. There we were accorded a hearing before the full Platform Committee of which Judge Alton B. Parker was chairman. We were subjected to considerable questioning and exchange of views, with the result that the committee did include most of the requests that we presented.

After the party conventions began the real fight. As the campaign progressed, the opposition again attempted to discredit our activities with ridicule and perversion and declared that, "Gompers had promised to deliver the labor vote to the Democratic Party." I knew full well that I could not deliver the labor vote nor did I make any such promise or pretense. The only vote which I controlled was my own. I did try as a citizen and as a man to exercise my right with all citizens to persuade people to vote for the principles in which I so firmly believed. Members of organized labor were identified with political parties for reasons similar to those that determined political affiliations of all other voters. Many were working in industries in which tariff was a determining influence. Many were influenced by sectional forces and others were simply under the sway of habit. To mobilize the latent political power of labor, organize political discipline, and to create political standards and agencies for independent political action was a task very similar to that of mobilizing economic power in trade unions for sustained and intelligent use in furtherance of enlightened self-interest. This political discipline I knew could not be established in one campaign. We could only establish precedents. I knew I had to make the directing control in labor's political program stronger than the opposition interests that would seek to discredit or to dissipate labor's activity.

Since the Democratic Party had clearly declared for labor's contentions, I knew there would be no difficulties with men who had been affiliated with the Democratic Party activity or with those of them who were not fully identified with any political party, but it was a serious question whether those who had been identified with the Republican Party organization could be brought to see that their interests as workingmen made it necessary for them to vote against that party because of its attitude on labor's paramount economic interests. Of course, party politicians were not blind to this opportunity.

When I brought the labor issue into the presidential campaign, I realized that the labor movement had entered a new sphere of activity and that henceforth its spokesman must state its policies in national terms. The 1906 campaign had involved only concentrated efforts in widely separated localities to defeat conspicuous enemies of labor. In the presidential election, we had to direct labor's opposition to a national party that had pronounced against measures necessary to the functioning of labor organizations.

While beyond question the interest was focused upon the election of President, there was another vital consideration which we dared not ignore: that was the election of members of Congress; for after all, the making of legislative decisions lay primarily in their hands.

The problem presented the difficulties arising from a firmly rooted two-party system with no traditions of independent voting. Party organizations had jealously guarded their jurisdiction against any tendency to non-partisanism. It was no easy undertaking. It meant an educational campaign in enlightening working people as to their interests in politics. The Federation had appealed to political parties for legislative relief, but in vain. Organized employers maintained a lobby at the Capitol to defeat our bills. The bi-party system had a strong grip upon the American people, including wage-earners. Independent voting was practically unknown, with the exception of the mugwumps.

Up to 1880, the American labor movement usually sought expression in partisan political action. Independent labor parties were organized, lasted a short time—a few years at the most—then disappeared to be replaced by others.

The Federation has maintained itself since 1881 as a purely voluntary association, and despite adverse conditions, great diversity of nationalities and languages and extent of the country, it has been able to maintain continuous progress and to promote fraternity and solidarity.

The secret of this continuous progress has been understanding of the nature and possibilities of economic power and concentration on mobilization of that power. The Federation has maintained that economic organization is adequate to deal with all of the problems of wage-earners. Its political action is simply to utilize the functions of the trade union in another field.

The Socialists contested this policy, for they regarded it as trespassing upon their field. They looked upon the political field as their domain and fiercely resented any difference in political tactics. They asserted that they had a party devoted to the promotion of the interests of labor and that organized labor ought to use the Socialist Party as its political expression.

We have been and are still confronted with prodigious obstacles in the path of the full activities of the trade unions in our general federation, and we felt and feel it our duty to disregard speculative philosophies to the greater need of concentrating our efforts in securing practical results. The Federation was facing an emergency which threatened its very existence. The Federal courts had been using injunction writs of such a drastic nature and such wide scope of application as to paralyze labor union activity. Anti-trust laws were invoked to serve the same purpose as the old conspiracy laws and to outlaw unions. The Socialist Party could not muster enough votes to give us needed relief. Experience with third parties in this country did not warrant our attempting that course.

Critics of the non-partisan political policy of the Federation were not lacking. There were many who thought it impossible for the Federation to make any headway unless a labor party were formed. The "intellectuals" of the country made our problem doubly difficult by flooding magazines with articles on the British Labor Party and exhorting American labor to go and do likewise.

However, many of us had a very clear understanding of the pitfalls connected with party organization. I was regarded as its spokesman and personally responsible for the effectiveness of the aggressive non-partisan political action. The results were not conspicuous and were not readily appreciable by those not closely connected with political affairs. To those of us who had occasion frequently to go to Legislatures and among elected persons results were evident in the changed atmosphere and the increasing respect paid to labor legislation. One by one, those who had been conspicuous enemies of labor met with political misfortunes.

Although the Republican Party won the election of 1908, confidence in the party was considerably shaken, and in the congressional election of 1910 they met a decisive defeat. The results of those campaigns demonstrated the practical efficiency of the political policy inaugurated in 1906. In 1912 the Republican Party, which had repeatedly ignored labor legislative demands, lost control of both the legislative and executive branches of the national government.

The achievements of the non-partisan policy thus far were not sufficient to put constructive legislation on the statute books. The situation was discussed in Executive Council sessions, and although all members were convinced that the non-partisan policy was based upon sound fundamentals, several expressed the opinion that unless some achievements could be shown after the 1912 election we would be forced to modify our policy.

I went to the Republican Convention in Chicago in 1912 where with my colleagues I again submitted labor's legislative demands to the Platform Committee. The Old Guard was in full control, and Mr. Taft was renominated with practically no change in the labor planks over what had been pronounced in 1908.

When the progressive element in the Republican Party revolted against the arbitrary and reactionary policies of party leaders, they formed the nucleus around which many independent voters rallied. During his term as President, Mr. Roosevelt had rendered a tremendous service by stimulating an attitude of mind among all voters known as progressive. The Roosevelt personality and the growth of progressivism were twin forces that produced the Bull Moose Party.

On Saturday afternoon after the close of the Republican Convention, I went to the Baltimore Convention with other representatives of labor to submit proposals upon labor planks in the platform. Those were given cordial consideration. After many ballots were taken the nomination finally went to Woodrow Wilson. After I got back to Washington, Representative Hughes called me up by telephone and asked me if labor would have any objections to the nomination of Thomas R. Marshall for Vice-President. I assured him that I knew of no reason that would make him objectionable.

I confess I felt very much disheartened at the outcome of the political conventions in the summer of 1912. Experience in the previous presidential campaign after the attacks were made against my associates, and particularly against me, indicated that I could best help in this campaign by counsel and assistance rather than conspicuous service that would focus attacks upon me. I therefore made few engagements for public speaking. The Federation's widely distributed connections had by this time become accustomed to look to Washington for information and advice in political work. It had been no easy undertaking to develop the habit of securing congressional records from Washington so that the facts as developed by the votes of the candidates might determine the attitude of the local organized labor movement, but in the course of time this method and practice became firmly fixed. To accomplish this, it was necessary that records at headquarters be absolutely accurate and that all information be impartial. When local organizations found that they could depend upon information sent them, it was not difficult to get response. The campaign of 1912 was marked by intensive labor activity in the congressional elections. When the vote came in November, Woodrow Wilson was elected President, and the Democratic Party carried both Houses of Congress. The verdict was clearly interpreted by members of Congress and in the short session of the 62d Congress labor measures received unprecedented attention.

Labor's Magna Charta

When Senator Sherman proposed to forbid by law the development of industrial combinations, I felt that his theory was fundamentally wrong. The greater efficiency that follows unification of control and management benefits society through increased production. Sustained progress of industry requires freedom from legislative prohibition, and non-social tendencies can best be curbed by intelligent regulation. However, there ought to be inhibitions against the unlawful activities of the industrial and trust combinations—that is, the brazenness with which these financial and business corporations control not only elections but the administration of affairs, the judicial interpretation, and congressional action.

I have often been amused by the declaration that the "law of supply and demand" was an "immutable, natural" law, that it not only controlled wages but prices. I have often pointed out that business co-partnerships and trusts in controlling output interfere with the so-called inexorable operations of the law of supply and demand and that the trusts had cornered prices to such an extent as to obtain higher profits during periods of industrial depression. Furthermore, so far as workers are concerned, the organizations of labor in the movement to reduce the hours of labor, to deal with common problems collectively, and pay union benefits were an estoppel to profiteers in the attempt to depress wages below standards established by the workers, necessary to absorb increasing national wealth. As for prices during normal conditions, whenever there has been a great demand for many articles, new and improved machinery, new tools, new processes, and the application of greater power have met demand, and through such improvements the prices of articles were reduced. Of course, if there is a limited natural supply of raw material, prices are maintained or enhanced according to the demand; but in respect to all other factors, when human labor and ingenuity can be applied to an increased demand for products they develop new tools, machine processes, and power to meet the increased demand, and thus, despite higher wages, the cost of production is lessened. This briefly set forth is the reason for my conclusion that the law of supply and demand is not an immutable law, but that it is amenable to human thought and action to overcome its most injurious results to the people. Economic factors are variables that respond to human control.

As the years went by, the scope and frequency of injunctions issued in labor disputes increased until the practice became a grave handicap in the necessary work of trade unions. Then we undertook to secure legislation to define the use of injunctions.

The first measure to limit and define the use of injunctions which had our approval was introduced by General Grosvenour of Ohio. This bill passed the House. By the time that the opposition to labor legislation became concentrated, a clear-cut measure had been formulated which at our request was introduced by Representative Pearre of Maryland. We were very anxious to have this bill enacted. The feeling was intense. We accomplished little.

The American labor movement did not organize its political power until we encountered political obstacles interjected into our economic activity. The Danbury Hatters' case and the Buck's Stove & Range Company injunction were typical of a general problem which labor encountered all down the line. Clear differentiation between things political and things economic has been a compass that has steered me in deciding many a difficult problem. The economic world is essentially scientific; politics is the field of contending forces. In order to rescue the labor movement from the field of force, I urged regulation and restriction of the use of the injunction in industrial disputes and removal of labor unions from the scope of anti-trust law.

Following the failure of the Pearre Bills, William B. Wilson, a union-card representative from Pennsylvania, formerly secretary-treasurer of the United Mine Workers, introduced both anti-injunction and anti-trust measures which were approved by labor. Defeat of those measures was the objective of the combined effort of manufacturers. There were repeated and extensive hearings before the Judiciary Committee, in which I always participated. Despite our activity, none of our bills in Congress were passed. Our task was much more difficult than that of the British labor movement in dealing with similar issues. England accepted class distinctions and was willing to enact legislation giving wage-earners relief without concerning herself closely as to the underlying philosophy that justified the action. In the United States, our institutions are founded upon the basic principle of equality, and American labor had to make plain that it did not request special privilege but equality of opportunity.

Fortunately, late in the closing hours of the 61st Congress, there developed a clear-cut issue upon which we secured a record vote which distinguished our friends from our enemies upon our fundamental issue. When the Sundry Civil Bill was under consideration in the House, our legislative committeeman suggested to William Hughes of New Jersey that he introduce the following amendment to that section of the bill providing money for the Department of Justice to be used in the prosecution of anti-trust cases:

> Provided, however, that no part of this money shall be expended in the prosecution of an organization or individual for entering into combination or agreement having in view the increasing of wages, shortening of hours, or bettering conditions of labor or for any act done in furtherance thereof, not in itself unlawful.

The amendment passed the House, but was defeated in the Senate. The bill went to conference, but because of the proviso or "rider" as it was called, the conferees were unable to agree and so reported to their respective houses. President Taft summoned the Republican Party leaders to the White House the next morning and plainly gave them orders. It was a personal triumph for President Taft when the House receded under the President's whip. However, responsibility for opposition to labor's fundamental demand was definitely fixed upon the Republican Party and its leading members. This was the issue which we carried into the congressional election of 1910.

When the Sundry Civil Appropriations Bill at the close of the 62d Congress was under consideration in the House of Representatives, labor's famous proviso was offered and adopted by the House. It passed the Senate and went to the President with the proviso still intact. The bill to create a Department of Labor had [also] been introduced by Representative Sulzer. The bill passed Congress in the last hours of the 62d Congress. On Sunday, March 2, I spent a good part of the day at the Capitol conferring with various congressmen, including William B. Wilson who was to be the first Secretary of Labor if the President signed the bill creating the Department of Labor. [He did.] That signature insured the presence of William B. Wilson, a representative of wage-earners, in President Wilson's cabinet which attended him at his inaugural. This achievement represented efforts extending over a period of thirty years.

Although it was then the fourth of March and his action meant serious difficulty for important government work, President Taft vetoed the Sundry Civil Bill and stated that his reason for failing to approve the measure was the labor proviso.

The situation made it imperative that President Wilson call an extra session of Congress soon after he assumed office. The inauguration of Woodrow Wilson was accompanied by Democratic control of both houses. It was a situation fraught with great possibilities, and there were many of us who confidently expected that the administration would inaugurate a national policy in which human welfare and social service would be the dominant purposes. Personally, I felt that the trade union movement and I as president of the Federation, had considerable at stake. If the Administration fulfilled its pledges in good faith, the political policies which I helped to inaugurate would have proved themselves. The Administration recognized that labor had been an effective agency in taking the political control out of the hands of reactionaries.

When the special session of Congress convened, a representative of the Federation requested the chairmen of the House and Senate appropriations committees to include the labor proviso with the anti-trust section in the bill which they were to report. Practically all of the discussion in both houses centered on the labor proviso and a similar proviso applying to farmers. These were included in the bill as reported, which passed both houses intact and went to the President.

I sent a letter to President Wilson on this subject, stating even more fully the reasons why labor urged his approval of the bill. The National Association of Manufacturers and similar organizations hostile to organized labor besieged the President to veto the bill. Notwithstanding, he signed it. This achievement indicated that there was hope that Labor might secure legislation which we so much desired. In the regular session bills were introduced both to define and regulate the use of the injunction and to establish the legality of trade unions. It seemed very difficult to get legislation that would assert positively what had been conceded in principle by the labor proviso. When in 1914 Congress undertook the revision of anti-trust law, Arthur Holder, our legislative committeeman, suggested we attempt to have labor sections included in the law instead of attempting to have separate bills passed. The suggestion was adopted.

The anti-trust measure was sponsored in the House by Congressman Clayton of Alabama and we had a number of conferences with him. In the formulation of the labor provisions of the trust bill, the leading members of the Judiciary Committee had frequent conferences with the labor group in the House. This labor group was organized after the 1906 congressional election. All members of Congress who held cards in bona fide trade unions were asked to co-operate for the enactment of labor legislation. Thus the organized labor movement secured direct representation on the floor of Congress without regard for party affiliation. This union-card group numbered only six the first year, but grew steadily with each election. It was organized with a chairman and held regular and special meetings both at the Capitol and in the office of the Federation. I usually attended the meetings of the group which in turn kept constantly in touch with my office while this bill was in the making.

When the labor measures were finally adopted by the Senate, my emotion well-nigh overcame me. It was a great hour for labor, when there was enacted into the law of our republic a basic fundamental declaration upon which humanitarian endeavor could be based. The law contained this section from which we hoped to secure protection from perversion of anti-trust law:

> That the labor of a human being is not a commodity or article of commerce. Nothing contained in the anti-trust laws shall be construed to forbid the existence and operation of labor, agricultural, or horticultural organizations, instituted for the purposes of mutual help and not having capital stock or conducted for profit, or to forbid or restrain individual members of such organizations from lawfully carrying out the legitimate objects thereof, nor shall such organizations or the members thereof be held or construed to be illegal combinations or conspiracies in restraint of trade under the anti-trust laws.

The Clayton Anti-Trust Law was signed by President Wilson, October 15, 1914.

Of course, I was not such a novice as to imagine that these labor sections constituted the end of our difficulties with the judiciary. Section 20 of the act, which deals with regulation and limitation of the use of injunctions in industrial disputes, was not the clear-cut formulation of policy that labor sought under the old Pearre bill. However, it was the best obtainable at the time and was intended, so the congressmen stated, to correct the abuse of the injunction writ in application to industrial relations. In view of the legislative intent of Congress, I felt justified in accepting the section as a frank response to labor's need and so interpreted the law in my editorial and public utterances. Of course, I, as everyone else, knew the effectiveness of the measure depended upon judicial action and interpretation. What the courts would do only time could tell. In the meanwhile, it was my duty to help educate public thought as to the intent of Congress. The purpose of Congress was plain. Sections 6 and 20 were intended as a guarantee of industrial rights to working men engaged in a conflict to establish better conditions of work. They constitute the charter of industrial freedom or, as I called it, "Labor's Magna Charta."

6

THE WAR YEARS

1914–23

I Abandon Pacifism

When on July 28, 1914, there flashed across the Atlantic the message that war had been declared in Central Europe. I did not believe it was possible for civilized nations deliberately to undertake to settle differences through force of arms and to enter into the destructive horrors of war made possible by human inventions and our increased knowledge of science. A war of aggression was abhorrent to the spirit of America. The American wars which had occurred during my lifetime were wars for a great principle.

Like all men not personally familiar with the details of the problems of foreign relations, I had some very idealistic notions. So far as my attitude on foreign relations was concerned, I was a pronounced pacifist. When the United States declared war on Spain in behalf of Cuba, I felt again that our country was rendering necessary service as the champion of freedom and the protector of a weak and struggling people. It was not the sort of war in which the industrial basis was conspicuously obvious; hence, there was no great need for a large-scale mobilization of industries in support of the American flag. The whole engagement occurred in the interim of conventions; hence, there were no decisive pronouncements of organized labor upon the war. However, in my capacity as a private citizen and as a representative of what I knew to be the spirit of the American labor movement, even before our troops reached Spanish soil, I joined with a large representative group of liberal American citizens in a memorial to the Senate protesting against any policy of imperialism. When the Hawaiian issue was telescoped into the situation by the annexation of Hawaii, I wrote to Speaker Reed, vehemently protesting.

I opposed retention of conquered territory and pointed out that the whole moral effect of the acquisition of the Philippine Islands with their semi-savage population would undo what had been accomplished by organization and education upon the line of social, economic, political, and moral reform, particularly in raising the standard of living for the wage-earners of the United States.

However, the peace that was signed between Spain and the United States left us in possession of the colonies that had cost Spain so much turmoil with the exception of Cuba which was given its independence with certain guarantees to the United States under the Platt amendment.

The American labor movement then set itself to the task of establishing higher standards of life and work in these new American possessions. We realized that in order to protect our standards within the states we must help the Island workers to develop their higher political, social, and industrial problems. The only possible agency through which this could be accomplished was an organized labor movement within the territories.

Just before the World War broke upon us in 1914, the Carnegie Peace Foundation had requested me to furnish them with copies of all my articles and addresses on international peace to be published as one of their series. In July 1914, when I learned my hopes and dreams for world peace were ruthlessly destroyed, I hastened to the Carnegie Peace Foundation and withdrew the manuscript I had given them authority to publish. I was no longer a pacifist.

The propaganda carried on by Austrian and German representatives in this country, even in high official places, convinced those who were accustomed to watch the forming of public opinion that our government could not remain neutral. The American people were anti-military, so much so that we had not maintained a policy of adequate defense in proportion to our country's increased participation in world-affairs. The basis for our international policies was radically different from that of Europe. This was both a reason and a result for our policy of aloofness.

In order to focus public thought on this problem, we arranged that the annual meeting of the Civic Federation held in New York in January 1916, should present various aspects of the problem of national preparedness. A number of our most influential citizens were invited to participate in that conference and accepted. Among them were Theodore Roosevelt, William Howard Taft, Henry Stimson, and General Leonard Wood.

I made my first public preparedness speech. In view of the uncertainty which the public felt as to the attitude of labor in the approaching war, that speech of mine was important news and was carried in great length by the metropolitan press. In this speech, as in my letter to the Carnegie Hall meeting of the Friends of Peace, I was speaking directly to the wage-earners of the country. I did not anticipate great difficulties in mobilizing labor opinion in defense of the issue I saw involved in the European War—the defense of democratic institutions.

In the next few months I was to learn that it was not possible for any important world power to remain neutral. I was convinced that Germany was the real aggressor. I had many German friends whom I loved dearly. Notwithstanding my great admiration for German science and technology, I understood to what an extent autocratic regimentation of the German people had extended so that their conditions of life and work, daily intercourse and even the information taught in schools and disseminated by publications were directed by a system of "Verboten."

Millions of American citizens were of German origin. They were good citizens, industrious, thrifty, and progressive. That the Germans were pronounced in their fealty to their "fatherland," even though they were good American citizens, was fostered by the "Turnvereins" and "Saengerbunds" and German-American leagues. I had for years been a member of the Washington Saengerbund—a relationship which terminated with the war.

As it became obvious that the United States could not escape becoming involved in the European War, I began to consider the possibilities of German-American societies being utilized for German propaganda. I also was conscious that there were thousands of Germans and German-Americans in the American Federation of Labor. Some few organizations and certain local units were practically made up of Teutonic members.

[In 1915] German propaganda began to make its influence felt in this country. I was convinced that the real issues of the war concerned those who believed in democratic institutions and that the time had come when the world could no longer exist part democratic and part autocratic. It was an issue upon which there could be no real neutrality, and therefore propaganda for neutrality was propaganda to maintain autocracy. Those not actively for democracy were in effect against it. Germany planned to control American public opinion and to get us committed to policies helpful to them before we awoke to the fact that we were involved in the war. I felt that even though we were technically neutral we could not permit German propaganda to intrench itself and prejudice our decisions. This propaganda made its appearance in the labor movement among the longshoremen of New York. It came first in the guise of I. W. W. preaching the doctrine of sabotage. They urged strikes that would tie up shipping, taking care that the ships to be involved were for British or French ports carrying munitions of war. Mysterious fires made their appearance on such vessels shortly after leaving port. There were "accidents" in munition factories and in industries producing basic articles from which war munitions and foodstuffs were to be made.

Gradually, this propaganda became more open, and the subject of neutrality was injected. German propagandists sought to make it appear that selling munitions to one or the other contesting armies in the war was a breach of neutrality. I held that American workmen were not concerned with the destination of the products they made, but that they were concerned only with the processes of production for which they were paid.

A more subtle form of propaganda made its appearance early in 1915. This again was an appeal to the workmen who constitute the major proportion of our population. It was largely in the form of pacifist movements and therefore subtly dangerous, for the labor movement had for years been committed to anti-militarist ideals. Certain influential men in various groups were interested in movements to promote pacifism. One of these efforts known as the Friends of Peace was inaugurated with the prestige of a number of well-meaning prominent citizens including William Jennings Bryan who as Secretary of State made a record in negotiating arbitration treaties. Soon another endeavor was under way. Labor men throughout the country were deluged with invitations to form labor peace councils. There is in practically every community a fringe to the labor movement consisting of those who are "professional" labor men. This fringe can readily be converted to new causes and movements if sufficient financial incentives are offered. In New York and in Washington a few were induced to assume leadership. Labor Peace Councils were formed in Chicago, in Washington, and in Baltimore. I was much concerned to find that a number of valuable labor men had been caught in this net.

It was in this period that the United States began to appreciate the price of permitting our immigration policies to be written in the interests of industries that wanted to maintain a surplus of cheap labor. That policy was a gamble with fate, and many an anxious hour it caused me in war-time. The labor movement had done what it could to Americanize this "cheap labor," but it was a struggle against powerful trusts. The corporations tried to restrict immigrant workers by language barriers and by foreign language papers, which were subsidized by the Hamburg-American and German-American Steamship lines as well as by the corporations themselves. Through these papers the most bitter attacks were made against the American labor movement and its leaders, and any sort of anti-Americanism might be promulgated and their home country institutions idealized. Anything was resorted to, to keep the men from organizing upon purely American trade union lines, because they feared the labor movement would educate their "cheap laborers" to American standards of life and work. With war-time appreciation of national unity came an epidemic of Americanization work. It went the way of all spasmodic endeavors used as substitutes for sustained activity based upon an intelligent program. Shortly before war was declared, an immigration restriction law was passed over the second veto of President Wilson. That measure will be, I hope, the beginning of immigration policy based upon intelligent regard for national welfare. America's destiny depends upon her conserving her virility.

In the fall of 1915, the Grand Jury of New York began investigating so-called sedition cases—various attempts that had been made to violate neutrality and put our government in the position of supporting or aiding one of the groups of contestants in the European War. The grand jury began to inquire into the activities of the Friends of Peace and the Labor National Peace Council and also the origin of certain strikes in New York harbor and in munition factories. I had foreseen before others in the labor movement that the United States had entered a period when all activity, whether individual or group, would be interpreted in the light of its effect upon the one great world-issue, the struggle between the European nations led by Germany and the group which represented more liberal conceptions of government and personal relations.

Upon an issue of this character I did not see how the United States could long remain neutral. American citizens I knew even then were not neutral in their sympathy. I thought that I knew conditions better than the majority of wage-earners—I had felt keenly my responsibility in helping to direct the labor movement and to protect individuals. We all had to shift from the freedom of action, thought, and speech that belongs only to peace over to the circumspection and control made imperative by war dangers. I had been able to direct a number of labor men who had not realized that things that can be done safely in time of peace arouse suspicion and condemnation in time of war. Because of my intimate knowledge of what was taking place in the economic world, I was subpoenaed to appear before the grand jury. Later, I was subpoenaed as a witness in the trials of Buchanan, von Rintelen, the Wolf of Wall Street, Schulteis, and others.

There were only a few of the labor men that I had not been able to convince that the so-called peace and neutrality movements were for the purpose of aiding the Central Powers. These men found themselves in the most uncomfortable position of having their loyalty to our government under suspicion.

Labor to the Fore

During 1916, the consequences of a German victory in the European War became increasingly obvious to Americans. The possibility of a German super-government was apparent to those who loved our personal freedom and democratic institutions. German domination was based upon a system of subordination of individual initiative to a central plan and purpose. I admire efficiency, but I do not wish it if established by force but rather coming as the product of individual development. There were many other Americans who had this same point of view.

[In 1916,] a bill providing for a Council of National Defense and an Advisory Commission was introduced in Congress. The bill provided a council consisting of Cabinet members—the Secretary of War, Secretary of Navy, Secretary of the Interior, Secretary of Agriculture, Secretary of Labor, and the Secretary of Commerce to be given authority to co-ordinate industries and resources for national security and welfare. An advisory commission to the council consisting of seven private citizens was to be appointed by the President.

While this bill was before Congress, the Secretary of Labor called me over the telephone and explained to me that the measure was an Administration proposal and that it was the President's intention to include in the Advisory Commission a representative of labor. The Secretary had urged the President to appoint me as that representative. After considering the proposal over-night, I informed Secretary Wilson that I would serve upon the Advisory Commission if the President desired to appoint me. After the bill became law, President Wilson appointed the following to serve on the commission: Daniel Willard, Julius Rosenwald, Howard E. Coffin, Bernard M. Baruch, Dr. Hollis Godfrey, Dr. Franklin Martin, and Samuel Gompers. I received notification of my appointment in October. The Council of National Defense held its first meeting in December, but was not fully organized until March 3, 1917, although several meetings were held in the interim.

All during the pre-war period I had been turning over in my mind how I could best perform my duty to the American wage-earners to lead them aright and to protect their interests. To remove uncertainty as to labor's position and to protect wage-earners by providing them with a definite constructive program, I sent out a special call for a conference of official representatives of American labor that we might confer and determine what should be the position of labor in the impending crisis. We owed to our movement and to the government to make our position known in advance. That conference met in Washington on March 12, 1917, and after one day's deliberations adopted a declaration expressing American labor's position in peace or in war. The declaration was a frank presentation of those fundamental principles which must be the basis for co-operative action either upon peace or wartime production. It was an offer of service by labor and a statement of conditions which would make possible fullest co-operation with war administration. Labor felt that if we as a nation were going into a war in defense of democratic institutions it was important to insist that basic mobilization at home be firmly grounded upon principles of democracy and human justice, and tendered our services on such conditions.

The mandate from the labor movement strengthened my position in the Advisory Commission and in the Council of National Defense. I never made the mistake of presuming to speak for American labor without possessing necessary authorization. This practice was of telling force in many a difficult situation. The Council of National Defense and the Advisory Commission were both new political agencies without precedent and were confronted by huge problems in inaugurating their work. The nature and scope of our work were essentially to be determined by us. Untrammeled by bureaucratic precedents, we established a going machine upon a basis of business efficiency.

Our commission had advisory power only and no executive or administrative responsibility. We commissioners were chosen because we represented groups essential to mobilization. We were to advise as to how the field which we represented could best be mobilized. It was agreed that each should constitute a committee and should organize as he thought best to do his particular piece of work. Our chairman, Mr. Willard, was to be responsible for transportation; Mr. Coffin for munitions and manufacturing and industrial relations; Mr. Baruch, raw materials, minerals, and metals; Mr. Rosenwald, supplies, including clothing, etc.; Dr. Martin, medicine and surgery, including general sanitation; Dr. Godfrey, engineering and education; and I, labor, including conservation of health and welfare of the workers.

In the beginning I was conscious that other members of these committees regarded me with suspicion or reservations, but after we had been working together for a while they all accepted me as genuinely eager to serve my country.

The work of the commission was fascinating to me. We were in reality getting reports on national resources in the basic fields. I was deeply interested in the immense possibilities for service in such mobilization of information.

There were two aspects to the problem of mobilizing labor in support of the war which were phases of the old problem of establishing good will. There were no new principles in the war labor problem. In fact, the problem was simplified by having practically but one employer and by the dominance of one all-pervading motive—to win the war. Mutuality of interests promoted good will. I am confident that the passage by Congress of the Seamen's Law and labor provisions of the Clayton Anti-Trust Act contributed much toward the crystallization of the patriotic spirit of labor. Labor, I knew, wanted to offer co-operation and efficient workmanship. Something must be done to assure reciprocal action by management, for labor alone could not guarantee continuity of war production. Major responsibility rested upon management. Working agreements must be determined on a basis of equity and mutual advantage. The first step in this direction I felt was some objective form of getting together in support of the common cause. I invited to assist me on the War Committee on Labor a group of representatives of organized labor, prominent employers, important financiers, publicists, and technicians.

My Committee on Labor mapped out certain divisions of activity necessary to safeguard the life and health of wage-earners in war production. There were committees on wages and hours, mediation and conciliation, welfare work, industrial training, housing, women in industry. These were volunteer committees with no authority save desire to serve.

Only two full meetings of the Committee on Labor were called. The work of the committee proceeded under division committees and under direction of an executive committee which in the first months of the war met weekly. The executive committee consisted of representatives of organized labor and of management. Some of those representing management were groups that were not familiar with the organized labor movement, and I felt that permanent constructive results could be accomplished by giving them opportunities to acquaint themselves with the work of organized labor. Perhaps the greatest purpose these committees furthered was to indicate the kind and nature of permanent labor administrative agencies that the government must establish for wartime production, and despite all handicaps these early committees accomplished an enormous amount of work and made genuine contributions.

On a larger scale the same evolution was taking place in the work of the Council of National Defense and the whole Advisory Commission.

The regular governmental departments became organized to assume éx-ecutive war duties and additional war agencies were authorized. Among the organizations that resulted from the recommendations of the Advi-sory Commission of the Council of National Defense were the War In-dustries Board, Aircraft Production Board, the Food Administration, the Fuel Administration, the Munitions Board, the Emergency Fleet Cor-poration, the Railroad Administration. There was no man who gave greater service than Daniel Willard. It was his duty to secure co-opera-tion and co-ordination of transportation and communication agencies of the country. His efforts reached an impasse when it was found that the Sherman Anti-Trust Law forbade the very thing that he had undertaken to accomplish. The railroad executives were willing to co-operate, but when they found that consolidating the service of parallel lines and pool-ing equipment, etc. was in plain violation of the provisions of the anti-trust law, they were not willing to place themselves and their liberty in jeopardy. The government, finding itself in that position, had no alter-native but to take over railroad control and administration. Steps were taken accordingly, and under government management Mr. Willard continued to render service.

Through my committee there was developed the first plan for a national board of labor adjustment. This plan proposed a board of seven, three of whom should be representatives of organized labor and three representatives of employers, while the seventh was to represent the public. It was further proposed that the eight-hour day should be the standard for all war production work and that in cases of disputes con-cerning wages the standards should be those established by organized labor in the vicinity. This proposition I submitted to my colleagues on the Advisory Commission. There was considerable discussion and objec-tion to the eight-hour day as well as to the acceptance of union condi-tions and scale of wages as of June 1, 1917. The proposal was taken to the Council of National Defense and discussed in joint conference. A committee was appointed consisting of Secretary Wilson, Secretary Red-field, Daniel Willard, and me. This committee had many meetings which did not result in unanimous findings. The other three members of the committee proposed a certain modification of the plan, changing the number of members from seven to nine, omitting reference to organized labor and union standards. In this form, the measure was reported to a joint meeting of the council and commission. In the discussion I entered protest. However, the proposal was adopted but never put into effect.

One of the first declarations made by my committee was against the deterioration of working conditions established by economic organizations and the enforcement of labor legislation for the protection of life, health, and limb. It required vigilance on my part to forestall attacks on our labor laws, but we came through the war with our standards unlowered and the spirit of all citizenship buoyed to the highest pitch.

At no stage of our work was there time for indecision. Those of us who knew what had really been happening in both France and England appreciated the imperative need of putting an American army in the field with the least possible loss of time. Things happened very quickly in the war executive branch of the government, and even Congress curtailed its deliberation. A political truce between parties and deference to the judgment of experts facilitated results. The first few months were a period of policy formation. Many decisions were a complete reversal of prevailing thought and practice. Many of us who had been most resolute in advocacy of voluntary principles found it necessary to assume responsibility for initiating policies which placed control in the hands of the government. One of the first of such problems that developed was decision as to the basis for mobilization for military service. I knew that American thought was at variance with the draft principle. Organized labor had been distinctly anti-military and had opposed compulsory service, but labor's position I knew had been reached with consideration of a very different set of conditions from what faced us in the worldwide war. The war made it necessary for central authority to assume responsibility for defense of the principles of our Republic and to utilize national resources for that purpose. The most important national resources were the citizens of the country. The most essentially democratic method of mobilizing human resources was universal draft. Viewed in this light, I knew that this draft was in harmony with the principles of organized labor and that organized labor, after it had had the opportunity to consider the new situation, would approve the policy. I therefore assumed responsibility as representative of labor on the Advisory Commission of co-operating in the development of plans for the draft.

As far as American participation in the World War was concerned, American workers felt that the war was their war. The cause for which our government had declared war upon the Imperial German Government was one which we felt was righteous and wholly necessary. The issues of that War were stated by the spokesman of our Republic in a way that proclaimed to the world the spiritual reasons that made us willing to give our sons, our personal service, and our money to the War. So far as the duties of citizenship are concerned, American wage-earners have never felt that their identification with organized labor has built up any class lines that separate them from other groups of citizens. Organized labor realized that the most valuable service it could contribute to winning the War was to help maintain and raise production levels. The same psychological conditions that promoted production under private agreements would in an intensified degree promote production of war projects. The problem was to establish collective agreements with the government covering war production.

The first big war contracts were for cantonment construction. The War Department plunged into this herculean job, mobilizing as rapidly as it could the necessary technical ability in administrative service. Secretary Baker was fortunately the type of man who attracted persons with such ability.

The first step was the letting of the contracts to construction companies which was placed in the hands of an able assistant who had volunteered for war work, Louis B. Wehle. It happened that, in addition to being a lawyer, Mr. Wehle had a broad sympathy with labor problems. He realized that one of the big problems for which the government had to provide was the adjustment of industrial relations. He came to my office where we discussed the problem and finally developed the following simple agreement to be signed by Mr. Baker and me:

> For the adjustment and control of wages, hours, and conditions of labor in the construction of cantonments, there shall be created an adjustment commission of three persons, appointed by the Secretary of War; one to represent the Army, one the public, and one Labor; the last to be nominated by Samuel Gompers, member of the Advisory Commission of the Council of National Defense, and President of the A. F. of L.
>
> As basic standards with reference to each cantonment, such commission shall use the union scale of wages, hours, and conditions in force June 1, 1917, in the locality where such cantonment is situated. Consideration shall be given to special circumstances, if any, arising after said date which may require particular advances in

wages or changes in other standards. Adjustments of wages, hours, or conditions, made by such boards are to be treated as binding by all parties.

Newton D. Baker
Samuel Gompers
June 19, 1917

No one knew whether the War Department had authority to enter into collective agreements, but Newton D. Baker and I as individuals assumed responsibility for a course that we knew was indispensable. Shortly afterwards, additional memoranda were signed extending this agreement to all construction work done during the war-time by the War Department, the Navy Department, and the Emergency Fleet Corporation.

I shall always feel that Secretary Baker performed a very courageous and patriotic part in sharing responsibility for this initial project. Later agreements were made between various war agencies and the divisions of organized labor directly concerned with the specific undertakings. These agreements were modified in the light of experience under the Baker-Gompers agreement.

When it was finally determined that the Secretary of Labor was to be war labor administrator, Secretary Wilson asked me to appoint labor representatives to assist in the development of a war labor policy. I appointed such representatives who helped to draft the fundamental principles upon which the work of the War Labor Board was established.

From the time that our participation in the war was inevitable, there were serious misgivings in the minds of many as to what would be the attitude of foreign-born groups. America had let in foreigners without concern as to whether they had become really Americanized. We had no war cloud threatening us. We were working, conserving, and performing our duties as a people—as citizens. It is true that we had groups such as the German-American citizenship, the Irish-American citizenship, the "over-seas Americans," and these in turn frequently exercised a political power among nations; but in so far as our every-day lives were concerned there was a complacency, for there was no apprehension of any real division, or disunity of our people in an emergency which was then foreign to our state of mind. War brought troubled questions as to the allegiance of the foreign-born, the hyphenated citizens, as we came to call them. Not without reason, we wondered if America were really a nation or only an agglomeration of nationalities.

The military struggle itself was on such a gigantic scale that complete national co-operation for action was indispensable. The first problem of mobilization was to assure unity in the national mind. There were many groups that might have held aloof or given only half-hearted co-operation. This was in some aspects a labor problem. The great majority of the foreign born were wage-earners.

Perhaps the most important disrupting agency among them was the Socialist Party organization which was "international." It subordinated nationalism to internationalism, and as the Socialist Party largely emanated from Germany, the sympathy of its devotees was with that country. I have no substantial authority for the statement, but I was and am convinced that the officers of our government deferred their action upon the acute relations between the United States and Germany by reason of their apprehension of the possible lack of national sentiment and unity among the diverse nationalities in our country. War experiences led me to wonder if Socialism, in addition to its philosophic and economic short-comings, had not been manipulated to further sinister purposes. Un-Americanized workers proved especially susceptible to Socialist propaganda. There were several hundred foreign-language publications within the United States, formulating and directing opinion among the foreign born. Whether these papers were aiding their readers to a better understanding of America was a matter to which little thought was given in pre-war time. There was a sort of complacent confidence that America was a melting pot in which all manner of diverse nationalities could be gathered, and inevitably, without planning or consideration on our part, Americans would finally emerge. In the absence of constructive efforts on the part of the community, the trade union movement had undertaken to teach foreign workers the economic bases of American standards of life, work, and ideals.

I held that if these foreign-born workmen, lured and brought into our country by big business or with profit as the primary purpose, were good enough to be brought here for this purpose, they were good enough for us to try to organize them to make better citizens and make better men of them.

In July 1917, the Socialist Party met in regular convention in St. Louis in which they adopted declarations in support of internationalism and pacifism. Pacifism at that time was substantial aid to Germany and the Central Powers and therefore tantamount to avowed hostility to the cause of the Allies. From the time that policy was endorsed by the Socialists, it was no longer possible for loyal Americans to continue membership in the party. The declaration resulted virtually in the dissolution of the Socialist Party. This situation left thousands, and especially foreigners who had looked to that organization for leadership, without intellectual guidance. Not only was there need of establishing an agency for mobilizing sentiment among these foreign-language groups in support of national policies, but there was an opportunity to bridge over the more superficial differences that had separated groups within the labor movements.

I called into these conferences representatives of the National Labor Publicity Organization so that the work planned for New York could be extended wherever the foreign problem was acute. At these conferences we developed a plan for bringing together in one organization representatives of the American trade union movement and representatives of what were known as radical organizations. Members of this organization agreed to lay aside for the period of the war whatever differences they might have upon procedure and to rally in defense of the fundamental principles for which our government stood. This organization we called the American Alliance for Labor and Democracy. The Alliance was national in scale, and under it were gathered the most influential Socialist leaders of the country, prominent trade unionists, and noted publicity persons.

As, of course, was necessary under war emergencies, I first submitted this proposition to the Advisory Commission and Council of National Defense and to George Creel who was chief of the Committee on Public Information. The plan was approved.

After our government formally declared war on Germany, the nature and method of German propaganda became more subtle and therefore much more dangerous. It assumed the form of ultra-internationalism and extreme "democracy." In America the medium for disseminating this teaching was a People's Council in which there was a Workingmen's Division. It was about this division that I was chiefly concerned.

In the summer the People's Council announced that a National Conference would be held in St. Paul which would be "truly representative of labor and would reflect the real mind of labor." That was one way to refute that claim once and for all time, and I accepted the challenge. I called a national conference of the American Alliance for Labor and Democracy to be held at the same time in St. Paul. I had no official authority for my course in organizing the Alliance and serving as its president, but I had the intrinsic authority arising out of great national need and opportunity to serve.

The American Alliance for Labor and Democracy became one of the unofficial agencies through which the National Committee on Public Information operated. It did splendid publicity work serving not only the radical press but all the labor press. Its speakers' bureau organized numbers of public meetings. After the Stockholm propaganda started in Europe, the Alliance planned a country-wide labor loyalty program for the week in which February 22 fell.

By the fall of 1917 the mind of American labor had disclosed itself with reassuring definiteness. Even constant agitation from Stockholm made little impression. I felt that the one thing needful to assure our coalition till the end of the war was a personal message from President Wilson to the representatives of American trade unionism assembled in convention. I presented this thought to my colleagues in the Executive Council, and when they approved, requested Secretary Wilson to convey the invitation to the President. The President accepted and declared he wanted to give his message in person. It was arranged for him to go to Buffalo for the opening day of the convention. Our honor was all the more distinctive from the fact that the President had not left Washington since the beginning of the War and had made no public addresses except his messages to Congress. He spoke surrounded by the significance of a grim cordon of soliders, but his words breathed the uplift of high human purpose at war with principles of unfreedom. A reference he made to me cheered me in some of the hard places where I had to contend against less appreciative understanding.

I look backward in bewilderment at the work I did. The work of the labor movement was unusually heavy. I felt it imperative to maintain personal contact with all regions. I had personal knowledge of the immense work which the American Alliance for Labor and Democracy was doing. Then I had my official work as Advisory Commissioner. By way of diversion, I gave many evenings to selling Liberty Bonds, on the street, in public gatherings, or special drives. I seemed to be always on a train or in a conference.

I have no overweening conceit as to my service in connection with the World War, but I tried to do all that was possible for me to do. So I record in what may be regarded as too much detail some of the things I did for the information which it may give and because during the years of the world-struggle I was absorbed with the one object that it was labor's war as much as it was the war of any other group of our people; that labor had to make good in helping to win the war and to emerge from the war with freedom and democracy safeguarded and its honored name and high ideals maintained.

Stockholm

After the United States had plunged into the depths of war preparations and had completed our organization, I became conscious of a new form of German propaganda which made a powerful appeal to sentiment and humanitarianism. It argued that because of the destruction and waste of the war, every possible agency should be used to end fighting by securing agreement between peoples upon the issues involved in the war. It built upon the foundations laid by international Socialism and held that all peoples were the victims of their capitalistic governments. According to this interpretation, no one knew the causes of the war or which country was the real aggressor. All were equally responsible, and therefore the quickest way to end the war was for the peoples of the warring countries to reach an agreement upon peace terms.

On May 24, 1917, I received a cablegram from Oudegeest inviting the Federation to participate in an international congress of trade union centers to be held in Stockholm June 8, to determine a trade union program for peace negotiations. I discussed the Stockholm proposal with Frank Morrison and John Alpine, members of our Executive Council who were then in Washington, and then I sent Oudegeest a cable stating that before the United States entered the war we had proposed an international labor congress to meet after the war and at the time and place where the representatives of each government were to meet in peace congress. Our proposal was rejected, and we did not see how any good could come out of our participation in the Stockholm Conference during the war. Oudegeest and those he represented continued their efforts to induce our Federation to be represented at an international congress at Stockholm. From various sources of information I learned that the proposal to settle and end the war by negotiations was gaining favor.

A few days later I received a cablegram from Lindquist, the Swedish labor leader who was president of the Stockholm conference of neutrals and Central allies, telling me that the trade union centers represented in the Stockholm conference of trade unions would meet to discuss peace demands September 17 in Switzerland and inviting the United States to send representatives. The Executive Council decided that all such conferences as the one proposed were premature, untimely, and could lead to no good purpose. We were apprehensive lest such a conference would place obstacles in the way of democratizing institutions of the world and would hazard the opportunities for liberty and freedom of all people.

In the fall came the news of the Russian collapse. It was a staggering blow to the Allies both for military and sentimental reasons. The whole world had rejoiced in the overthrow of czardom. In our country where there had long been sympathy with Russian revolutionary movements, the news brought a feeling of great uplift. At the time, we were on the verge of war and were about to enter a period of terrible sacrifices. There was cheer in the feeling that the war had brought to that land of oppression a new and wonderful opportunity.

Our Executive Council sent an official cablegram conveying fraternal greetings and pledging the support of America's workers to Russia's efforts to secure freedom. In every message—and there were many of them—I urged them to build practically and constructively. I knew Russian workers, and I knew the dangers of newly acquired rights and freedom.

Our government felt that as an older republic it owed a duty to Russia that had shaken off despotism in a period when its problems were made extreme by war difficulties. President Wilson sent a commission to Russia personally to assure the people of our sympathy and desire to help and to make arrangements to give them such practical assistance as they could. But all our efforts to prevent the second Russian revolution failed.

The Russian nation had made stupendous sacrifices in the war only to find that hundreds of thousands of her young men had been needlessly killed because of the dishonesty of officials responsible for munitions and supplies. The revolutionists had made promises to fulfill which would necessitate an economic revolution. When the Kerensky régime hesitated to precipitate the second revolution while at the same time maintaining an army in the field in co-operation with the Allies, the Bolsheviki seized control. These pirates ran up the black flag over helpless Russia and declared war upon the established order about which the fabric of civilized life had been woven, and Russia was transformed from an Ally into a menace.

The coming of Communism in Russia gave world-wide revolutionary propaganda an impetus—an incalculable menace to war production. Realizing that labor's clear thinking was the key to the war, I lost no opportunity to get first-hand information of Russian matters—official or unofficial. I met practically every group of Russian representatives that came to this country as well as Americans who returned. It was no great surprise to me when the Bolshevik dictatorship was established on the ruins of the Russian revolution. I had years before predicted to William English Walling what would happen if there should be an attempt to establish a Socialist commonwealth. Since there was in Russia no middle class, no working class movement as such, when the storm broke it would not bring progressive, upward steps, but tyranny would be followed by unbridled license.

The Communist propaganda of Lenine reinforced German propaganda for a negotiated peace. Both railed against "capitalist" governments and urged the "people" to take matters into their own hands. There followed a world-wide Socialist offensive to control public opinion. Should labor be lured by the Russian will-o'-the-wisp, the gains of years would be lost. No one knew the tactics of Socialists better than I, and I had no choice but to assume leadership to protect American labor and American institutions. I found on a pretty broad scale the truth of what Ferdinand Laurrell had said years before, "It is not a pleasant task to destroy men's dreams." I redoubled my efforts to prevent our being lured to Stockholm.

Since I gave unreserved approval to the Fourteen Points of President Wilson, I could find no good reason why I should attempt to mobilize a group within our nation to hold conversations with the enemies of our country. My conception of internationalism was altered by my war experiences—the alteration of one of addition, not subtraction. I learned that one had to be a nationalist before one could be an effective internationalist. It was characteristic of the individualism of America ex-

pressed in genuine absence of class stratification, that financiers, indus-
trialists, farmers, wage-earners, and every group were solidly behind
the President, and that allegiance to the government took precedence
over all other relationships. Each felt that his country was in danger and
responded accordingly. We did not feel that we had to connive with
wage-earners of other countries to forge a club against our own republic.

Peace

[In November 1918,] I went to Laredo, Texas, for a conference to organize a federation of Pan-American labor. The members of our Executive
Council and a number of representative labor men were in Laredo to
take part in that conference. On the way we heard the premature report
of the Armistice. On November 11 soon after my arrival in Laredo, I
bought a small printed sheet issued as an extra of one of the local papers. It contained a dispatch from Washington stating that the Secretary
of State early that morning had given out the official statement that the
Armistice had been signed. I hastened back to my colleagues and gave
them the information. We were all overjoyed.

Immediately following the Pan-American Congress, our Executive Council held a meeting in San Antonio. We discussed labor problems growing out of the truce. The Council anticipated that the Peace
Congress would be called shortly and planned to put the Federation in a
position to carry out our various declarations and to have a part in shaping the peace treaty. It had been our thought, even before the United
States entered the war, that a labor congress ought to be called for the
same time and place as the Peace Congress. It was obvious that if constructive leadership did not at once assume the responsibility, "radical"
groups would take the initiative.

I was anxious that American labor should be represented in the
Peace Commission. The recognition was due because of the service labor had rendered in making peace possible. It was expedient because
our representation would present labor interests as economic problems,
whereas otherwise the emphasis would be upon political aspects only.
In addition, the distinction would help us in our own struggle. There
were two groups eager for reaction to overtake American labor—reactionary employers and the Bolsheviks and near-Bolsheviks of all lands.

Predatory employers had already launched an "open shop" campaign with its proposed wage reductions. Throughout the war the American labor movement had been the tireless foe of propaganda that served autocracy under another guise. War had created favorable conditions for revolutionary propaganda in all countries. Organized labor saw no reason why our government should suddenly change its policy of recognizing the constructive representative character of the American labor movement.

Upon my return East, people with whom I came in contact from all walks of life assumed as a matter of course that I was to be named on the Peace Commission. This was also true of those from diplomatic circles and distinguished foreign representatives. The situation grew exceedingly embarrassing for me as the President seemed to be thinking apart from the rest of us. There were many rumors, but the announcement of the personnel of the Commission definitely ended labor's expectation.

The political or "Stockholm" group in Europe were revising their program to adapt it to the changed situation. Pacifist propaganda was still used for ulterior purposes. Arthur Henderson sought the leadership of that movement. He believed that the obstacles to a war-time international labor conference vanished with the truce.

[In January 1919,] I received an official announcement from Secretary Lansing that President Wilson had appointed Edward N. Hurley of the U.S. Shipping Board and me to represent the United States on the Commission on International Labor Legislation. The designation of this commission to assist the Peace Congress made it imperative for labor to be in a position to submit a unified program. I therefore renewed my request for agreement upon some definite line of action. The inter-Allied conference was not held. However, a separate conference between the American delegation and the Belgian labor organizations was arranged to take place at their headquarters in Brussels.

Upon my appointment as a representative of the United States on the International Labor Commission I was assigned an office in official headquarters in the Hotel Crillon. The Commission convened February 1. M. Colliard, French Minister of Labor, opened the sitting. Mr. Barnes proposed the appointment of me as president which was seconded by all delegations. Arthur Fontaine was made secretary-general and Harold Butler assistant secretary-general.

The British delegation had prepared proposals which had been circulated in both French and English before the second meeting, and these served as the basis for discussion. In a perfectly obvious way that draft controlled the thinking of the conference, and it certainly made my task more difficult and unpleasant. At once and continuously there was apparent the difference between the Old World and the New. Our political, social, and economic philosophy and methods are in sharp contrast as they have grown out of different environments and national characteristics. New World individualism and initiative have shaped our thinking and activity.

The Old World was accustomed to dealing with labor problems through legislation, and it was natural for Old World representatives to think of international labor problems only in the terms of international legislation. They had in mind the development of a super-government that should develop standards for the workers everywhere.

In the New World, in addition to regarding labor problems as a part of the economic field in which methods are essentially different from those of the political field, we had the problems arising out of a written constitution and our Federal form of government. It is very difficult for the average person of continental Europe to understand the spirit and the practical methods of America. The representatives from France and Italy were frankly in favor of a super-government, and they could not understand that the objections I advanced were based upon facts and concrete obstacles.

I opposed with vigor and persistence that part of the draft that proposed giving two votes to the government delegate, on the ground that there are really only two groups in society—the employed and the employing. I believed that the make-up of an international conference thus weighted against labor would militate against confidence in the new body. I proposed one delegate, one vote. This I won, but the advantage was lost when the government was given two representatives. Having in mind the effectiveness of the use of the advisory powers of governmental agencies, I was not in favor of giving an international labor bureau mandatory powers. My experience had convinced me that legislation cannot accomplish that which is contrary to the general will and that far better results can be secured by reaching unanimous agreement after having made a survey of the facts in a case. It was impossible to convince the advocates of super-government that they were planning to defeat their own purposes. Perhaps there is no one who is so intolerant as the theorist who wants to do good. Time and time again I felt that the situation within the International Labor Commission was impossible and that no constructive results could be secured, but, on the other hand, I felt constrained to stay by the work because my withdrawal would react to the detriment of the purposes of President Wilson.

The second big fight I made was for the principle that the International Labor Office or its annual assembly shall not propose to any country a law, convention, or treaty which contains lower standards than obtain in that country. After the acceptance of the American proposals safeguarding the rights of federated governments (such as ours), this proposal was the crux upon which our commission was about to split. I announced that unless that proposal was adopted by the commission, [the United States] would be forced to refrain from signing the report, and we would submit a minority report to the Plenary Council. After the die had been cast by my statement to the commission, they adopted the principle by practically a unanimous vote, the Japanese delegation again refraining from voting.

In addition to the Draft Convention which provided for the organization and operation of an International Labor Bureau and conferences, there was drawn up a declaration of labor principles to be inserted in the Peace Treaty. These principles constituting a Bill of Rights for Labor were to write into the treaty an extraordinary recognition of certain common principles of relations between men in the affairs of daily life. The basis for this charter was the principles which the American Federation of Labor submitted to the Inter-Allied Conference in London in September 1918. In substance the principles to be approved by the countries signing the treaty were:

> In right and in fact the labor of a human being should not be treated as merchandise or an article of commerce.
> Employers and workers should be allowed the right of association for all lawful purposes.
> No child should be permitted to be employed in industry or commerce before the age of fourteen years.
> Between the years of fourteen and eighteen gainful employment permitted at work not physically harmful and on condition that technical or general education be continued.
> Every worker has a right to a wage adequate to maintain a reasonable standard of life.

Equal pay should be given to women and to men for work of equal value in quantity and quality.

A weekly rest, including Sunday, or its equivalent for all workers.

Limitation of the hours of work in industry on the basis of eight hours a day or forty-eight hours a week.

The commission designated Washington as the place for the first International Labor Commission to be held under the treaty and adopted an agenda providing for an organizing committee. The last meeting was held on March 24.

Problems after Armageddon

It had been my hope that the principles of co-operation and co-ordination effective during the war would serve as a foundation for industrial reorganization after the war. It was a hope that did credit to my optimism. Instead, there have been big battles to maintain pre-war standards.

When I returned from Amsterdam in 1919, I found confronting the labor movement gigantic problems in steel and transportation. Steel, a basic industry, while consolidating under trust control had arbitrarily and ruthlessly opposed the organization of its workmen. It was the only big industry to which the war did not bring constructive progress in industrial justice. Even during the war, steel companies refused to deal with bona fide organizations of wage-earners and created company-owned unions. At its 1918 convention the A. F. of L. authorized a committee to organize steel workers. That committee selected as its secretary a man whom I had seen but once.

When sometimes before I was attending a meeting of the Chicago Federation of Labor one of the delegates in the body of the hall made a strong speech, declaring that he was converted from the old ideals he had, that he supported in full the fundamental principles, the ideas, the methods, philosophy, and policy of the American Federation of Labor which at that meeting I had enunciated. I was much impressed. I did not know the man nor even his name. I had never seen him before. A few days after my return to Washington I wrote to John Fitzpatrick, president of the Chicago Federation of Labor, and asked the name of the man who made the talk in support of the A. F. of L. I was informed that it was William Z. Foster. It was my desire to give this man the opportunity to be helpful to the bona fide labor movement. He had declared himself to be so thoroughly changed.

Whether the reports which came to me were truthful or otherwise, I knew that he had been working in the stockyards organization which resulted in much improvement in the conditions of the workers in the industry. Then when the convention of the American Federation of Labor in St. Paul in 1918 decided to undertake the campaign to organize the workers in the steel industry I was made chairman of the committee, and Foster secretary. I was really pleased with his selection as secretary of the organizing committee. The committee was made up of the representatives of all unions within whose jurisdiction steel workers came. This was a working plan that provided unity of effort with flexibility necessary to retain trade alignments.

After the Armistice, the strength of the steel unions increased materially. Agitation against the twelve-hour day gained impetus. The resistance of U.S. Steel to labor unions became more aggressive. In a number of steel towns, free assemblage and free speech were denied as effectually as though no constitutional guarantees existed. Acts of violence against our organizers followed. On behalf of our committee I wrote Judge Gary, asking for a conference. Not even the courtesy of an acknowledgment was received. This was in conformity with the United States Steel Corporation policy of refusing to "recognize" the union. Refusing to recognize the obvious leads to complications.

Because my official duties had necessitated my absence from the country, I resigned as chairman of the committee, and Fitzpatrick had been selected for that position. When I returned from Amsterdam, I learned that a strike vote had been taken and strike authorized. The committee personally applied at Judge Gary's office for a conference. Judge Gary though in his office refused to see the committee but asked them to submit their business in writing. This was done, and the reply received was that United States Steel would not "recognize" representatives of organized labor.

After the situation had been considered by our Executive Council, it was decided that we appeal to President Wilson to use his good offices to secure an adjustment of the situation. Fitzpatrick, Davis, Foster, Hannan, and I laid the situation before President Wilson who manifested sincere interest and who endeavored to bring about a conference.

However, he failed. He had just started to secure popular support in favor of the treaty ratification.

I then called a conference for the full organizing committee in my office (September 8). I told the men that according to confidential information at a meeting of the "open-shop" interests held in New York City, it had been decided that the U.S. Steel should make the fight against further organization of workers. The Corporation was prepared for the contest and welcomed an opportunity to force aggressive action upon labor. Both Foster and Fitzpatrick assured me that it was impossible to prevent the strike on the appointed day.

As a committee, we sent a telegram appealing to President Wilson. The President replied, urging in view of his inability to arrange satisfactory mediation at that time, that strike be postponed until after the industrial conference which he had called for October 6 to develop national agreement upon fundamental principles of industrial relations. The steel strike was set for a date just preceding the conference of September 22. If it were deferred, there was a possibility that differences could be adjusted upon the basis of agreements reached in the conference; if it took place according to schedule, the background of conflict would render very difficult that spirit of conciliation and deliberation necessary to make the President's Industrial Conference effective.

When I received the President's telegram, I communicated with Fitzpatrick at Pittsburgh urging compliance with the President's request. The organizing committee met to consider the situation. With the assistance of William Johnston, president of the Machinists' organization, I made an insistent struggle to postpone action. After a two days' session, the committee decided to abide by their strike program and sent a letter to President Wilson stating the reasons for that course. Though I knew that the strike would fail, the best I could do was to suggest and advise, for it must be understood that as president of the American Federation of Labor I had neither the right nor the power to call the strike or to countermand the strike order.

In these conferences, Foster had been so insistent that the strike should take place upon the day set that I began to doubt his sincerity and to believe, as I am now convinced, that his whole conciliatory policy toward the American Federation of Labor and the trade union movement was for no other reason than to gain some foothold by which he could undermine and destroy the bona fide labor movement of America and to try to reconstruct it upon the Soviet revolutionary basis.

I had no sympathy with the attitude of Judge Gary. On the contrary, if an effective movement could have been brought about to teach him a lesson in industrial history, I was not unwilling that it should be administered to him; but for me to have interposed or to have declared publicly that in my judgment the strike should not take place would simply have brought about chaos among the men who had been organized to the number of over one hundred thousand, and the result would have been even more injurious than it turned out to be.

However, the years of educational work in furtherance of the eight-hour day of the A. F. of L. and intensive efforts to establish eight hours as the maximum work-day in many industries, had made conspicuous the brutality of the twelve-hour day and the seven-day week. There were many who deplored the two-shift system in steel. Under the leadership of Morris L. Cooke, the Philadelphia Engineers' Club initiated a study of the technique of changing from a twelve to an eight-hour shift in continuous industry. The study challenged interest and finally led to an engineering report on the twelve-hour day in industry by the Federated American Engineering Societies, which was submitted to the heads of the United States Steel Corporation by President Harding. Public opinion was roused to the social problem by the Inter-Church Steel Report. At last the end of the twelve-hour day seemed at hand, and the organization of the steel workers was again put under way.

The Industrial Conference called by President Wilson was peculiarly constituted. There were representatives of employers, labor, and the public. The group representing the employers was 100 per cent employers; the group representing labor was 100 per cent labor; the representatives of the public were fully 90 per cent employers and among them some of the largest employers in the country, including Judge Gary and Mr. Rockefeller. It seemed to my associates and me that if the conference was to reach constructive conclusions, the best means to test it was an effort to have the conference recommend mediation for the purpose of reaching some cordial entente between the Steel Corporation and the workmen on strike. Our resolution for mediation came before the conference in its original form and was rejected. After a vote was called, I stated that rejection of our proposals on the steel strike and collective bargaining legislated us out of the conference. We left the conference in a body.

The government can supply counsel and information on industrial problems, but industries and all elements concerned must finally work out the solution.

In transportation, the situation had been complicated by unwise propaganda. Organization of workers in the railway shops had progressed tremendously under the Federal railway administration. As the time to return the railroads to private operation drew near, came the Plumb Plan episode. This plan, sponsored first by some of the Brotherhoods, was presented to the shop crafts, and an attempt made to commit them to the plan.

The proposal, which had the appearance of progressive thought, concealed many fundamental weaknesses. My name had been printed among the sponsors of the plan. As the situation was critical for the shopmen, I did not want to embarrass them by asking for explanations, so I held my peace publicly.

In the meanwhile, a Railway Labor Board was established under Federal law, and the experiment of government control over personnel was under way. Before long, the unions were forced into strike, and there began the revulsion against government operation and in favor of private operation and collective bargaining. And so men learn.

Through the transitional war period and the industrial storms of the past years, the labor movement emerged intact, stronger than at our entrance into the war. The past years have been a revealing test, sharply distinguishing the permanent from the ephemeral. They have demonstrated again the dependability of voluntary institutions assuring individual initiative. They reveal that genuine growth and progress do not come from above or the outside. They do not come through formulas or declarations but from the educational self-imposed discipline of the life process and are manifest in self-revealing work.

We American trade unionists want to work out our problems in the spirit of true Americanism—a spirit that embodies our broadest and highest ideals. If we do not succeed, it will be due to no fault of ours. We have been building the A. F. of L. in conformity with what we believe to be the original intent and purpose of America. I have an abiding faith that we will succeed, and with that success are involved the progress and the welfare of the great mass of American citizenship.

I have no overwhelming conceit of the value or the importance of what I have recorded in this book, nor do I wish to underestimate it. From my observations and experience I have reached the conclusion that over-modesty is after all in itself a species of vanity. So I have in these pages written a faithful record of what I have seen and done with such comment as seemed necessary for clear understanding of the subjects and facts with which I have dealt.

Perhaps, what I have not included may be as important or more so than what these pages contain. So much which exists in the archives of the labor movement and elsewhere for the time being baffles gathering and research. Perhaps if life, time, and opportunity afford, I may again attempt to devote myself to further presentation of facts of life and work. This I say without fear of dispute or refutation, that the World War changed me only in one respect. That is, when the war demonstrated that pacifism in which I believed and which I faithfully advocated was a vain hope, I realized that the struggle in defense of right and freedom must ever be maintained at all hazard. In all other things, I have steadily held to the faith.

Thrice since Armistice Day I have looked death in the face very closely. But my seventy-third birthday and then the 42d anniversary of the A. F. of L. (November 15, 1923) found me as usual at my desk, doing the work that I love best—work that is such a privilege to do that I sometimes feel selfish because of my opportunity to do so much. The work of the labor movement does not grow less for it has its roots in vital needs. That gives it the same intrinsic power to interest that life holds, and to me the two are inseparable. I hope to keep on with my work until I go out into the silence.

SELECTED
BIOGRAPHICAL GLOSSARY

The following abbreviations are used: AFL, American Federation of Labor; BLF, Brotherhood of Locomotive Firemen; CMIU, Cigarmakers International Union; FOTLU, Federation of Organized Trades and Labor Unions; IWW, Industrial Workers of the World; ILGWU, International Ladies Garment Workers Union; ITU, International Typographical Union; IWA, International Workingmen's Association; K of L, Knights of Labor; MBIU, Machinists and Blacksmiths' International Union; NLU, National Labor Union; NTU, National Typographical Union; UMWA, United Mine Workers of America.

ARTHUR, PETER M.   B. Scotland, 1831; to U.S., 1842; railroad worker and locomotive engineer; joined Brotherhood of Locomotive Engineers, 1863; elected Chief Engineer, 1874–1903; d. 1903.

BARONDESS, JOSEPH   B. Russia, 1867; to U.S., 1888; union organizer in New York City, 1890s; important force in founding ILGWU, 1900; a Socialist and Zionist; d. 1928.

BERGER, VICTOR L.   B. Austria, 1860; to U.S., 1878; teacher and newspaper editor in Milwaukee; member, ITU; co-founder, Socialist Party of Amer-

217

ica, 1901; elected to Executive Board, 1901–23; first Socialist Congressman, 1911–12; reelected 1918 but denied seat for opposition to World War I; reelected 1922–28; d. 1929.

BOYCE, EDWARD   B. Ireland, 1863; to U.S., 1882; miner, joined K of L, 1884; led Coeur d'Alene, Idaho, strike of 1892; elected president Western Federation of Miners, 1896; led Western Federation out of AFL, 1897; cofounded Western Labor Union (1898) and American Labor Union (1902) to challenge AFL; supported IWW; d. late 1930s.

BUCHANAN, JOSEPH   B. Missouri, 1851; journalist and editor; member, ITU and K of L, 1880s; published *Labor Enquirer* (Denver), 1882–86; organized workers into K of L; member K of L executive board, 1884–86; expelled, 1886; d. 1924.

CAHAN, ABRAM   B. Russia, 1860; to U.S., 1882; union organizer and Socialist; editor, *Jewish Daily Forward* (New York City) and novelist; d. 1951.

CAMERON, ANDREW C.   B. Scotland, 1836; to U.S., 1851; printer and editor; leader of NTU in Chicago; editor, *Workingmen's Advocate*, 1864–80; president, Chicago Trades Assembly, 1866–70; cofounder, NLU; delegate to IWA convention, 1869; d. 1890.

CARL, CONRAD   B. Bavaria; to U.S., 1854; leader of German tailors in New York City; member of IWA; later a journalist; d. 1890.

CARTER, W. S.   B. Texas, 1859; locomotive fireman; editor, *Locomotive Firemen's Magazine*, 1894–1904 (succeeded Eugene V. Debs); general secretary, BLF, 1904–8; president, 1909–22; director, Division of Labor, U.S. Railway Administration during World War I; d. 1923.

COHEN, FANNIA   B. Russia, 1888; to U.S., 1904; joined ILGWU, 1909; became first woman vice president, 1916–25; executive secretary of union's education department, 1918–61; cofounder of Workers' Education Bureau and Brookwood College, 1921; d. 1962.

DEBS, EUGENE V.   B. Indiana, 1855; locomotive fireman; elected Democratic politician, Indiana, 1879–85; joined BLF, 1875; editor of journal and national secretary-treasurer, 1880–94; cofounded American Railway Union, 1893, first president; jailed in aftermath of Pullman strike; cofounded Socialist Party of America, 1901; five-time presidential candidate, 1900–1920; jailed for opposition to World War I, 1919–21; d. 1926.

DELEON, DANIEL   B. Venezuela, 1852; to U.S., 1874; lawyer; Columbia University professor, 1883–89; supported Henry George in 1886; joined K of L, 1888; Socialist Labor Party, 1890; editor, *The People*, 1892–1914; founded Socialist Trade and Labor Alliance, 1895; cofounded IWW, 1905; expelled in 1908 over political differences and founded rival union; d. 1914.

DREIER, MARY E.   B. New York City, 1875; labor reformer and prominent suffragist; member, Women's Trade Union League, 1903–50; president,

1906–14; member, New York State Factory Investigating Commission, 1911–15; chaired New York State Committee on Women in Industry, 1917–19; d. 1963.

DUNCAN, JAMES   B. Scotland, 1857; to U.S., 1880; granite cutter; president, Granite Cutters International Association, 1885; member, executive board, AFL, 1894–1928; member of American Labor Mission to Paris Peace Conference, 1919; d. 1928.

EVANS, CHRISTOPHER   B. England, 1841; to U.S., 1869; miner; president, Miners National Association, 1873; secretary, AFL, 1889–94.

FINCHER, JONATHAN   B. Pennsylvania, 1830; machinist; cofounder, MBIU, 1858; cofounder, Philadelphia Trades Assembly, 1863; editor, *Fincher's Trades Review*, 1863–66; elected to state legislature from Hazelton (Luzerne County), 1876.

FITZPATRICK, JOHN   B. Ireland, 1871; to U.S., 1882; horseshoer; president, Chicago Federation of Labor, 1901, 1906–46; leader in 1919 steel strike; d. 1946.

FORAN, MARTIN A.   B. Pennsylvania, 1844; cofounder, International Coopers' Union, 1870; edited *Coopers' Journal*, 1870–74; became lawyer in Cleveland, 1873; U.S. Congressman (Democratic), 1882–88; d. 1921.

FOSTER, FRANK   B. Massachusetts, 1855; printer; delegate of ITU to founding convention, FOTLU, 1881; secretary of latter union, 1883; joined K of L, 1882; chairman of executive board, 1883; leader of Boston K of L, 1881–87.

FOSTER, W. H.   B. England, 1847; to U.S., 1873; printer, president, Typographical Union No. 3 and Cincinnati Trades Assembly, 1878; secretary, FOTLU, 1881–83, 1885.

FOSTER, WILLIAM Z.   B. Massachusetts, 1881; industrial worker; joined Socialist Party of America, 1900–1909; member, IWW, 1910–12; founded Syndicalist League of North America, 1912; led 1919 steel strike; joined American Communist Party, 1921; national chairman, 1932–57; d. 1961.

FURUSETH, ANDREW   B. Norway, 1854; to U.S., 1870s; merchant seaman; secretary, Sailors' Union of the Pacific, 1887; president, International Seamen's Union, 1908–38; d. 1938.

HAYWOOD, WILLIAM D.   B. Utah, 1869; miner; joined Western Federation of Miners, 1894; member, executive board, 1899; chaired founding convention, IWW, 1905; active Socialist agitator, 1908–12; rejoined IWW, 1912–21; arrested for antiwar activities, 1917; sentenced to prison; jumped bail to live in Soviet Union, 1921; d. 1928.

HILLQUIT, MORRIS   B. Russian Latvia, 1869; to U.S., 1886; admitted to New York bar, 1893; member of Socialist Labor Party, 1890s; withdrew to help found Socialist Party of America, 1901; member, national executive committee, 1907–12, 1916–33; general counsel, ILGWU, 1913–33; d. 1933.

HOWARD, ROBERT   B. England, of Irish parents, 1844; to U.S., 1873; textile worker; secretary, Fall River (Mass.) Spinners' Association, 1878; elected state representative, 1880–82; state senator, 1885; teasurer, FOTLU, 1881–85; secretary, Fall River K of L, 1885.

JARRETT, JOHN   B. England, 1843; to U.S., 1862; iron puddler; president, Sons of Vulcan, 1873; president, Amalgamated Association of Iron and Steel Workers, 1879–83; chairman, FOTLU, 1881–83; later a lobbyist for Tin Plate Association; d. 1918.

JESSUP, WILLIAM   B. New York City, 1827; ship joiner; vice president, NLU (for New York State), 1866; officer, Workingmen's Union (New York) and president, New York Workingmen's Assembly, 1867–72.

JOHNSTON, WILLIAM   B. Nova Scotia, 1874; to U.S., 1885; machinist; joined International Association of Machinists in Rhode Island, 1895; district leader, 1905–11; national president, 1912–26; served on War Labor Board during World War I; d. 1937.

LEFFINGWELL, SAMUEL   B. Ohio; printer; led printers' unions in Cincinnati (1850s) and Indianapolis (1870s); joined K of L, 1875; delegate to K of L national conventions throughout 1880s; president, 1882 convention, FOTLU; organized and first president of Indiana State Federation of Labor.

LENNON, JOHN B.   B. Wisconsin, 1850; tailor; organized Denver Tailors' Union, 1883; general secretary, Journeymen's Tailors Union of America, 1886–1910; national treasurer, AFL, 1890–1917; editor, *The Tailor*, 1886–1910; d. 1923.

LYNCH, JAMES   B. New York, 1867; printer; joined Syracuse local, ITU, 1887; president, 1890; national president, ITU, 1900–1914, 1924–26; commissioner, New York State Industrial Commission, 1914–21; d. 1930.

MCBRIDE, JOHN   B. Ohio, 1854; miner; joined Miners' Union, 1870; president, 1883–86; Democratic representative to Ohio State Assembly, 1883–86; president, National Progressive Union of Miners; helped found UMWA, 1890; president, 1892–95; president, AFL, 1895; strong People's Party advocate, 1896; newspaper editor, Ohio, 1896–1917; d. 1917.

MCDONNELL, JOSEPH P.   B. Ireland, 1840; Fenian activist, embraced Marxism, 1869; Irish delegate to IWA, 1872; to U.S., 1872; editor and publisher, *Labor Standard*; chaired New Jersey State Federation of Labor, 1883–98; remained an active Socialist; d. 1906.

MCGUIRE, PETER J.   B. New York City, 1852, of Irish parents; wood-joiner; organizer for Socialist Labor Party, 1874–79; founded Brotherhood of Carpenters and Joiners, 1881; instrumental in founding of both FOTLU and AFL; vice president, AFL, 1889–1900; ousted from Brotherhood in internal political dispute, 1902; d. 1906.

McNEILL, GEORGE   B. Massachusetts, 1837; writer; leader of Boston Eight Hour League, International Labor Union; deputy chief, Massachusetts Bureau of Labor, 1869–74; joined K of L; treasurer, District 30, 1884–86; active in AFL; d. 1906.

MITCHELL, JOHN   B. Illinois, 1870; miner; joined K of L, 1885; delegate to founding convention, UMWA, 1890; vice president, 1897; president, 1899–1908; vice president, AFL, 1898–1914; with Gompers supported organized labor's participation in National Civic Federation, 1900; resigned UMWA presidency over Civic Federation affiliation, 1908; d. 1919.

MORGAN, THOMAS J.   B. England, 1847; to U.S., 1869; machinist (1875–95) and lawyer; cofounded Chicago Trades and Labor Assembly, 1870s; author of the famous Plank 10 rejected by Gompers in 1894; member of Socialist Labor Party and later Socialist Party of America; d. 1912.

MORRISON, FRANK   B. Canada, 1859; to U.S., 1872; printer; joined ITU Chicago local, 1886; graduated law school, 1894; ITU delegate to AFL, 1896; elected secretary, AFL, 1897–1939; d. 1939.

O'CONNELL, JAMES   B. Pennsylvania, 1858; machinist; joined K of L and International Association of Machinists, 1880s; member, executive board, IAM, 1891; president, 1893–1911; vice president, AFL, 1895–1918; president, AFL Metal Trades Department, 1911–34; d. 1936.

PARSONS, ALBERT   B. Alabama, 1848; printer; Confederate Army veteran; employed by U.S. Internal Revenue Bureau, 1869–71; editor and printer in Chicago, 1871–86; member, ITU, K of L, Socialist Labor Party; became an anarchist, 1881; convicted of Haymarket bombing; executed 1887.

POWDERLY, TERENCE V.   B. Pennsylvania, 1849, of Irish parents; machinist; joined MBIU, 1870s; joined K of L, 1874; Master Workman, 1879–93; elected mayor of Scranton, 1878–84; vice president, Irish Land League, 1883; U.S. Commissioner General of Immigration, 1897–1902; d. 1924.

SARGENT, FRANK   B. Vermont, 1854; locomotive fireman; Grand Master, BLF, 1885–1902; U.S. Commissioner General of Immigration, 1902; member, National Civic Federation; d. 1908.

SORGE, FRIEDRICK A.   B. Saxony (now East Germany), 1828; active in German revolutionary movement, 1848; to U.S., 1852; music teacher; member, New York Communist Society, 1858; joined IWA, 1869; general secretary, 1872; close friend of both Karl Marx and Frederick Engels and popularizer of their ideas in America; d. 1906.

STEWART, IRA   B. Connecticut, 1831; machinist; joined MBIU, 1850s; national leader of the Eight Hour League; cofounder of International Labor Union, 1878; d. 1883.

STRASSER, ADOLPH   B. Austria-Hungary; to U.S., 1871 or 1872; cigarmaker; helped organize Social Democratic Party, 1873, and Socialist Labor

Party, 1877; joined CMIU, 1872; international president, 1877–91; cofounded AFL, 1886; served on executive council, 1904–7.

SYLVIS, WILLIAM   B. Pennsylvania, 1828; iron molder; founder, Iron Molders International Union, 1859; president, 1863–69; president, NLU, 1868–69; d. 1869.

TROUP, ALEXANDER   Printer; secretary-treasurer, NTU, 1866–68; vice president, NLU, 1868; Connecticut legislator; d. 1908.

TROUP, AUGUSTA LEWIS   B. New York City, 1848; reporter and typesetter; first president, Women's Typographical Union, 1868; won charter from ITU for women's union, 1869; corresponding secretary, ITU, 1870; d. 1920.

WILKINSON, JOSEPH   B. Ireland, 1856; to U.S.; 1872; tailor; cofounder, Amalgamated Trade and Labor Union, New York City; secretary, Journeymen Tailors' National Union.

WILSON, WILLIAM B.   B. Scotland, 1862; to U.S., 1870; miner; joined local miners' union in Pennsylvania, 1877; member, K of L, 1878; District Master Workman, K of L, 1888–94; cofounder, UMWA, 1890; member, general executive board, 1891–94; left K of L, 1894; international secretary-treasurer, UMWA, 1900–1908; Democratic congressman, Pennsylvania, 1906; first Secretary of Labor, 1913–21; d. 1934.

WOODHULL, VICTORIA C.   B. Ohio, 1838; reformer and clairvoyant; editor, *Woodhull & Claflin's Weekly*, 1870–76; strong advocate of feminism, world government, free love; member, IWA (Section 12), 1871–72; presidential candidate, Equal Rights party, 1872; editor of British eugenics journal, *Humanitarian*, 1892–1901; d. 1927.

SUGGESTED READINGS

Brody, David, ed. *The American Labor Movement.* New York: Harper and Row, 1971.

Buchanan, Joseph. *The Story of a Labor Agitator.* New York: Outlook Company, 1903.

Christie, Robert A. *Empire in Wood: A History of the Carpenter's Union.* Ithaca, N.Y.: New York State School of Industrial and Labor Relations, 1956.

Commons, John R. *Labor and Administration.* New York: Macmillan, 1913.

Commons, John R.; Saposs, David J.; Sumner, Helen L.; Mittelman, E. B.; Hoagland, H. E.; Andrews, John B.; and Perlman, Selig. *History of Labor in the United States.* 2 vols. New York: Macmillan, 1918.

Dick, William M. *Labor and Socialism in America: The Gompers' Era.* Port Washington, N.Y.: Kennikat Press, 1972.

Fink, Gary, ed. *Biographical Dictionary of American Labor Leaders.* Westport, Conn.: Greenwood Press, 1974.

Fink, Leon. *Workingmen's Democracy: The Knights of Labor and American Politics.* Urbana, Ill.: University of Illinois Press, 1983.

223

Gompers, Samuel. *The American Labor Movement: Its Makeup, Achievements and Inspirations.* Washington, D.C.: American Federation of Labor, 1914.

Green, Marguerite. *The National Civic Federation and the American Labor Movement, 1900–1925.* Washington, D.C.: Catholic University of America Press, 1956.

Grob, Gerald. *Workers and Utopia: A Study of Ideological Conflict in the American Labor Movement.* Evanston, Ill.: Northwestern University Press, 1961.

Grubbs, Frank L. *The Struggle for Labor Loyalty: Gompers, the A.F. of L. and the Pacifists, 1917–1920.* Durham, N.C.: Duke University Press, 1968.

Jacobson, Julius, ed. *The Negro and the American Labor Movement.* Garden City, N.Y.: Anchor Books, 1968.

Karson, Marc. *American Labor Unions and Politics, 1900–1918.* Boston: Beacon Press, 1965.

Kaufman, Stuart Bruce. *Samuel Gompers and the Origins of the American Federation of Labor, 1848–1896.* Westport, Conn.: Greenwood Press, 1973.

Livesay, Harold G. *Samuel Gompers and Organized Labor in America.* Boston: Little, Brown and Co., 1978.

McNeill, George, ed. *The Labor Movement: The Problem of Today.* New York: M. W. Hazen, 1888.

Mandel, Bernard. *Samuel Gompers, A Biography.* Yellow Springs, Ohio: Antioch Press, 1963.

Morris, James O. *Conflict within the AFL: A Study of Craft versus Industrial Unionism, 1901–1938.* Ithaca, N.Y.: New York State School of Industrial and Labor Relations, 1958.

Perlman, Selig. *A Theory of the Labor Movement.* New York: Macmillan, 1928.

Powderly, Terence V. *The Path I Trod.* New York: Columbia University Press, 1940.

Reed, Louis S. *The Labor Philosophy of Samuel Gompers.* New York: Columbia University Press, 1930.

Salvatore, Nick. *Eugene V. Debs: Citizen and Socialist.* Urbana, Ill.: University of Illinois Press, 1982.

Swinton, John. *Striking for Life: Labor's Side of the Labor Question.* Philadelphia (?): American Manufacturing and Publishing Co., 1894.

Taft, Philip. *The A.F. of L. in the Time of Gompers.* New York: Harper and Row, 1957.

Trant, William, ed. *Trade Unions: Their Origin and Objects, Influence and Efficiency.* Washington, D.C.: American Federation of Labor, 1915.

Ware, Norman. *The Labor Movement in the United States, 1860–1895: A Study in Democracy.* New York: D. Appleton, 1929.

Zieger, Robert H. *Republicans and Labor, 1919–1929.* Lexington, Ky.: University of Kentucky Press, 1969.

INDEX

Loeb, Daniel. *See* DeLeon, Daniel
Loewe v. *Lawlor*. *See* Danbury Hatter's case
Lynch, James, 66, 69, 220

McBride, John: as AFL president, xxiv, 107–8, 109, 117, 156, 220; mentioned, 81, 82, 116
McBryde, Patrick, 107
McCarthy, P. H., 136
McCloskey, M. J.,35
McCraith, August, 107–08
McDonnell, J. P., xvii, xxiii, 30, 35, 44–45, 66, 113, 136
McDowell, Mary, 128
McGuire, Peter J.: and Gompers, xiv, 12, 31, 46, 104; and IWA, 35–36, 44; and Tompkins Square Riot, 32, 35; and Social Democratic Party, 36; and eight-hour day, 72–73; and AFL, xxiii, 82, 85, 104; and British Trade Union Congress, 109; and Irish nationalism, 109; mentioned, xix, 78, 80, 151, 156
McGlynn, Edward (clergyman), 99, 101, 102
McGregor, Hugh, 35–36, 44–45, 66
McMackin, John, 102
McNeill, George E., 22, 66, 79, 95, 221
Maine State Federation of Labor, 174
Mann, Tom, 139
Marshall, Thomas R., 180
Marti, José, 141
Martin, Howard (doctor), 193, 194
Marx, Karl, xi, xiiii, xvii, xviii, 19, 27, 28–29, 30, 60, 113
Marxism: influence on Gompers, xiii–xiv, xvi, xxiii, 19, 27; and trade unions, 19, 27, 29, 35–36; and International Workingmen's Association, xiii–xiv, 29–30
Massachusetts State Federation of Labor, 86
May Day demonstrations, 96, 98
Menche, Adam, 98–99
Metcalf, R.H., 107–8
Miller, Henry, 162
Miller, Hugo, 74
Mitchell, John, 151, 153, 164, 169, 176, 221
Monckton, J.H., 35, 66
Moore, Mark, 67
Morgan, J. Pierpont, 151, 153, 154
Morgan, Thomas J., 107, 115–16, 221
Morrison, Frank, 169, 203, 221
Murch, Thomas, 18, 72

National Association of Manufacturers: and immigration, 166; and eight-hour law, 172; anti-union philosophy, xxvii–xxviii; mentioned, xxx–xxxi, xxxii, 168, 175, 185
National Civic Federation: Gompers's involvement in, xxxi, xxxiv, 131, 149–52; and preparedness campaign, 189; attitude toward unions, xxxi–xxxii, xxxiv, xxxix; mentioned, xxxv, 118
National Committee on Public Information, 202
National Federation of Miners, 28, 81
National Labor Publicity Organization, 201
National Labor Tribune, 28
National Labor Union: and William H. Sylvis, xiii, 18; and politics, 18, 45; and International Workingmen's Association, 19, 29; and Independent Party, 45; mentioned, xiii, 28, 67
National Union of Cigarmakers, 16
New York City: immigrants in, 12, 22, 136, 138–39; and trade unionism, xviii, 22, 28, 75–80, 136, 138–39; and eight-hour movement, 95–96
New York Evening News, 13
New York State Factory Investigating Commission, 145
New York State Workingmen's Assembly, xxxiii, 44, 83–84, 100
New York Union Printer, 83
New Yorker Volkszeitung, 59, 142
Nickelsberg, Kaufman, 43
Nugent, John, 107
Number 10 Stanton Street group. *See* Economic and Sociological Club

O'Connell, James, 118, 140, 157, 221
Olney, Richard, 122
Open-shop campaign, xxvii–xxviii, xxxix, 207, 211–13

Pacific Coast Trades and Labor Union, 71
Panic of 1873, 31
Paris Peace Conference, 4. *See also* Versailles Peace Conference
Parker, Alton B., 143, 177
Parnell, Charles S., 109
Parry, David, 175
Parsons, Albert, 96, 221
Pasco, David, 83
Pearre, Matthew (Representative), 182
Pearre Bill, 176, 183, 186
Peckham, Rufus, 61
Penna, Phil H., 107